POLITICAL INSTITUTIONS IN
CONTEMPORARY FRANCE

POLITICAL INSTITUTIONS IN CONTEMPORARY FRANCE

Robert Elgie

OXFORD
UNIVERSITY PRESS

OXFORD

UNIVERSITY PRESS

Great Clarendon Street, Oxford OX2 6DP

Oxford University Press is a department of the University of Oxford.
It furthers the University's objective of excellence in research, scholarship,
and education by publishing worldwide in

Oxford New York

Auckland Bangkok Buenos Aires Cape Town Chennai
Dar es Salaam Delhi Hong Kong Istanbul Karachi Kolkata
Kuala Lumpur Madrid Melbourne Mexico City Mumbai Nairobi
São Paulo Shanghai Taipei Tokyo Toronto

Oxford is a registered trade mark of Oxford University Press
in the UK and in certain other countries

Published in the United States
by Oxford University Press Inc., New York

British Library Cataloguing in Publication Data
Data available

Library of Congress Cataloging in Publication Data
Data available

ISBN 0–19–878266–7

3 5 7 9 10 8 6 4 2

Typeset in Minion and Congress Sans
by RefineCatch Limited, Bungay, Suffolk
Printed in Great Britain by
Biddles Ltd, King's Lynn, Norfolk

PREFACE

I am indebted to a number of people who have helped me during the course of this book. In the first place, I would like to thank Peter Mair for asking me to contribute a book to his series and for his comments and advice throughout the project as whole. I would also like to extend particular thanks to Sue Dempsey and her predecessor at Oxford University Press, Angela Griffin, both of whom were very patient, courteous, and helpful. I would also like to thank Katy Plowright at OUP. I am also grateful to Shane Martin and two anonymous reviewers who read through a number of draft chapters and made some extremely helpful comments. I have tried to take their concerns on board, but, of course, the responsibility for the final version is entirely my own. Finally, I would like to thank my parents as well as my immediate family, Etain, Matthew, and Michael, for all their support over the years.

R.E.

CONTENTS

LIST OF FIGURES

LIST OF TABLES

LIST OF BOXES

INTRODUCTION

The aim of this book is threefold. First, it serves as a core text for under-graduates studying contemporary France. It contains basic information about the legal and constitutional powers of the country's political institutions, the procedures and practices of the decision-making process, the behaviour of political figures, and the general development of the political system since 1958. In short, it provides an introduction to the government and politics of contemporary France by focusing on the institutions of the Fifth Republic. Secondly, the book also puts forward a clear argument. The French system continues to create the expectation of strong leadership, but increasingly it constrains the coordinating and leadership capacity of senior political actors. Thirdly, this argument is placed in the context of an overall framework that stresses the interaction of institutions, actors, and ideas. This framework helps us to understand why institutions are formed, why they change, and why certain choices are made within any given set of institutional structures. Overall, there is both a descriptive and an analytical element to the book. The reader will be provided with information about the main institutions in the French political system. The reader will also be provided with an account of why these institutions exist and why they operate in the ways that they do.

The popular image of the Fifth Republic has been that of a State-centred, presidentialized, and highly centralized regime. The system was Statist in the sense that there was a widespread belief that change could only come about by way of the State and its structures. The system was presidentialized by virtue of the fact that the presidency was the focus of the political process and was deemed to be the only institution which could set the direction of change. The system was centralized on the grounds that the centre dominated the periphery both financially and legally with the effect that change could be implemented throughout the country as a whole. However, the popular image of the Fifth Republic was always somewhat misleading and now this is increasingly the case. The State system is compartmentalized, which diminishes its transformative capacity (see Chapter 3). There are countervailing powers within both the executive itself and the wider governmental and party political system that challenge the position of the presidency (see Chapter 4). There are strong sub-central pressures to which those at the centre have to respond (see Chapter 8). Thus, there are strong elements of institutional concentration in the system that have profound historical roots (see, for example, Chapter 6). At the same time, there are, and have always been, elements of institutional fragmentation which have been amplified by recent developments, such as the growth of the European Union (see particularly Chapters 1, 3, 5, 7, and 8) and the rise of the rule of law (see Chapter 7). Overall, the French system is one in which the myth of 'heroic' leadership remains a powerful mobilizing force, but where the capacity for central direction is increasingly constrained.

An institutional focus helps us to explain this situation. In recent years, institutions have become a particular subject of academic attention. Here, the term 'institution' refers to 'the formal rules, compliance procedures, and standard operating practices that structure the relationship between individuals in various units of the polity and the economy' (Hall 1986: 19). The so-called 'new institutionalism' (for example, March and Olsen 1984; Shepsle and Bonchek 1997) has stressed the importance of institutions and for two reasons. First, institutions are the product of political competition. For example, the Fifth Republic was itself the outcome of a political contest. The main actors in the Fourth Republic were unable to agree on a resolution to the problem in Algeria and the institutions of the Fourth Republic were unable to provide a context within which the Algerian problem could be resolved. As a result, the political class turned to General de Gaulle for leadership and the Constitution of the Fifth Republic was the product of this leadership (see Chapter 1). Thus, institutions are important because they reflect the outcomes of wider political struggles. Secondly, institutions are important because they help to shape these self-same struggles. Institutions provide the context in which some of the most important aspects of political competition take place. In particular, as one observer famously wrote, institutions affect both the degree of pressure that political actors can bring to bear on the decision-making process and the likely direction of that pressure (Hall 1986: 19). So, for example, once the institutions of the Fifth Republic were established, they provided a strategic context in which subsequent political competition was played out. In short, they established the rules of the game. Needless to say, the institutions of the 1958 regime have themselves been changed and amended over the years. Indeed, many of the chapters in this book outline the process and consequences of institutional change during this period. The fact remains, though, that in the period since 1958 political competition has been shaped by the individual and collective configuration of the institutions of the Fifth Republic. These are the reasons why political institutions are the main focus of this book.[1]

All the same, an exclusive focus on institutions can be misleading. It is a truism, but one that is sometimes overlooked by political scientists, that only actors act. Institutions do not. To put it another way, institutions do not make decisions. Only people make decisions. The decisions people make are influenced by the institutional context in which they find themselves (see above). Moreover, these decisions are shaped by the ideas, beliefs, and values that people hold (see below). However, we must not lose sight of the fact that people and their preferences should be a prime focus of political attention. This means that even though this is a book about political institutions, we need to concentrate on people, parties, and social movements when we want to provide an account of the role of institutions in the contemporary political system. Thus, it is important that we know something about the most important figures in French political life (see Chapter 1). Equally, it is important that we know the basic details of political parties, because parties remain the most important actors in the political system (see Chapter 2). In fact, throughout the course of this book we will see that party competition shapes the outcomes of the Fifth Republic's institutions in a very fundamental way. For example, we will see that presidential politics is conditioned by the nature of party political competition at any one time (see Chapter 4). We will find that the same is true for legislative politics. The National Assembly is a weak institution because political parties have no particular incentive for it to operate otherwise (see Chapter 6). We will also see that party forces use the judiciary to protect and promote their own interests (see Chapter 7). What all this means is that we can only fully understand the importance of political institutions if we focus on the interaction between actors, their preferences, and institutions.

At the same time, we also need to focus on the role of ideas in the political process. Actors are important because they have preferences. Politics is a complicated business because different people have different and competing preferences. In some types of studies, academics often treat these preferences as 'given'. In other words, it suits the purposes of certain writers to ignore the issue of why people think the things they do in order to concentrate on the task of determining what happens given that they think these things.[2] This approach has its place, but it leaves out a key aspect in the study of political life, namely why people have particular preferences in the first place. This book at least starts to address this question. It does so by examining the role of political ideas. Ideas help to constitute some of the most basic preferences of political actors in the system. Some ideas have very deep roots. These ideas help to establish a body of shared and often quasi-sacred political beliefs. In France, the idea of the Republic has this sort of status (see Chapter 1). The same is true for the idea of the State (see Chapter 3), the public service (see Chapters 3 and 5), and the equal provision of public service across the national territory (see Chapter 8). Thus, long-standing ideas are a source of institutional stability. By the same token, long-standing institutions are a source of ideational stability. In short, institutions and ideas can be mutually reinforcing. By contrast, other ideas are more ephemeral. They come and go. As the salience or understanding of ideas changes, institutional structures may also change (see above). In other words, even if institutions are 'sticky', ideational change can be a motor for institutional reform. In the context of this book, ideas such as new public management (see Chapters 3 and 5), the rule of law (Chapter 7), and decentralization (Chapter 8) have all become increasingly salient over time and have helped to bring about institutional change.

Against this background, the book is structured as follows. Chapters 1–3 inclusive set the scene. Chapter 1 provides information about the origins of the current political system, the Fifth Republic, and the politics of the regime since its creation in 1958. In so doing, this chapter helps to identify the key personalities, events, and ideas in contemporary French political life. Chapter 2 identifies the main political parties in the system and outlines the basic features of their historical development, organizational characteristics, and ideology. Chapter 3 examines the role of the State in French political life. In France, the State is more than just a collection of institutions. It is also a powerful mobilizing idea. This chapter identifies the institutional and ideational foundations of the State-centric model as well as the limitations to this model. In these ways, Chapters 1, 2, and 3 outline the general institutional, ideational, and party political situation in the Fifth Republic. By contrast, Chapters 4–8 inclusive focus on particular institutions. Chapter 4 examines the dual executive, outlining the role of the President and Prime Minister. Chapter 5 looks at the bureaucracy and the issue of technocracy. Chapter 6 focuses on the legislature and explains why the National Assembly and the Senate are so weak. Chapter 7 considers the changing role of the judiciary and the increasing importance of judicial politics. Chapter 8 addresses the topic of centre–periphery relations and the impact of recent decentralization reforms. Together, these chapters provide factual information about the main political institutions in the French system as well as an analysis of the way they operate in practice. Finally, the book concludes with a short chapter that summarizes the main themes of the text.

NOTES

1 In academic parlance, the new institutionalism treats institutions as both endogenous and exogenous (Carey 2000: 754–5). This is the equivalent to saying that new institutionalists focus on both equilibrium institutions and institutional equilibrium (Shepsle 1986).

2 For example, Shepsle and Bonchek (1997: 16–17) write: 'We do not pretend to know why people want what they want—we leave that to biologists, psychologists, and sociologists . . . For us, preferences are one of the givens of the situation . . . In short, we take people as we find them.'

1

The Origins and Politics of the Fifth Republic

Overview

This chapter provides a brief political history of the Fifth Republic. It begins by sketching the background to the 1958 regime, focusing on the Third Republic (1875–1940), the Vichy government (1940–4), the post-Liberation governments (1944–6), and the Fourth Republic (1946–58). It then introduces the political system of the Fifth Republic by examining the main events of the de Gaulle, Pompidou, Giscard, Mitterrand, and Chirac presidencies. This chronological approach helps to set the scene for the thematic approach that is adopted throughout the rest of the book. It also highlights the role of ideas in the political process. This issue is addressed in the conclusion.

Introduction

French history can be divided into two distinct periods: the period before the Revolution in 1789 and the period after it. In the post–1789 period, France has experienced no less than thirteen different Constitutions. That is to say, in slightly more than 200 years the French political system has been organized in thirteen often radically different ways—from absolute monarchy to liberal democratic republics, passing through empires, constitutional monarchies, autocracies, and absolute republics.[1] If this situation is compared with the situation in, for example, Britain or the United States, both of which have operated within a single constitutional system over a similar period of time, then the contrast between the instability of the French constitutional system and the stability of British and American systems is striking. Against this background, the Fifth French Republic stands out. The Fifth Republic was created in 1958. Although it is not yet the most long-lived constitutional arrangement in French political history and even though there continue to be calls for the creation of a Sixth Republic,[2] the Fifth Republic has provided considerable institutional stability for more than forty years now and it will probably prove strong enough to resist the calls for fundamental change at least for the foreseeable future. Even so, as we shall see, the Fifth Republic had a turbulent beginning and it continues to be the context in which dramatic political events occur. At no time was this point illustrated more clearly than in the events surrounding the 2002 presidential election. Thus, within the stable institutional framework that has existed since 1958, there has been and there continues to be political and institutional change.

The background to the Fifth Republic

The modern-day French political system is usually taken to begin in 1870 with the surrender of Louis-Napoléon Bonaparte, Bonaparte III, following French military defeats in the Franco-Prussian war. Although for the next few years the French political system was still in turmoil, this point marks the beginning of contemporary French politics. This is, first, because it represents the end of the Second Empire and, hence, at least the beginning of the end of bonapartist, plebiscitary politics and, secondly, because it was also the time when the monarchists finally proved to be too weak to regain power and restore a king to the throne. French history from 1789 to 1870 had seen a fairly regular alternation between republics, constitutional monarchies, and bonapartist empires. (see Box 1.1). In 1875, at the time of the effective creation of the Third Republic, hopes of reinstating the monarchy were dashed. In 1877, when a republican majority was returned following the premature dissolution of the legislature by the President of the Republic, a former bonapartist and monarchist sympathizer, Marshal MacMahon, hopes of another monarchical restoration disappeared altogether. In this sense, the early years of the Third Republic mark a watershed in French constitutional history in that they saw the basic acceptance of the republican form of government.

BOX 1.1	French constitutional regimes, 1789–2002
1789–91	Constituent Assembly
1791–2	Legislative Assembly (limited monarchy)
1793–4	The Convention (authoritarian Republic–Constitution never applied)
1795–9	The Directory (pluralist Republic)
1799–1814	The Consulate and the Empire (bonapartist authoritarianism)
1815–30	The Restoration (limited monarchy)
1830–48	The July monarchy (limited monarchy)
1848–51	The Second Republic (pluralist Republic)
1852–70	The Second Empire (bonapartist authoritarianism)
1870–5	Provisional governments (pluralist Republic)
1875–1940	The Third Republic (pluralist Republic)
1940–4	The Vichy regime (authoritarian State)
1945–58	The Fourth Republic (pluralist Republic)
1958–	The Fifth Republic (pluralist Republic)

That said, the history of the Third Republic was far from glorious. True, it lasted until 1940. As such, it holds the record for being the most long-lived of all the post-revolutionary political regimes in France to date. Even so, its sixty-five-year history was punctuated by a series of crises and scandals. The early years of the regime were marked by threats to the very existence of the Republic itself. For example, in 1888–9 there was a fear that a populist general, Georges Ernest Boulanger, would win power and install a pseudo-bonapartist regime. Ultimately, though, these fears were unfounded and the rule of law prevailed. Boulanger fled, leaving his supporters embarrassed and leaderless. More importantly, in the period 1894–9 the Dreyfus affair split the country. A Jewish army officer, Captain Alfred Dreyfus, was accused of espionage. He was entirely innocent, but he was convicted. The importance of the subsequent campaign for his release went far beyond the issue of whether or not Dreyfus was really guilty. The anti-Dreyfusards believed that the country was threatened by anti-national forces, including Jews, freemasons, and the left generally. Those who supported Dreyfus feared that the Republic was in danger from a mixture of the army, the Church, and anti-Semites. In the end, Dreyfus was pardoned. The Republic survived and was perhaps even strengthened by the affair.

Thereafter, the politics of the Republic were increasingly marked by the confrontation between the left and the right over economic issues. On the left, there was a sense that the forces of capital, or the 'wall of money', would never let a democratically elected left-wing government legislate freely. On the right, there was the feeling not only that the left was not competent to govern, but also that its policies threatened the basic economic and financial interests of the country. For example, in 1924 a centre-left government was elected, the so-called 'Cartel des gauches'. In fact, the government was only mildly reformist. However, the business class reacted unfavourably and the Prime Minister, Édouard Herriot, soon resigned in the face of an increasingly difficult financial situation. Similarly, in 1936 the Popular Front government was elected. The government was a coalition of Socialists and radicals with the communists supporting the coalition in parliament. This time, the government, under the leadership of Léon Blum, did pass a number of important reforms. There were wage increases, the introduction of a maximum 40-hour working week, and the right to two weeks' paid holiday per year, the structures of the Bank of France were democratized, and the nationalization of the railway system was prepared. However, once again, the government quickly experienced severe economic problems. In June 1937, little more than a year after coming to power, Blum stepped down. In this way, the Popular Front experiment merely reinforced the entrenched attitudes of both the left and the right regarding the prospects for governance under the Third Republic.

In fact, the fate of the Third Republic was sealed soon after. In 1940 the parliamentarians of the Third Republic capitulated ignominiously in the face of the Nazi threat. In July of that year, following the rapid advance of Hitler's troops through France, the Third Republic's parliament voted itself out of existence. The Republic was dissolved and full powers were given to a former First World War military hero, Marshal Philippe Pétain, as the leader of the French State. Only 80 parliamentarians voted against Pétain, while 569 voted in favour. The government was sited at Vichy and had unequivocally fascist overtones. It established what it called a New Order. It replaced the revolutionary motto 'Liberty, Equality, Fraternity' with a new slogan 'Work, Family, Fatherland'. Only officially sanctioned social groups were allowed to work with the government in a corporatist-style arrangement. Political opponents were arrested, while political parties and free trade unions were abolished. Worst of all, Vichy officials implemented Nazi deportation policies, rounding up French Jews and sending them to concentration camps in Eastern Europe.

Thankfully, the Vichy regime lasted only a short period of time. In

August 1944, Paris was liberated by the Allies and the French leader in exile, General Charles de Gaulle, returned to head a provisional government. The post-Liberation governments mainly comprised communists, Socialists, gaullists, and social Catholics, who soon formed the Christian Democratic party (Mouvement républicain populaire, MRP). These governments passed a series of important reforms. For example, women were given the right to vote. The elite administrative training school, ENA, was created to train future generations of technocrats (see Chapter 5). A number of key industries and firms were nationalized. These included the Bank of France, the coal, gas, and electricity industries, the car manufacturer Renault, as well as a range of credit and insurance companies (see Chapter 3). Also, the tradition of State economic planning was introduced and the growth of the French economy in the post-war years is usually accredited to the series of five-year plans that began at this time. This involved the State, through the office of the Planning Commission, identifying the immediate economic needs of the country and organizing economic policy to meet those needs.

In addition to the economic and social reconstruction of the country, the post-Liberation governments had to reconstitute the political system. In this context, one point on which everyone could agree was that there should be no return to the Third Republic. In October 1945 this proposition was overwhelmingly approved by the people in a referendum (see Table 1.1). Instead, the election of a Constituent Assembly was approved and it was given the task of drawing up a Constitution for a new Republic, the Fourth Republic. This task, though, proved to be very difficult. There was fundamental disagreement about some of the most basic principles on which the Constitution was to be founded. In short, de Gaulle wanted strong presidential leadership, whereas the other parties wanted a parliamentary regime. Among the latter, the communists and to a lesser degree the Socialists wanted a strong parliament, whereas the other forces preferred a more balanced relationship between the executive and the legislature. In January 1946 de Gaulle resigned as head of government, when it became clear that his proposals would be rejected. In May 1946 a draft Constitution, which was backed by the communists and the Socialists, was defeated in a referendums. As a result, in June 1946 a second Constituent Assembly was elected. In October of that year a second draft Constitution, which was the result of a compromise between the Socialists and the MRP

TABLE 1.1	Referendums in France, 1945–1946 (%)			
Date	Issue	Yes	No	Turnout
21 Oct. 1945	End of the Third Republic	96.4	3.6	79.1
21 Oct. 1945	Approve a Constituent Assembly and referendum on a new Constitution	66.5	33.5	79.1
5 May 1946	Approve draft of new Constitution	47.2	52.8	79.6
13 Oct. 1946	Approve draft of new Constitution	53.2	46.8	67.6

Source: Morel (1996: 71).

and which was opposed by the communists, was put to a referendum and was approved, but only just. The process had been difficult but the Fourth Republic could begin.

The Fourth Republic was one of the most short-lived and unloved of all the country's post-revolutionary regimes. In fact, there was a great deal of progress under the Fourth Republic. Most notably, there was strong economic growth. By 1958, GDP had grown by 33 per cent since 1951 and industrial production had increased by no less than 54 per cent (Sowerwine 2001: 275). There were social advances too. The number of annual weeks' paid holiday was increased from two to three and a universal pension scheme was established. French officials also played a key role in the development of the European Economic Communities (EEC) and the Treaty of Rome was signed in 1957.

All the same, the Fourth Republic faced a number of problems. First, powerful political forces were opposed to the very existence of the regime. For example, the communists, who had been in government 1944–7, were now out in the cold. They were opposed not just to the Constitution of the Fourth Republic, but to the system itself, denouncing it as a capitalist regime. The gaullists, too, were hostile to the system. More accurately, de Gaulle was implacably opposed to the assembly-dominated structure of the Republic and withdrew from the political process altogether. Also, the extreme right re-emerged (see Chapter 2). In January 1956 the *poujadistes*, so called because they were led by Pierre Poujade, won 11.6 per cent of the vote. The *poujadistes* were an anti-system party that included among their number Jean-Marie Le Pen, the current leader of the extreme right-wing National Front party. All told, there were powerful anti-system forces.

Secondly, the country's political institutions were criticized. In particular, there was a lack of political leadership. The President was a figurehead with no powers and Prime Ministers were reliant for their survival in office on highly unstable majorities in the National Assembly. In total, there were twenty-five different governments and fifteen different Prime Ministers in the period 1946–58. Only two heads of government held office for more than a full year and in 1948 one government held office for just two days before it was brought down. In addition, parliament had considerable law-making capabilities. There were two working chambers of parliament, the National Assembly and the upper house or Council of the Republic, and parliamentary committees were extremely strong. In short, for governments, just surviving was difficult and passing meaningful legislation was scarcely any easier. Thirdly, and most importantly, political leaders were faced with the issue of decolonization. In the early 1950s there was a war in Indo-China (the future North and South Vietnam) that the French effectively lost. The fact that the war was fought at all was criticized by some. The fact that it was lost was traumatic for others. In 1956, Morocco and Tunisia were both given their independence, without war but still with a great deal of resentment both within France and outside. The real problem, though, was Algeria. At that time, Algeria was a department of France (the administrative equivalent of a British county). By 1954, the nationalist movement in Algeria had reached the conclusion that only force would bring about independence. However, there were around a million expatriate settlers who shared the idea that Algeria was an integral part of France and that it should remain so. These people had seen that independence had been granted to colonies elsewhere and had come to the belief that the governments of the Fourth Republic were not to be trusted. These attitudes were present on mainland France as well. The result was an armed conflict between Algerian nationalists and the French army as well as the very real threat of a *coup d'état* in France by people who wanted Algeria to remain French.

By May 1958, the prospect of military rule and/or civil war seemed very close. The governments of the Fourth Republic no longer appeared able to cope with the crisis. On 13 May there was a *coup d'état* in Algeria and generals loyal to Algeria remaining French took power. On 24 May the rebellion spread to Corsica. On 29 May the President of the Fourth Republic, René Coty, called upon General de Gaulle to return to politics as Prime

Minister. De Gaulle accepted on condition that he would be given full powers for a period of six months and that he would oversee the creation of a new Republic, the Fifth Republic. On 3 June parliament in effect approved these terms. Following numerous meetings between de Gaulle and his key advisers, most notably Michel Debré, a draft Constitution was ready by 29 July. Following some minor amendments, the draft was agreed by the government on 3 September. A referendum took place on 28 September and the new Constitution was overwhelmingly approved. On 4 October 1958 the Fifth Republic came into being.

The Fifth Republic

Charles de Gaulle: the founding father (1958–1969)

In May 1958 Charles de Gaulle was the natural person to call upon to constitute a new regime as he had the greatest political standing of anyone in the country. His authority was derived from several sources. First, in the 1930s he had opposed official government policy and argued that the country should prepare for war against Germany by rearming massively, especially by investing in tanks. In retrospect, following the debacle of France's defeat in 1940, he was proven to be right. As such, de Gaulle was seen as someone who might have prevented defeat and national humiliation in 1940 and who might be able to prevent a new defeat in Algeria as well as a civil war in France in 1958. Secondly, de Gaulle was the Leader of the Free French forces during the Second World War and was recognized by the Allied leaders, albeit somewhat reluctantly (certainly by the Americans), as the overall head of the French resistance movement. He set up a French government in exile and reorganized what remained of the Free French forces with the aim of retaking the country again when the occasion arose. Therefore, he was a war hero in his own right. Thirdly, the General was untainted by the failures of the Fourth Republic. As noted above, he had withdrawn from the Liberation government in January 1946 and he had played no further part in any of the governments of the Fourth Republic. As a result, he was not seen to be responsible for any of the Republic's failures. Fourthly, and perhaps most importantly, de Gaulle had the support of much of the army. As a result, the threat of a *coup d'état* receded. All told, as a general, de Gaulle had the support of the pro-French Algeria lobby and, as someone who might be able to prevent a military takeover, he had at least the conditional support of the political class generally.

The General, though, was not just a military man. He was also a man of ideas and he had a vision of how the new Republic should be organized and how its Constitution should be worded. De Gaulle argued that the Third and Fourth Republics had failed because they were too dominated by political parties. He believed that parties necessarily acted in their own interests and not in the national interest. This was a classical republican vision of the French national interest (see Chapter 3). Moreover, de Gaulle believed that the political institutions of the previous republics had merely encouraged the role of political parties. The new Republic, de Gaulle believed, had to put a stop to this practice. To this end, the General's main aim was to establish a strong presidency. The President, de Gaulle believed, should be the incarnation of the national interest, providing the means by which French national grandeur could be restored. At the same time, de Gaulle also wanted to strengthen the role of the Prime Minister and the government at the expense of parliament. The Prime Minister should be free to carry out the job of governing the country. The legislature, the playground of political parties with their petty bickering and point-scoring so he argued, had to be tamed.

The Constitution of the Fifth Republic reflected these basic principles. In essence, the Constitution established a hybrid system. The President and the Prime Minister were both given certain independent powers (see Chapter 4). The President, who was elected by a college of local notables and who was secure in office for seven years, was responsible for high politics—defence, foreign affairs, and the respect for constitutional authority. The Prime Minister, who would be appointed by the President but who remained responsible to an albeit much less powerful National Assembly, was charged with the day-to-day running of the country. Given his constitutional principles, it was no surprise when in December 1958 de Gaulle stood for election as President of the Republic. He saw himself as the person whose destiny was to lead France back to greatness and what he considered to be the country's appropriate place in the world. The General was triumphant. In the Fifth Republic's first presidential election on 21 December 1958, de Gaulle received 62,394 electoral college votes. His main opponent, Georges Marrane, the PCF candidate, received only 10,355 votes and Albert Chatelet, the candidate of the non-communist left, received just 6,721 votes. On 8 January 1959 de Gaulle officially assumed office and the next day he appointed his first Prime Minister, Michel Debré. (For a list of Presidents and Prime Ministers since 1959, see Table 1.2).

Once elected, de Gaulle's main priority was the Algerian crisis. There is still a debate as to whether de Gaulle came to power with the unspoken intention of giving Algeria its independence, knowing that this was the only way to end the war, or whether he decided that this was the proper course of action when he was in office. Whichever version of events is correct, he soon articulated this policy publicly. On 16 September 1959 de Gaulle declared that Algeria would be given the right to self-determination. In so doing, he angered the most senior ranks of the army and the French settlers in Algeria who believed that they had been abandoned. On 24 January 1960 the situation in Algeria boiled over. Generals loyal to *l'Algérie française* tried to seize power. They failed, but the event

TABLE 1.2	Presidents and Prime Ministers in the Fifth Republic (1959–2002)	
President	**Prime Minister**
Charles de Gaulle, 1959–69 (gaullist)	Michel Debré, 1959–62 (gaullist)
	Georges Pompidou, 1962–8 (gaullist)
	Maurice Couve de Murville, 1968–9 (gaullist)
Georges Pompidou, 1969–74 (gaullist)	Jacques Chaban-Delmas, 1969–72 (gaullist)
	Pierre Messmer, 1972–4 (gaullist)
Valéry Giscard d'Estaing, 1974–81 (centre-right liberal)	Jacques Chirac, 1974–6 (gaullist)
	Raymond Barre, 1976–81 (centre-right, but no official party affiliation)
François Mitterrand, 1981–95 (Socialist)	Pierre Mauroy, 1981–4 (Socialist)
	Laurent Fabius, 1984–6 (Socialist)
	Jacques Chirac, 1986–8 (gaullist)
	Michel Rocard, 1988–91 (Socialist)
	Edith Cresson, 1991–2 (Socialist)
	Pierre Bérégovoy, 1992–3 (Socialist)
	Édouard Balladur, 1993–5 (gaullist)
Jacques Chirac, 1995– (gaullist)	Alain Juppé, 1995–7 (gaullist)
	Lionel Jospin, 1997–2002 (Socialist)
	Jean-Pierre Raffarin, 2002– (centre-right)

was significant. When de Gaulle denounced the insurrection, he showed that he supported the rule of law and that he was serious about his policy of self-determination. There was no going back. In France both support for de Gaulle and condemnation of the rebel generals were overwhelming. The tide had changed. The threat of civil war had disappeared. Algerian independence was now merely a matter of time. On 8 January 1960 the French massively approved the policy of self-determination in a referendum (see Table 4.1). On 22 April 1961 there was a *coup d'état* in Algiers and this time the generals took power. De Gaulle immediately assumed emergency powers and the rebellion did not last long (see Chapter 4). Finally, on 8 April 1962 the French overwhelmingly supported a further referendum that agreed the terms of Algerian independence. To all intents and purposes, the Algerian problem had been resolved. This is not to say that the issue was completely closed. On 22 August 1962 de Gaulle was nearly assassinated by French Algerian rebels and anti-gaullist hostility lingers on to this day amongst a certain section of the population, particularly on the extreme right, who feel that they or others were betrayed by the General. It is merely to say that the 'normal' business of democratic politics could resume.

In the period 1958–62, the day-to-day business of government was run by the Prime Minister. Debré was an interventionist head of government who headed a reformist administration. For example, the country's economic situation was stabilized with the so-called Pinay-Rueff Plan and important legislation was passed in areas such as education. However, Debré wanted Algeria to remain French. Consequently, when de Gaulle announced the policy of Algerian self-determination, Debré's political position was undermined. In this context, the fact that he chose to remain in office at all was testimony to his loyalty to de Gaulle and his desire to avoid any further institutional crises at such a delicate time. All the same, in April 1962, when the Algerian issue was finally resolved, Debré resigned. He was replaced by Georges Pompidou. At the time, Pompidou was largely unknown to the general public. He had been a loyal gaullist supporter and adviser for a long time. However, he had pursued a career in banking and was not part of the established political class. This, in some respects, was an advantage and Pompidou still holds the record for being the longest-serving Prime Minister under the Fifth Republic.

In the early years of his presidency, de Gaulle largely confined himself to foreign and defence policy and the Algerian war. Indeed, throughout his presidency foreign affairs was a major preoccupation. Once the Algerian problem was resolved, though, de Gaulle turned his attentions to domestic policy as well, intervening closely in the areas of economic, cultural, and local government policy amongst others. De Gaulle was a very inter-ventionist President and his impact upon the French political system can hardly be overestimated. He created the expectation that there should be presidential leadership in France. In this context, de Gaulle believed that even if he was able to exercise strong leadership, because of his wartime record and his triumphal return to power in 1958, those who followed him as President would not be able to do so as things stood. For de Gaulle, only a constitutional amendment would secure presidential leadership. This amendment would replace the election of the President by an electoral college with the direct election of the President by universal suffrage as in the USA. After the failed assassination attempt in August 1962, de Gaulle took steps to bring about this change. In October 1962, an amendment to reform the Constitution was overwhelmingly approved in a referendum (see Table 4.1). In retrospect, this was a turning point in the French pol-itical system. It marked the end of the debate over whether France should have a presidential or a parliamentary system. It also marked the high point of de Gaulle's presidential career. He was popular, the Algerian problem was resolved, presidential authority was secure and, following the National Assembly elections in November of that year, both the government and parliament were controlled by the gaullists.

Things could only go wrong. The first sign of trouble was in 1965. At that time, the presidential term of office was seven years. So, the second presi-dential election in the Fifth Republic, the first by universal suffrage, was held in 1965. Initially, everyone expected de Gaulle to win easily. However, in the end he was run quite close by a Socialist and former Fourth Republic Minister, François Mitterrand (see Table 1.3). The General was expected to win more than 50 per cent of the vote at the first ballot. In this case, he would have been elected without the need for a second ballot. However, he failed to do so and, at the second ballot, where the top two candidates of the first ballot compete against each other, de Gaulle defeated Mitterrand by 55.2 per cent to 44.8 per cent, still a wide margin but nonetheless a much smaller one than many people had initially predicted. Then, in May 1968, the stability of the regime and the authority of both the President and the

TABLE 1.3	The presidential election of 5 and 19 December 1965 (%)	
	First round	Second round
Charles de Gaulle (gaullist)	44.65	55.20
François Mitterrand (Socialist)	31.79	44.80
Jean Lecanuet (centrist)	15.57	
Jean-Louis Tixier-Vignancour (extreme-right)	5.20	
Pierre Marcilhacy (independent)	1.71	
Marcel Barbu (independent)	1.15	

government were called into question by a wave of unrest. Students and workers demonstrated, sometimes violently, against the system and the government. At one point, de Gaulle thought about calling in the army to stop the strikes by force. But, wisely, he decided not to. Although agreement between the protesters and the government was soon reached, the impact of the events of May 1968 was profound. They were a reflection of the changing nature of French society. Increasingly, people were concerned with issues of citizenship and self-expression, rather than institutional or personal security matters. Moreover, even though the gaullists won a crushing majority in the June 1968 National Assembly elections, for a growing proportion of the electorate de Gaulle himself was increasingly seen as a figure from the past, holding up social and political change. Finally, in April 1969 and against the advice of his closest collaborators, de Gaulle organized a referendum to reform the structure of local government and the Senate. He called the referendum in order to restore his flagging popular authority. He believed that, if he won, then his legitimacy would be restored, and he announced that if he lost, then he would resign. This was the same tactic that he had used in previous referendums. This time, though, it backfired. The proposal was defeated and, true to his word, de Gaulle resigned immediately, playing no further part in politics. He died in 1971.

Georges Pompidou: the short presidency (1969–1974)

The resignation of de Gaulle meant that an early presidential election had to be held. There is no Vice-President in the French system and when the presidency is vacant the President of the Senate merely deputizes on an interim basis (see Chapter 6). The 1969 presidential election was an unusual affair. The communists did very well on the first ballot and the Socialists were trounced. The overwhelming favourite and the eventual winner was Georges Pompidou (see Table 1.4). Little more than a year earlier Pompidou had in effect been sacked as Prime Minister by de Gaulle when he dared to suggest that he might be presidential material himself. With the General's abrupt resignation, the way was now clear for Pompidou to take up the mantle. At the second ballot of the election, Pompidou easily defeated the centre-right candidate, Alain Poher, in a contest that scarcely fired the public's imagination, so similar were the candidates' visions of the country.

The Pompidou presidency was marked by the continuation of presidential supremacy and problems of domestic policy reform. As noted above, Pompidou was a gaullist and he had been de Gaulle's Prime Minister for six years. As a result, he had basically the same vision of the country as the General and he certainly had the same vision of the presidency. So, for example, Pompidou continued to exercise the same level of control over foreign and defence policy as de Gaulle had done previously. It was Pompidou personally who, in 1969, reversed his predecessor's decision and lifted France's veto on Britain's entry to the Common Market. Similarly, in economic affairs, Pompidou, as an ex-banker, was well placed to take decisions himself and, in 1969, decided that the franc had to be devalued. In short, there was little change in the style of government during the Pompidou years. The same was true for the content of policy, but here there was a problem. Pompidou was a conservative. He was wary of change. By contrast, France was undergoing a period of profound social

TABLE 1.4	The presidential election of 1 and 15 June 1969 (%)	
	First round	Second round
Georges Pompidou (gaullist)	44.47	58.21
Alain Poher (centre-right)	23.31	41.79
Jacques Duclos (communist)	21.27	
Gaston Defferre (Socialist)	5.01	
Michel Rocard (unified Socialist)	3.61	
Louis Ducatel (independent)	1.27	
Alain Krivine (extreme-left)	1.06	

transformation and there were demands for reform. Pompidou responded to these demands by appointing Jacques Chaban-Delmas as Prime Minister. Chaban was a long-time gaullist. However, he had the reputation of wanting to introduce major changes to the French system of government. He called these changes the 'New Society' reforms. A number of reforms were passed. For example, there was the beginning of regional government (see Chapter 8) and there was a reorganization of the State-controlled media. However, conflict between the President and the Prime Minister soon came to a head. In July 1972 Pompidou effectively sacked Chaban and replaced him with a loyal subordinate, Pierre Messmer (see Chapter 4). Presidential supremacy was reasserted, but the reform process stalled.

In fact, Pompidou's main problem was that he was not de Gaulle. Much as Pompidou tried to recreate the same popularity for himself as de Gaulle had enjoyed, he was unable to do so. For many people, de Gaulle was a charismatic leader. Pompidou was not. Although he enjoyed the legitimacy of being directly elected by the people in 1969, he did not have the same sort of political authority as the General previously. The gaullist party was loyal to de Gaulle and not to Pompidou. The party never showed the same sort of allegiance to Pompidou as it had to the General. Pompidou was simply de Gaulle's successor. True, he was one of the most senior people in the gaullist party, but there were other figures who challenged his position and Chaban-Delmas was one of those people. Therefore, when Pompidou sacked Chaban it was more a sign of weakness than strength. In fact, Chaban's departure marked the beginning of the end of the Pompidou presidency in more ways than one. Through the course of 1973 it became clear that the President was ill and he died in April 1974.

Valéry Giscard d'Estaing: the single-term presidency (1974–1981)

The 1974 presidential election was very different from the contest five years earlier. This time the left was a real force. The communists and the Socialists fielded a common candidate at the first ballot, François Mitterrand, who campaigned on what would today be considered a radical left-wing programme of nationalizations and State-centred economic planning. The gaullist candidate was Chaban. However, his campaign was undermined by the fact that a section of the gaullist party refused to support him. In particular, certain Pompidou loyalists, led by Jacques Chirac, opted to support the centre-right candidate and former Finance Minister, Valéry Giscard d'Estaing. At the first ballot, Mitterrand was well ahead of everyone else, while Giscard easily outpaced Chaban. At the second ballot, though, it proved difficult for the left to win the support of floating, centrist voters. As a result, Giscard sneaked home, winning by the smallest of margins (see Table 1.5).

For many people, Giscard's election represented a new start. From 1958 to 1974 the regime had been dominated by two gaullist patriarchs, the General himself and Pompidou. Giscard, though, represented something different. First, although he had been a government Minister since the early 1960s, at the age of 49 he was still young. Secondly, he was not a gaullist, but a centre-right liberal. Thirdly, he had campaigned at the presidential election on a reformist platform, promising to change society and create a modern France. All told, after sixteen years of gaullist rule, there was a feeling that the system was on the point of renewal and public expectations were high. To a degree, these expectations were met. The beginning of Giscard's presidency saw a number of policy changes. For example, the minimum voting age was reduced to 18; there was a liberalization of both the abortion and divorce laws; the country's television and radio systems were also reformed; there were constitutional changes so as to allow the Constitutional Council to play a fuller role (see Chapter 7); finally, there was a pronounced Europeanization of the policy process, with

TABLE 1.5	The presidential election of 5 and 19 May 1974 (%)	
	First round	Second round
Valéry Giscard d'Estaing (centre-right)	32.60	50.81
François Mitterrand (Socialist)	43.25	49.19
Jacques Chaban-Delmas (gaullist)	15.11	
Jean Royer (right)	3.17	
Arlette Laguiller (extreme-left)	2.33	
René Dumont (ecologist)	1.32	
Jean-Marie Le Pen (extreme-right)	0.75	
Emile Muller (social democrat)	0.69	
Alain Krivine (extreme-left)	0.37	
Bertrand Renouvin (monarchist)	0.17	
Jean-Claude Sebag (federalist)	0.16	
Guy Héraud (federalist)	0.08	

Giscard being instrumental in the decision to introduce direct elections to the European Parliament.

However, the hopes that people had entertained at the start of Giscard's term in office gradually disappeared. The beginning of the Giscard presidency coincided with the oil price rises of the mid-1970s. At the time, France was heavily dependent on foreign energy resources. Consequently, the cost of industrial production increased rapidly. This had severe consequences for inflation, the value of the franc, interest rates, and the budget deficit. While it is a moot point as to whether the left would have fared any better or, indeed, much worse, the fact remains that public confidence in Giscard's management of the economy declined. In addition, Giscard's political situation was deteriorating. In 1974, he appointed Jacques Chirac as Prime Minister, a reward for the latter's act of electoral *lèse-majesté* in regard to Chaban. However, the relationship between Giscard and Chirac was difficult. The President made it clear that he was in charge of the government's policy-making agenda. Soon Chirac objected, and in August 1976 he resigned. In his place, the President appointed Raymond Barre, who could at least be relied upon to be loyal. However, Chirac had his sights set on the next presidential election. As a result, even though the government was a coalition of gaullists and centre-right *giscardiens*, there was trench warfare between the two groups for the next five years. This damaged the right as a whole and it certainly weakened Giscard's position (see Chapter 4). Worse still, some of the laws that were passed towards the end of Giscard's term in office seemed to betray the spirit that had been present immediately after his election. In particular, there was the infamous *Sécurité et Liberté* reform of 1980, which increased the powers of the police and appeared excessively repressive. Finally, Giscard's personal reputation was tainted because of various scandals with which either he personally, or his government, was associated. A government Minister, Robert Boulin, apparently committed suicide in mysterious circumstances. Giscard himself was accused of having received a host of diamonds from the dictator and then self-proclaimed Emperor of the Central African Republic, Jean-Bedel Bokassa, presumably in return for some sort of political favour. The allegations were never corroborated, but the political mud stuck.

In this context, the country went to the polls. In contrast to 1974, the left was divided. However, the Socialists, for the third time in the form of

François Mitterrand, were now dominant and the communists were left trailing far behind. The right was also divided. Once again, though, Giscard, who had built an efficient electoral machine in the form of the Union for French Democracy, outdistanced the gaullist candidate, Jacques Chirac. Thus, the second ballot pitted the same two candidates against each other as in 1974 and, as before, the result was extremely close. On this occasion, though, the left won (see Table 1.6). The economic situation clearly cost Giscard dearly. More than that, the political situation had changed. It was easier now for Mitterrand to win the support of undecided, centrist voters. The communists were no longer a serious threat and Mitterrand had toned down some of his left-wing rhetoric. Just as importantly, Chirac committed another act of electoral treachery. Immediately prior to the second ballot, he announced that personally he would vote for Giscard, but he gave the impression to his gaullist supporters that they should not necessarily feel obliged to do so themselves. By itself, this pronouncement may not have changed the course of the election. However, it certainly did not help the President's cause. Giscard was defeated and, to this day, he continues to nurse a grudge against his former Prime Minister.

François Mitterrand: the long presidency (1981–1995)

The feeling in the period immediately following Mitterrand's election was one of euphoria. The left was in power for the first time since 1958 and there were great celebrations. One of Mitterrand's first acts was to dissolve

TABLE 1.6	The presidential election of 26 April and 10 May 1981 (%)	
	First round	Second round
François Mitterrand (Socialist)	25.85	51.76
Valéry Giscard d'Estaing (centre-right)	28.32	48.24
Jacques Chirac (gaullist)	18.00	
Georges Marchais (communist)	15.35	
Brice Lalonde (ecologist)	3.88	
Arlette Laguiller (extreme-left)	2.30	
Michel Crépeau (left-radical)	2.21	
Michel Debré (gaullist)	1.66	
Marie-France Garaud (gaullist)	1.33	
Huguette Bouchardeau (unified Socialist)	1.11	

the National Assembly. In the ensuing election in June, the Socialists were triumphant once again. Despite their own relatively poor electoral showing in the presidential election and despite pressure from the newly elected Reagan administration in the USA, for the first time since 1947 communist Ministers were appointed to the government. This was a reward for supporting Mitterrand at the second ballot of the election. The communists held four relatively minor posts in the government, Transport, Public Service and Administrative Reforms, Health, and Training.

The first year of the new government saw the passage of a number of significant reforms. For example, in the field of civil liberties, the death penalty was abolished along with the Court of State Security. In terms of centre–periphery relations, greater responsibilities were given to locally elected representatives and the powers of State officials at the sub-national level were reduced (see Chapter 8). Social reform measures included a reduction in the working week to 39 hours without a loss of salary, the introduction of a fifth week of paid holiday, and an increase in the level of the minimum wage. The rights of individuals in the workplace were also reformed. In the economic sphere, the government embarked upon an increase in public spending equivalent to 0.5 per cent of gross national product (GNP). Over 100,000 jobs in the public sector were created. There were also increases in the basic rates of income tax, and a new wealth tax was introduced. Perhaps most strikingly, a comprehensive programme of nationalizations was instigated. A total of eleven industrial groups, thirty-six banks, and two finance companies were nationalized. What is more, with the exception of Dassault and Matra, the State took a 100 per cent stake in all of the newly nationalized companies (see Chapter 3).

The reformist zeal of the newly elected government was evident. However, there were problems. The 1981 reflation had resulted in a growing balance of trade gap, a large budget deficit, and an increasingly uncompetitive rate of inflation when compared with France's main trading partner, Germany. To remedy this situation, the French government sought a realignment of the exchange-rate parities of the European Monetary System (EMS). In October 1981 the franc was devalued for the first time. In June 1982, there was another devaluation. This time, the franc was devalued by 5.75 per cent and the mark was revalued by 4.25 per cent, and on this occasion there was also a prices and wages freeze and supply-side measures designed to encourage investment. However, the key economic indicators failed to improve. Consequently, a further devaluation was agreed upon in March 1983. On this occasion, the franc was devalued by 2.5 per cent, the mark was revalued by 5.5 per cent, and the French government was obliged to adopt a much harsher dose of financial austerity than before. In the space of slightly less than two years the government had made a complete 180-degree U-turn in its economic policy.

Even at the time, it was clear the March 1983 devaluation was a key turning point for the left. Previously, the left had contented itself with the idea that its reforms would have been successful if it were not for the pernicious influence of the 'wall of money' (see above). In 1983, similar arguments were heard. This time, the blame was laid at the door of international capital. France had reflated at a time when other countries, most notably the United States (USA) and Britain, were in the grip of neo-liberal economics with Reagan and Thatcher respectively at their strongest. Thus, it was not France's fault or the Socialists' fault that there were economic difficulties, so the argument went, but the fault of foreign right-wing governments. Moreover, the EMS, it was argued by some, was a further part of the problem. The franc, they suggested, should be allowed to float freely. If it were permitted to do so, then the government's reflationary policy would succeed. For a period in March 1983 President Mitterrand was clearly tempted by this line of reasoning. In the end, though, he rejected it. Mitterrand chose to keep the franc in the EMS. In so doing, he made the strategic and historic decision that France's future lay in Europe. The importance of this decision can hardly be overestimated. From this point on, Socialist governments abandoned any pretence that the capitalist system could be revolutionized, or even fundamentally reformed. Instead, they were committed to the careful management of its exchange rate (later to be known as 'le franc fort'), even if such a policy meant that there had to be reductions in public spending and increased social security contributions in order to try and balance the state budgets. More than that, the importance of the 1983 devaluation also lay in the fact that France was unequivocally committed to the policy of European integration, and Mitterrand personally championed this policy for the remainder of his time in office.

In the event, the austerity programme did little to revive the government's fortunes as the level of unemployment continued to increase and the economic gloom failed to lift. In addition, the government was hit by a further crisis in the spring of 1984 when it tried to reform the education system. The Education Minister, Alain Savary, proposed to reduce the subsidy that the State gave to private schools, something which in many cases threatened their existence. As most private schools in France are Catholic schools, this reform was seen by both the opposition and the public as being an attack on the Catholic Church. Over one million people demonstrated in Paris against the reform. Faced with this opposition, Mitterrand decided to drop the bill, even though he was sure that this would provoke the resignation of Savary and Mauroy. He was right. Following Mauroy's departure, Mitterrand appointed Laurent Fabius, a young Socialist technocrat and former Budget Minister. It was, however, too late. The communists took the opportunity to leave the government. Their support was falling and the party's strategists assumed that this was because they were being blamed for the economic problems with which the government was associated. They were partly right, but the reasons for the communists' decline were much more complex and intractable. Even though Fabius was relatively popular, the Socialists were still in difficulty. At the March 1986 parliamentary elections the right-wing coalition won, but with a majority of only three seats in the National Assembly.

The 1986 election brought about a new situation: cohabitation (see Chapter 4). The hybrid nature of the Fifth Republic means that presidential government is dependent upon the President's ability to appoint a loyal Prime Minister who has the backing of the majority in the National Assembly. After the 1986 elections, the left-wing President was faced with a right-wing majority. Consequently, Mitterrand had to appoint someone who could command the support of this majority. He appointed Jacques Chirac, the leader of the gaullists. To the extent that the Constitution indicates that the Prime Minister is responsible for the day-to-day running of the country, cohabitation meant that for the first time in the history of the Fifth Republic the Prime Minister was in full control of policy-making. The President was only able to intervene sporadically in foreign and defence matters, although he still represented France, often with Chirac alongside him, at summit meetings. There were those, such as former Prime Minister Raymond Barre, who argued that cohabitation undermined the very foundations of the Fifth Republic. Moreover, the relationship between Mitterrand and Chirac was difficult. Both wanted to stand at the 1988 presidential election and neither wanted the other to gain the political upper hand. The public, though, seemed to approve of cohabit-ation, and the opinion poll ratings for both the President and the Prime Minister were strong.

The incoming government tried to mimic their British and American counterparts. They cut taxes, embarked upon a process of privatization (see Chapter 3), made it easier for firms to make workers redundant, and liberalized price controls. In short, they extolled the virtues of the market and criticized the role of the State. At first, the policies were popular. However, soon problems started to appear. The stock market crash in 1987 effectively put an end to the programme of privatization. A number of reforms, such as the privatization of prisons and a strict immigration bill, proved to be unpopular and were dropped. Mitterrand's popularity, by contrast, continued to increase. Because of his opposition to the govern-ment's policies, none of the government's unpopularity rubbed off onto him. Also, as he confined himself solely to foreign and defence matters, he increased the image of himself as an elder statesperson, in contrast to Chirac's image of an embattled Prime Minister. As a result, in the first round of the 1988 presidential election, Mitterrand polled well, while Chirac saw off the challenge of his centre-right rival Raymond Barre. At the second ballot, though, Mitterrand was re-elected by a handsome margin (see Table 1.7).

The second Mitterrand presidency was very different from the first. In 1981, he won with the support of the communists on the basis of a commitment to restructure French social and economic life. In 1988,

TABLE 1.7	The presidential election of 24 April and 8 May 1988%	
	First round	Second round
François Mitterrand (Socialist)	34.10	54.02
Jacques Chirac (gaullist)	19.94	45.98
Raymond Barre (centre-right)	16.54	
Jean-Marie Le Pen (extreme-right)	14.40	
André Lajoinie (communist)	6.76	
Antoine Waechter (ecologist)	3.78	
Pierre Juquin (dissident communist)	2.01	
Arlette Laguiller (extreme-left)	1.99	
Pierre Boussel (extreme-left)	0.38	

Mitterrand ignored the communists and campaigned for the support of the centrist electorate. He also made very few specific policy commitments. He won because he was a popular, reassuring figure. He did not win because he supported any radical, transforming programme. As a result, very few high-profile reforms were introduced. Instead, Mitterrand's main aim was the promotion of European integration. He cemented the Franco-German alliance, particularly in the period after the fall of the Berlin Wall in 1989, and he played a major role in the negotiations that led to the Maastricht Treaty. At home, though, there were problems. The Socialist party became involved in a series of scandals and internal divisions that damaged the image of the government. More importantly, unemployment continued to increase. Unable to control events, Mitterrand went through three Prime Ministers in five years. The first, Michel Rocard, was quite popular, but was a long-time presidential rival whom Mitterrand dismissed in 1991. The second, Edith Cresson, the country's first woman Prime Minister, was an unmitigated disaster. She lasted little more than a year. The third, Pierre Bérégovoy, was faced with a hopeless situation and could do nothing to lift the government's fortunes.

At the March 1993 legislative election, the Socialists were routed. Once again, therefore, there was a period of cohabitation. Chirac announced that he would not serve as Prime Minister, preferring to cultivate his presidential ambitions outside government. Instead, he recommended another leading gaullist and seemingly a loyal supporter, Édouard Balladur, who was duly appointed. In contrast to the first period of cohabitation, on this occasion the relationship between the President and Prime Minister was much less fraught. This was mainly because Mitterrand was a lame-duck President who was seeing out his time in office. More than that, he was also terminally ill and by the end of his presidency he was extremely weak. The Prime Minister, by contrast, was very active. He embarked on another wave of privatizations (see Chapter 3) and his reforms proved to be very popular. In this context, Balladur discovered presidential ambitions of his own. In the absence of a credible candidate from their own organization, many of the leading figures in the non-gaullist right supported the Prime Minister. This time it was Chirac's turn to be betrayed. Initially, Balladur's presidential bid seemed unstoppable. However, Chirac cleverly portrayed himself as the outsider who was challenging the incumbent. The French wanted a change and Chirac benefited. Consequently, at the first ballot

TABLE 1.8	The presidential election of 23 April and 7 May 1995 (%)	
	First round	Second round
Jacques Chirac (gaullist)	20.84	52.64
Lionel Jospin (Socialist)	23.30	47.36
Édouard Balladur (gaullist)	18.58	
Jean-Marie Le Pen (extreme-right)	15.00	
Robert Hue (communist)	8.64	
Arlette Laguiller (extreme-left)	5.30	
Philippe de Villiers (right)	4.74	
Dominique Voynet (ecologist)	3.32	
Jacques Cheminade (independent)	0.28	

Chirac beat Balladur and went through to the second round (see Table 1.8). More surprisingly still, the candidate of the left, Lionel Jospin, topped the poll. The Socialists were back. At the second ballot, Jospin performed creditably, but Chirac, who was once portrayed as the eternal loser, scored an easy victory. Like Mitterrand before him, Chirac had finally been elected.

Jacques Chirac: the difficult presidency (1995–   )

In his first term of office Chirac faced a series of problems, some of which were purely self-inflicted. In the first place, the President failed to forgive the people who had campaigned for Balladur. Thus, he did little to heal the wounds of the divided right. More importantly, the economy was in bad shape and Chirac, even in the period immediately after his election, did not seem to have any policies which would make things better. The new Prime Minister, Alain Juppé, was loyal, but unremarkable. In the autumn of 1995 plans to reform public-sector pensions (the so-called Juppé plan) resulted in the biggest set of social protests since May 1968 and had to be modified. Worse still, the government appeared to break its electoral pledges right from the start. During the election, Chirac appeared to promise tax cuts. After the election, taxes were raised. Finally, on the vital issue of Europe Chirac had to decide whether or not France wanted to join Economic and Monetary Union (EMU). If it did, the country faced the prospect of more spending cuts and further increases in taxes. If it did not, then it risked the wrath of the world financial markets and European isolation. Late in 1995, Chirac finally announced that France would join EMU. In its own way, Chirac's decision was almost as important and historic as Mitterrand's decision to remain in the EMS twelve years previously (see above). It reassured the markets. More significantly, it confirmed France's position as a leading player in the process of European integration. All the same, it left many of the President's supporters very disillusioned. The much hoped-for change had failed to materialize.

Against this background, Chirac gambled. In April 1997, he decided to dissolve the National Assembly a year early. His closest advisers were convinced that the right would win a narrow majority and that Chirac would be safe in office for five more years. They were wrong. The left won. More accurately, a broad-ranging coalition of Socialists, communists, Greens, and left-wing nationalists won power. The right was shattered and divisions that had only just started to mend reopened once again (see Chapter 2). More than that, to all intents and purposes the Chirac presidency seemed over. The President was condemned to a five-year period of cohabitation with the person whom he had beaten just two years earlier and he had no one to blame but himself.

In power, the so-called 'plural left' government, headed by Lionel Jospin, was popular. It introduced a number of key reforms, such as the introduction of a 35-hour working week without loss of pay, a parity law designed to increase women's representation in political life, so-called PACS (*pacte civil de solidarité*) legislation that allowed unmarried couples and same-sex couples to enjoy the same rights as married couples, and the creation of more than a million public-sector jobs for the long-term unemployed and for those just leaving school. There was also a major constitutional reform. The President's term of office was reduced from seven years to five years, beginning in 2002. The aim of the reform was to ensure that presidential and legislative elections would be held during the same period so as to lessen the likelihood of cohabitation in the future. Finally, and perhaps most notably of all, the economic situation improved. The left benefited immediately from an upturn in the world economy that made the country's difficult economic choices somewhat easier to make. Overall, for the first three or four years of the plural left government there was a general sense of optimism. The Prime Minister's poll ratings were high.

Paradoxically, though, the President's situation also started to improve. Like Mitterrand before him, Chirac had responsibility without power. He benefited from his position on the world stage, particularly after the attacks on the USA on 11 September 2001, while at home he was the focus for opposition to the government of the day. Chirac regained control of the gaullist party and he made plans for the creation of a new broad-ranging party of the right (see Chapter 2). What is more, this time there would be no dissident gaullist party candidates and the two other moderate right-wing candidates were no real threat. Chirac was the best-placed candidate on the right. To complete the picture, Jospin's poll ratings began to fall as the economic downturn in the autumn of 2001 began to take hold. In November 2001 for the first time since the onset of cohabitation more people had confidence in Chirac than Jospin as the person best placed to solve the country's political problems (**www.php.sofres.com**, accessed 6 November 2001). This turnaround in Chirac's political fortunes was all the more remarkable because the President was the subject of a series of corruption allegations. He was accused of involvement in the scandals surrounding the operations of the Paris city council. He was accused of using secret government funds to pay for private holidays. His wife and daughter were summoned to testify before prosecuting magistrates (see Chapter 7) and the President himself was only able to avoid the embarrassment of having to testify because he could claim immunity as part of his presidential prerogatives. For Chirac, re-election was imperative not least because otherwise he would be likely to face a number of very serious charges.

The 2002 presidential election was remarkable. It was like no other presidential election before it. At the first ballot, there were sixteen candidates, a record, and the polls showed that a large proportion of the public were not likely to make up their minds until the last minute. Media attention was overwhelmingly focused on Chirac and Jospin. The President was running a safe, but unspectacular campaign. In retrospect, though, the Prime Minister's position was fragile. One problem was that each element of the plural left coalition presented a candidate.[3] In addition, there were no fewer than three extreme-left candidates. So, there were plenty of alternatives for left-wing voters who were disgruntled with the government's performance. Furthermore, the economic situation was not improving, so there was little to attract floating voters to the Jospin camp. Finally, the main campaign issue was law and order. The President was quick to criticize the government's policies in this regard and the Prime Minister had little to say in reply. Thus, in the run-up to the first round of the election the polls consistently showed that Chirac would beat Jospin by a narrow but convincing margin at the second ballot.

This scenario never occurred (see Table 1.9). The result of the first-round of the 2002 presidential election was the biggest political shock in the Fifth Republic's electoral history. Chirac topped the poll, but Jospin was beaten into third place by Jean-Marie Le Pen, the leader of the extreme right National Front party. This was a traumatic result for Jospin. He immediately announced his retirement from politics and he played no part in the second-ballot contest or the subsequent campaign for the legislative elections. This was also a traumatic result for France. In the country that is the home of the Declaration of the Rights of Man and whose motto is 'Liberty, Equality and Fraternity' voters in their millions had supported a neo-fascist candidate who proposed racist policies and who had once declared that the gas chambers were a mere detail in the history of the Second World War. Le Pen benefited from a relatively low turnout. Some of Jospin's voters had simply stayed at home. He had also capitalized on the law and order issue. This was one of the National Front's long-standing preoccupations. More than that, Le Pen had mobilized large numbers of people who felt alienated from the political system, who believed

TABLE 1.9	The presidential election of 21 April and 5 May 2002 (%)	
	First round	Second round
Jacques Chirac (gaullist)	19.88	82.21
Jean-Marie Le Pen (extreme-right)	16.86	17.79
Lionel Jospin (Socialist)	16.18	
François Bayrou (centre-right)	6.84	
Arlette Laguiller (extreme-left)	5.72	
Jean-Pierre Chevènement (republican pole)	5.33	
Noël Mamère (ecologist)	5.25	
Olivier Besancenot (extreme-left)	4.25	
Jean Saint-Josse (hunting and fishing)	4.23	
Alain Madelin (neo-liberal right)	3.91	
Robert Hue (communist)	3.37	
Bruno Mégret (extreme-right)	2.34	
Christiane Taubira (left-radicals)	2.32	
Corinne Lepage (right-wing ecologist)	1.88	
Christine Boutin (pro-life)	1.19	
Daniel Gluckstein (extreme-left)	0.47	

established politicians were all corrupt, who felt that their livelihood was threatened by Europeanization and globalization, who believed that their culture was threatened by forces beyond their control. People who lived in villages where there were no law and order problems voted for Le Pen. People who lived in places where there were no immigrants voted for Le Pen. The leader of the extreme right was a natural home for people who wanted to protest about the current state of affairs and send out a clear signal to the political class that things had to change. They were not necessarily racist themselves. They were simply anxious and angry.

In its way, the campaign for the second round of the presidential election was also remarkable. Right from the moment when the first-round result was known, left-wing politicians, reluctantly but almost unanimously, announced that they would support Chirac. More than that, there was an incredible manifestation of civic responsibility. There were hundreds of anti-Le Pen demonstrations, including many organized by schoolchildren who did not have the right to vote. The belief that the French were indifferent to politics was shown to be unfounded. Quite the opposite, the French showed that they were very attached to the fundamental values of the Republic, democracy and civil rights, and these were the values that they believed Le Pen threatened. Chirac refused a televised debate with Le Pen. The leader of the extreme right was isolated and ineffectual. At the second ballot, the turnout increased dramatically and Chirac was returned with the highest second-round score that a candidate has ever achieved and is ever likely to achieve. For his part, Le Pen increased his percentage of the vote and he increased the number of people who voted for him. However, as far as he was concerned, it was a disappointing result. The extreme right was not able to establish itself as a serious contender for political power. While Le Pen showed that he could win millions of votes, he also demonstrated that even in the most favourable circumstances he was still a marginal figure who had no appeal for the vast majority of the population.

The trauma of the 2002 presidential election was followed in quick succession by the campaign for the National Assembly election. For the first time, the right was mostly united and a large centre-right party, the Union for the Presidential Majority, was created to build on Chirac's victory. The President appointed a new Prime Minister, Jean-Pierre Raffarin, whose avuncular style was designed to give the impression that he was in touch with the ordinary French person. What is more, it is true that

Raffarin, a Senator who had made his name as the head of a regional council, was not from quite the same mould as some of his technocratic predecessors (see Chapter 5) and his popularity was immediately evident. By contrast, the left was divided and the Socialists were bereft of a clear message and a real leader. At the same time, without Le Pen as a focus for attention the extreme right was a shadow of the force that it had been just a few weeks earlier. In this context, the right won an overwhelming victory. The contrast with the situation less than a year previously was dramatic. In addition to the Senate, the Constitutional Council, and much of local government (see Chapters 6, 7, and 8 respectively), the right now controlled the National Assembly and the government, while the President, who had been tainted by corruption allegations and threatened with impeachment just a few months earlier, had been overwhelmingly re-elected and was the guiding force behind a new and large moderate right-wing party. In this regard, the right is now better placed than any government since the early 1970s.

Conclusion

This chapter has provided a chronological account of the French political system since 1870 and, in particular, the development of the current regime, the Fifth Republic. While it is tempting to dwell upon the mass of names and events in this chapter, the main point to take away is the fundamental importance of certain political ideas. In this regard, in the period since 1870 the idea of the Republic itself has been fundamental. The onset of the Third Republic saw the final demise of imperial and monarchical politics, while the Vichy regime was traumatic for many reasons, not the least of which was because it was brought about by the dissolution of the Republic. The importance of the Republic as a political idea lies not just in the form of government with which it is associated (a President and an assembly), but in the bundle of norms that comes along with it. These include popular sovereignty, political equality, and the importance of the nation-State. Over the years, the interpretation of these values has varied. For example, Chapter 8 addresses the issue of the uniformity, or equality, of service delivery across the national territory and shows that this idea is no longer as dominant as it was previously. Whatever the interpretation of particular beliefs at a given time, what is important is that an overwhelming proportion of the population and the political class has shared a bedrock of beliefs relating to the fundamental values of the Republic. This consensus is vitally important because it helps us to understand better some of the otherwise rather confusing aspects of French political life. It is essential to an appreciation of why the main parties in the system, including most of the country's right-wing parties, have consistently promoted the need for State intervention in virtually all aspects of economic, social, and political life (see Chapter 3). It also helps to explain why there was such a tremendous popular outcry when Le Pen won through to the second ballot of the 2002 presidential election. In this case, the feeling of collective guilt came about at least partly because the leader of the extreme right was seen by the vast majority of people to be the antithesis of French republican values.

Another very clear instance of the importance of political ideas concerns the debate about the relative merits of presidential and parliamentary forms of government. This has been a long-standing debate in French political life. The terms of the debate have varied considerably, but the basic issue has remained the same. Should there be strong leadership via either a king, an emperor, or a President, or is it better to have a sovereign assembly? Until recently, the dominant ideational position frequently changed and reform followed. So, in 1877 the dissolution of the legislature by President MacMahon shifted the ideational balance in favour of an assembly system. However, the problems of the inter-war years led to the capitulation of the Third Republic and the installation of an authoritarian system under Marshal Pétain. In turn, the collapse of the Vichy regime meant that the main elements of the Liberation governments favoured an assembly-dominated system. Finally, the failure of the Fourth Republic led to the return of de Gaulle who promoted strong presidential leadership. In the end this debate was finally settled, or fudged, with the passage of the 1962 constitutional amendment. The Fifth Republic now has a semi-presidential system with a directly elected President and Prime Minister who is accountable to the National Assembly (see Chapter 4). The settlement of this debate is vital to our understanding of the stability of the Fifth Republic because it removed one of the long-standing divisions between the left, which traditionally promoted an assembly system, and the right, which had often favoured strong leadership. There are still ongoing concerns. Indeed, the shift from a seven-year to a five-year presidential term in

2000 is a good example of how there can be institutional change within the basic constitutional framework of the Fifth Republic (see Chapter 4). All the same, the absence of ideational competition over the very foundations of the regime has helped to stabilize the political system as a whole.

A final example concerns the rule of law. Even this most cursory examination of French political history has shown us that on occasion politicians and/or social groups have tried to circumvent the normal channels of the political and democratic process. On occasion, these actions have been unequivocally wrong. The Dreyfus affair is a case in point. On other occasions, a sense of romantic idealism is still attached to a particular situation. The events of May 1968 are a good example in this regard. Whatever the interpretation, these examples demonstrate that at times there has been only a partial acceptance of the rule of law. This idea is still embedded in the political system. For example, France remains a country in which groups as diverse as farmers and anti-McDonald's campaigners are willing to take the law into their own hands in order to publicize their beliefs. More than ever, though, the importance of the rule of law has come to be accepted as part and parcel of the political process. This can be seen most clearly in the increasing importance of the judiciary in recent years (see Chapter 7). In the context of this chapter, it was also seen in the massive mobilization against Le Pen between the first and second ballots of the 2002 presidential election. People reacted to Le Pen's performance by taking to the streets and demonstrating against him and his ideas, but they did so in a very calm and orderly, albeit noisy, manner. There was no violence. There was no so-called 'third round' of the presidential election, whereby those who had been defeated tried to take matters into their own hands. In the end, the leader of the extreme right was defeated by way of the ballot box, and overwhelmingly so. The conclusion to be drawn is that even if France remains an occasionally petulant democracy, it is nonetheless an increasingly mature one.

KEY TERMS

- Political Instability
- 1958 Constitution
- De Gaulle

- Political leadership
- Institutional change

NOTES

1 It might be noted that this figure does not include a number of constitutions that were drafted but never implemented, as well as a number of occasions when there were provisional arrangements, pending the introduction of a new system.

2 See, for example, the website of the Convention pour la 6ème République at **www.c6r-fr.org/**.

3 Jean-Pierre Chevènement's element of the plural left coalition had already left the government by this time.

GUIDE TO FURTHER READING

GILDEA, R., *The Past in French History* (New Haven, Yale University Press, 1994).
Good thematic introduction to the importance of ideas in French political life.

—— *France since 1945* (Oxford, Oxford University Press, 1994).
Perhaps the best political history of the post-war period available.

HAZAREESINGH, S., *Political Traditions in Modern France* (Oxford, Oxford University Press, 1994).
Thematic presentation of the major traditions in French politics.

MENDRAS, H., with COLE, A., *Social Change in Modern France: Towards a Cultural Anthropology of the Fifth Republic* (Cambridge, Cambridge University Press, 1991).
A thought-provoking book about the second French revolution.

TODD, E., *The Making of Modern France: Politics, Ideology and Culture* (Oxford, Basil Blackwell, 1991).
Provocative account by well-known French academic and social commentator.

2

....

The Party System

Overview

The aim of this chapter is to make sense of the French party system. It has two main parts. The first part briefly sketches the foundations and contours of the basic left/right division in French party politics. Even though the issues that divide the left from the right have changed over the years, the faultline between these two basic traditions still forms the basis of party competition to this day. The second part examines the various parties in each of these traditions. To provide a sense of coherence, each tradition, party, or group of parties will be examined in terms of its history, its basic ideology, its support over the years, its organization, and its political strategy. Organizing the chapter in this way will help us to understand both the derivation of contemporary party preferences—why they say what they say—and the strategic manifestation of these preferences—why they do what they do.

Introduction

At first sight, the French party system is extremely complicated. More than that, the casual observer could be forgiven for thinking that it is simply unfathomable. For example, there were sixteen candidates at the first-round of the 2002 presidential election (see Table 1.9). Moreover, unlike, say, Jacques Cheminade at the 1995 election, each of these candidates was treated as a serious political contender both by each other and by the media. True, there is little doubt that even in their heart of hearts some of these candidates never expected to poll more than 1 or 2 per cent of the vote at best. All the same, each one could also justifiably claim that she or he represented a distinct strand of opinion, thought, ideology, and/or historical tradition in French political life. What is more, if the situation in France is compared with the equivalent situation in certain other countries, then the seemingly confused nature of the French party system becomes even more apparent. After all, at the 2000 US presidential election there were only three serious candidates (the Democrats, the Republicans, and the Greens). Equally, in the 2001 British parliamentary election only four parties fielded candidates in virtually every constituency (Labour, the Conservatives, the Liberal Democrats, and the UK Independence party). The structure of the party system is so important because political parties are essential to the functioning of democratic institutions in European democracies, and France is no exception. The competition between their different preferences helps both to create the basic institutions of the political system and to determine the outcomes of the political process once those institutions have been established. As a result, it is crucial that any account of political institutions in France should outline the basic contours of party political competition in the system as a whole.

Political competition in France: the left and the right

The fundamental basis of the French party system is the competition between two opposing forces: the left and the right. In some senses, this classification is misleading and for a number of reasons. First, there have never been just two political parties in the system. On the contrary, there has always been a multi-party system. Secondly, there have often been parties or movements claiming that they belong to neither of these blocs. In particular, there is a long-standing 'centrist' tradition in French political life (Elgie 1994) while in the 1980s and 1990s the Greens pursued an independent political strategy (see below). Finally, in recent years the number of competitive parties has increased and, more importantly, there has been the emergence of a 'tripartite political space' (Grunberg and Schweisguth 1997). In particular, the results of the 1995 presidential election showed that left- and right-wing voters continue to hold separate beliefs and values. However, they also showed that a further distinction needed to be made between the values of moderate right-wing voters and extreme right-wing voters (ibid. 180–7). The dramatic events of the 2002 presidential election confirmed these findings (see Chapter 1). The fact that Le Pen's support failed to increase markedly between the two rounds of the election showed that by and large support for the extreme right was drawn from a discrete, but nonetheless significant, section of French society. Accordingly, while this chapter takes the competition between the left and the right as the most useful starting point when trying to make sense of the French party system, this chapter also treats the extreme right as a separate political entity, distinct from the parties and ideas of the mainstream or, perhaps more appropriately, the democratic right.

The salience of the basic left/right dichotomy in French political life is considerable. In historical context, the left/right divide dates right back to the period immediately prior to the French Revolution. At the time, the supporters of the king were seated on the right side of the parliamentary chamber, whereas the reformers were seated on the left. As a result, the right became associated with the forces that wished to preserve, or conserve, the status quo (hence, conservatives), whereas the left became associated with the desire for change. By the mid-nineteenth century these terms were in general use in both France and elsewhere. As a result, in both a French context and a wider context, the terms 'left' and 'right' are still helpful in delineating the basic division between the main forces in the political system.

In terms of ideology, the ideational distinction between the 'left' and the 'right' has changed considerably over the years. In the past, the two blocs were separated by their attitudes towards Church and State. In particular, the left fought for a secular system of education, whereas the right was associated with a Church-sponsored system. Now, though, this division has lost virtually all of its salience. More generally, the left and the right have always been, and continue to be, separated by their attitude towards the economy. Previously, the divide was very wide. For example, just thirty years ago the two main parties on the left, the communists and the Socialists, signed a Common Programme for Government in which they committed themselves to a 'break with capitalism', stated that marxism was the 'principal theoretical contribution' that inspired them, and proposed a wholesale programme of nationalizations with a strong emphasis on economic planning.[1] Needless to say, even though the right in France has been perhaps somewhat more State-centred in its beliefs than equivalent forces in other countries, it was vehemently opposed to the so-called union of the left. More recently, though, the economic policy differences between the left and the right have narrowed considerably. In this regard, the main change has come on the left. Since 1982–3, the left has promoted sound finances (see Chapter 1), it has accepted a free-market economic framework, and it has privatized various public-sector companies (see Chapter 3).

The transformation of the terms of the economic policy debate over the last twenty years has often led to the claim that in France, as in other countries, nothing separates the left from the right any more and that they both put forward essentially the same policies. This claim is unjustified. True, left- and right-wing governments both have to work within very specific constraints. For example, membership of European Economic and Monetary Union obliges French governments to meet a number of economic and financial criteria. All the same, left-wing governments put forward policies that would never be proposed by right-wing governments and vice versa. For instance, it is inconceivable that a right-wing government would have unilaterally introduced policies such a 35-hour working week and the so-called PACS legislation (see Chapter 1). Moreover, the evidence also clearly shows that the terms 'left' and 'right' still mean something to most people and that they still constitute the basic terms of political competition. For example, at the 1995 presidential election 98.1 per cent of people were able to place themselves somewhere on a seven-point left–right scale (Lewis-Beck and Chlarson 2002: 494). Moreover, 69 per cent of people were shown to believe that there was a difference between the left and the right in terms of the issues they promoted (ibid. 496).

In this context, what is the basic ideological difference between the left and the right in contemporary France? For the left, the difference is based on a belief that society can be improved. For example, Michel Rocard, the former Socialist Prime Minister, writes: 'What, at bottom, has distinguished, from the outset, the left from the right? It is a belief in man. We no longer believe, as we did a century ago, that man is naturally good: too many unhappy, dramatic experiences have shattered our illusions. But we continue to believe and always will believe that man is perfectible so long as an intelligent and generous social organization gives him the opportunity. And that the nobleness of political action, at the base as at the summit, in day-to-day militantism as in the exercise of power, consists of working tirelessly for this organization' (Rocard 1989: 23).[2] For the right, by contrast, the difference is based on a sceptical attitude towards the means by which the left is said to bring about social improvement. In particular, the right believes that the left continues to place too much emphasis on the State in this regard. For example, the former gaullist Prime Minister Édouard Balladur has written: 'What do statist systems stand for if not a mistrust of man and the use to which he can put his liberty? In a liberal system, by contrast, the State bases its relationship with citizens on respect and the guarantee of personal responsibility because they are capable of assuming it. At the same time, it is up to the State to define the rules of the game, in other words an order that everyone must respect' (Balladur 1989: 310). The fact that Balladur was willing to acknowledge that the State had a legitimate role to play in the decision-making process is just one sign that there are plenty of overlaps between contemporary left- and right-wing thought in France. At the same time, though, there remains a basic difference between them. At bottom, supporters of the two opposing forces do not believe the same thing.

As might be expected, the overall levels of support for the left and the right have changed over the years (see Table 2.1). In the immediate postwar period the left was by far the biggest bloc and the right was largely discredited. This changed with the onset of the Fifth Republic. At this time, the right became the strongest force and the left performed very badly. The next turning point was in 1981, when the left won a resounding victory. From this point on, the situation has become more complicated and for two reasons. First, since the mid-1980s the extreme right has done very well (see below). This has reduced the support for the democratic right. Secondly, the electorate has been extremely volatile. The left won in 1988, lost ignominiously in 1993, won again in 1997, and was routed in 2002. In short, there are no longer the clear trends in left/right support that were evident in the period up to the mid-1980s. Moreover, it must be appreciated that the overall figures for left/right support mask important changes within both the left and the right (see below). More than that, even when one or other bloc has been numerically superior, this does not necessarily mean that it has held power. For example, even though the left was the largest force in the 1940s and 1950s, the communists were excluded from office and governments invariably included the centrists and on occasions the gaullists as well. Thus, while the overall figures for left/right support show

TABLE 2.1	Left/right support at parliamentary elections, 1945–2002 (%)	
	Left	Right
1945	60.1	39.5
1946 (June)	58.6	41.0
1946 (Nov.)	57.1	41.8
1951	51.5	48.3
1956	52.4	30.3
1958	45.2	54.3
1962	43.7	56.2
1967	43.6	56.4
1968	40.5	58.9
1973	45.8	54.2
1978	52.3	47.5
1981	56.7	43.2
1986	45.2	44.6
1988	49.6	40.5
1993	42.1	44.1
1997	46.2	35.8
2002	40.7	43.4

Notes: The figures for the right include the support for the centrists, but exclude the support for the extreme right (1956 and 1986 onwards).

The figures for the left include the support for the ecologists from 1978.

the basic patterns of support within the country as whole, an understanding of party competition within the left and right is needed for a full appreciation of the significance of party politics as a whole (see below).

The list of competitive political parties in France is huge. For the purposes of this chapter, though, seven parties or groups of parties will be examined. On the left, there is a group of three trotskyite parties, Workers' Fight, the Revolutionary Communist League, and the Workers' party. In addition, there are the Communist party, the Socialist party, and the Greens. On the democratic right there are the Union for a Popular Movement and the Union for French Democracy. Finally, there is a set of two extreme right-wing parties, the National Front and the National Republican Movement. Other parties could have been included. Most notably, the Hunting, Fishing, Nature, Traditions party (Chasse, pêche, nature, traditions, CPNT) did well at the 1994 and 1999 European elections and the party's candidate at the 2002 presidential election, Jean Saint-Josse, also performed creditably. In addition, there is a group of three essentially anti-European groups, the left-wing Republican Pole (Pôle républicain) that is associated with the former Socialist Minister and 2002 presidential election candidate Jean-Pierre Chevènement, as well as two right-wing parties, the Rally for France (Rassemblement pour la France, RPF) and the Movement for France (Mouvement pour la France, MPF). There are also two dissident ecology parties, the Independent Ecology Movement and Ecology Generation, as well as a long-standing moderate left-wing party, the Left-Radical party (Mouvement des radicaux de gauche, MRG), which was part of the governing coalition 1997–2002 and which fielded a candidate, Christiane Taubira, at the 2002 presidential election. Finally, the list could also be extended to include regionally based parties in Corsica, the Overseas Departments and Territories, and mainland France itself, most notably in Brittany and Alsace, as well as quasi-parties, such as the Forum of Social Republicans (Forum des républicains sociaux), which was established by another 2002 presidential candidate, Christine Boutin, and pseudo-parties, such as the slightly ludicrous Natural Law party. These parties have been excluded either because they are small, or because they are regionally based, or because, like the CPNT, they are essentially single-issue parties.

The basic strategic question that these parties face is whether it is better to ally or go it alone. In general terms, there is no question of an alliance between the left and the right. True, at the second round of the 2002 election the left faithfully, if unenthusiastically, voted for Jacques Chirac in order to minimize the level of support for Jean-Marie Le Pen. This was a reflection of the fact that the left and the moderate right have a common concern for democratic values. Ordinarily, though, the basic characteristic of the French party system is the competition between the left and the right. Within both the left and the right, however, the issue of alliance or independence is always at the top of the electoral agenda. The various choices made by the different parties will be explored in the next section. Nonetheless, the fundamental point to note is that the institutions of the Fifth Republic encourage parties to adopt different strategies at different times. In general terms, European, regional, and the first-round of cantonal, municipal, legislative, and presidential elections encourage independent strategies. By contrast, the second rounds of the latter set of elections encourage alliances. (See the review of these systems in Chapters

4, 6, and 8 and Elgie 1996.) The conclusion to be drawn is that the large number of parties in France is at least partly a result of the wide variety of political opinion in the country. Even so, it is also partly a function of the electoral systems that operate at different levels of the polity and that encourage parties to adopt an independent strategy. This observation reinforces the theme of the interaction between ideas, preferences, and institutions that is central to this book.

The parties of the left and the right

The parties of the left

The trotskyite left

The origins of the trotskyite left in France go back to the schisms that occurred within the world-wide communist movement in the middle part of the last century. More specifically, they reflect the competition between Trotsky and both Lenin and, especially, Stalin. Trotsky believed that the Soviet Union (USSR) had not established a true communist system. As a result, in 1938 he founded the so-called Fourth International in an attempt to unite the communists who were opposed to the ideology and policies of the Communist Party of the Soviet Union (CPSU) under Stalin. The result is that one of the defining features of the trotskyite left in France has always been and remains its antagonism towards the French Communist party. The other main feature of the trotskyite left in France has been the highly sectarian nature of the movement. Over the years, this has led to frequent schisms and a bewildering number of parties and movements. The French section of the Fourth International was called the International Communist party (Parti communiste internationale, PCI). However, the PCI split in 1940 when David Korner, alias Barta, founded the Communist Union (Union communiste). This party is now the main element of the trotskyite left and is almost always known by the title of its newspaper, Workers' Fight (Lutte ouvrière, LO). The PCI split again in 1952. The two other elements of the trotskyite left in the contemporary party system are the descendants of this split. The larger of these two groups, the Revolutionary Communist League (Ligue communiste révolutionnaire, LCR), was officially founded in 1974. The other element, the Workers' party (Parti des travailleurs, PT), assumed its current form in 1991. It might be noted that the former Prime Minister Lionel Jospin was once associated with the forerunner of the PT (Askolovitch 2001). Indeed, revelations emerged in 2001 that his links with the movement continued until the 1980s when he was officially a high-ranking member of the Socialist party. These revelations did not help Jospin's presidential campaign.

The trotskyite left believes that it incarnates the true spirit and heritage of the communist movement, or rather each element individually believes that it is the true incarnation of the movement. It would serve absolutely no purpose to try to identify the ideological differences between LO, the LCR, and the PT. Their disputes have never amounted to anything more than the secular equivalent of the debate about how many angels will fit on the head of a pin. Moreover, it would serve scarcely any greater purpose to try to identify the ideological differences between these parties and the PCF itself. The reality is that the official policies of the various organizations are very similar. They are all resolutely anti-capitalist, anti-European, and support the anti-globalization movement. Instead, the main difference between the trotskyite left and the PCF is a matter of language and strategy. In short, the trotskyite left still talks the language of the revolutionary left and refuses to consider itself as a potential party of government. By contrast, the PCF has dropped, or at least de-emphasized, much of this language over the years and has been willing to assume political office (see below). Whatever the similarities or differences between the PCF and the trotskyite left, LO, the LCR, and the PT all aim to defend and promote the interests of workers and they all believe that the capitalist system needs to be radically transformed through the common ownership of the means of production.

The trotskyite left is a small political force. Indeed, some might question whether it warrants consideration as a serious competitor in the French party system at all. The fact remains, though, that in recent times it has become increasingly salient. Most notably, Arlette Laguiller, the LO candidate, has contested every presidential election since 1974 and in the last two elections she has performed very well (see Chapter 1). Similarly, while the PT remains a marginal grouping, the LCR has had some success in recent times. Indeed, the party's candidate at the 2002 presidential election, Olivier Besancenot, received 4.25 per cent of the vote. All told, the three candidates of the trotskyite left together polled 10.45 per cent of the vote in

April 2002 and helped ensure that Lionel Jospin failed to go through to contest the second ballot. Moreover, the various parties have had success at other elections as well. They have won representation on regional, departmental, and municipal councils. What is more, in 1999 the joint LO/LCR list won 5.18 per cent of the vote at the European elections and returned five MEPs to Strasbourg. Thus, support for the trotskyite left, while still small and fickle (the LCR won 1.27 per cent and LO won 1.20 per cent at the first round of the 2002 legislative election), should not be discounted.

Organizationally, the parties share a passion for secrecy and pseudonyms. For example, LO's organizational structure was only revealed for the first time in 1998. The party's best-known figure and perennial presidential candidate, Arlette Laguiller, is officially only the party's spokesperson. In fact, the guiding force behind the organization is Robert Barcia, a businessman in the pharmaceutical industry, who writes under the name of Roger Girardot and whose party name is Hardy. The party's annual conferences are not open to the public and there is a strict policy of expulsion (some might say excommunication) if members stray from the official party line. The party has around 2,000 members, but it publishes a weekly newspaper which has a much wider circulation. The party's electoral successes have meant that it receives state funding and its finances would appear to be relatively healthy for a small, anti-system party.[3] In sum, LO is a viable political organization with a strict internal code of discipline and a penchant for secrecy.

Even in the recent past, the trotskyite left did not have to worry too much about matters relating to electoral strategy. In the 1980s and early 1990s, the LCR and PT were unwilling to commit themselves fully to the electoral process and for its part LO was mainly content to register a protest voice at presidential elections. By the latter part of the 1990s, though, the electoral outlook improved as the PCF declined and the anti-capitalist movement strengthened. This meant that the parties were obliged to consider electoral tactics. In 1999, this led to a highly surprising move whereby LO and LCR agreed to run a joint list at the European elections. What is more, the list fared quite well (see above). While the parties failed to arrive at a common candidate for the 2002 presidential election and they also fought the 2002 legislative election separately, the fact remains that the prospect of a trotskyite alliance is much more likely now than it has been for a long time. Indeed, there is even some talk of some or all of the parties, especially the LCR, working with the communists. If this were to happen, it really would be a historic development on the left of the party system. All the same, the chances of such an alliance are very small and in all probability the various elements of the trotskyite left will continue to fight themselves, the communists, and the world in general.

The Communist party

The French Communist party (PCF) was formed in the wake of the 1917 Russian Revolution, which saw Lenin take power. In 1919, Lenin formed the Third International with the aim of bringing together Socialist and communist parties from around the world. Given Lenin's organizational principles and ideological beliefs, parties had to agree to certain conditions if they wished to join the Third International. In 1920, the French Socialist party, the French Section of the Workers' International (section française de l'Internationale ouvrière, SFIO), held its party congress at Tours.[4] The delegates to the congress debated whether or not to join the Third International. By a majority of 3:1, they voted in favour and formed a marxist-leninist party, the PCF, along the lines of the CPSU with the remainder of the delegates continuing to operate as the SFIO. This set of circumstances had two long-standing consequences. First, it meant that the left in France has been split between communist and non-communist, or Socialist, elements. As a result, rather like the different varieties of the trotskyite left, the communists and the Socialists have sometimes given the impression that they are keener to fight each other than the right-wing enemies that they have in common. Secondly, the events surrounding the formation of the PCF meant that the PCF was closely allied with Moscow from the time it was formed until the collapse of the USSR in 1991. The party did try briefly to dissociate itself from the Kremlin in the mid-1970s, but very soon it came back into line. In this context, the collapse of the USSR was traumatic for the party. Unlike many of its west European counterparts, the PCF did not disappear. Moreover, it decided that it would not even change its name. Even so, the party is no longer the same as it was little more than a decade ago. It is smaller, weaker, and poorer and the threat of political extinction is closer than ever.

Over the years, the PCF's ideology has shifted. For example, in 1972 it accepted for the first time that there could be alternations in power between parties. This was an attempt to reassure voters of its democratic credentials. For a similar reason, in 1976 it abandoned the notion of the dictatorship of the proletariat, one of the fundamental organizational principles of marxism-leninism. Moreover, in government it accepted spending cuts and rising unemployment during the early 1980s, and it was associated with a series of privatizations in the late 1990s. All the same, the party's rhetoric still harks back to a previous era of political competition. For instance, at the 31st party congress in October 2001 the official party programme asserted that 'The emancipation of workers will be the task of the workers themselves' and that '[o]ver and above all the wounds of history and in ways that are yet to be invented, this communist ambition is still relevant' (**www.pcf.fr**, *Résolution sur le Projet communiste*, accessed 30 October 2001). More concretely, the party declared that 'business is a range of powers that citizens must appropriate' (ibid.). All told, there is a growing gap between the official language of the party and its policies in office. The party still speaks the language of the old left. This partly accounts for the very tentative overtures that have been made between the LCR and the PCF in recent times (see above). However, in office the party has been obliged to defend policies that its supporters have found distasteful (see below).

Since its formation in 1920, the party has had a chequered electoral history. In 1932, the party won 8.5 per cent of the vote, while in 1936 it won 15.3 per cent and in 1945 it won 26.1 per cent. At this point, the communists were by far the biggest force on the left and support for the party peaked at the November 1946 legislative election when it won 28.6 per cent of the vote. From this point on, the party's vote began to decline. In 1958, the PCF won just 19.2 per cent of the vote, even though the party's support was remarkably stable throughout the 1960s and 1970s at around the 20–2 per cent mark. All the same, the 1978 legislative election marked a turning point. For the first time, the Socialists outpolled the communists. Thereafter, another decline started. In 1981, Georges Marchais, the party leader, scored only 15.5 per cent at the first ballot of the presidential election. In the 1988 presidential election, the PCF's candidate, André Lajoinie, won only 6.8 per cent, even though the party registered 11.4 per cent at the legislative election just a month or so later. Moreover, while Marchais's successor as party leader, Robert Hue, did quite well at the 1995 presidential election, winning 8.6 per cent, his performance at the 2002 election was a disaster and he was outpolled by both the LO and the LCR candidates. These results do not bode well for the PCF and for the first time there is the very real possibility that in the not-too-distant future the party will cease to be a significant political actor.

As with most matters relating to the party, the organizational structure of the PCF has changed over time. In the past, the party was organized along the lines of a classic marxist-leninist party. Here, the basic organizational principle was democratic centralism. In practice, this meant that internal dissent was forbidden at least publicly and that the leadership decided all matters of importance. However, following the collapse of the Soviet Union, the party has become somewhat more tolerant towards dissenting voices and criticism of the leadership can now be openly expressed. In some respects, though, the new-found openness of the party is becoming increasingly irrelevant as the number of party members continues to decline. As recently as 1978, the party claimed that it had no fewer than 632,000 paid-up members (Mair and van Biezen 2001: 17). However, by 1998 even the official party figures said that membership had fallen to 210,000. In reality, the figure is probably much smaller. Worse still, the party's finances are in a parlous state. The collapse of the Soviet Union was the first real problem in this regard. Previously, the party obtained an undisclosed, but undoubtedly considerable, amount of funding from Moscow. Now, this income has dried up. Moreover, the party's declining electoral performance means that it is obtaining less State financing than it used to do. Overall, the PCF has serious financial difficulties. There are real doubts whether the party's long-standing newspaper, *L'Humanité*, will survive. The party is going to have to lay off workers from the party headquarters and it cancelled its 2002 summer school for lack of funds. The PCF still maintains an impressive infrastructure relative to certain other parties in the system. For example, it still controls a large number of municipal councils which are an important source of political patronage in the French system (see Chapter 8). That said, the organizational future of the party is fragile and there is no doubt that in this regard the party is worse placed now than it has ever been in its history.

In this context, the issue of electoral strategy is still as salient as ever. From the moment the PCF was founded, the question of whether or not to ally with the Socialists has been debated. There were high-profile

arrangements at the time of the Popular Front and Liberation governments (see Chapter 1). However, the onset of the Cold War sent the PCF
into exile. The institutional structure of the Fifth Republic and, in particular, the presidentialization of the system and the two-ballot majority electoral system eventually forced the communists and the Socialists to work
together, even if the relationship has never been easy (Duhamel 1993). In
1972 the two parties formed the 'union of the left' at the heart of which was
the Common Programme for Government (see above). In fact, the Common Programme was abandoned less than five years later, but it did show
that the two parties could work together. Under the Mitterrand presidency,
there were communist Ministers in the government 1981–4 (see Chapter 1).
Moreover, the PCF was an integral part of the 'plural left' government
1997–2002. On both occasions, though, the party failed to gain any electoral benefit. Worse, its supporters were disillusioned by some of the policies that the party was obliged to defend in office. Following its disastrous
performance at the 2002 elections, the PCF would probably like to go it
alone and distance itself from the Socialists. However, it still relies on the
benevolence of the Socialist party and the support of Socialist voters to
ensure that its remaining deputies are returned to the National Assembly.
As a result, the two parties are likely to continue to work together in the
foreseeable future.

The Socialist party

The forerunner of the Socialist party (PS), the SFIO, was formed in 1905.
After the traumatic schism in 1920, the SFIO regrouped and was the leading force in both the Popular Front government in 1936 and the post-war
Liberation governments. Moreover, the party was a virtually indispensable
component of Fourth Republic governments. This, though, was one of the
main reasons for its eventual downfall. The party was closely associated
with the failure of the Fourth Republic and the trauma of decolonization.
As a result, at the beginning of the Fifth Republic in 1958 its support
slipped to 15.5 per cent and in 1962 it fell even further to 12.5 per cent.
Worse was to come. In 1969, Gaston Defferre, the Socialist candidate at the
presidential election, scored just 5.0 per cent of the vote. There was growing support for a variety of other moderate left-wing parties, most notably
François Mitterrand's Convention des institutions républicaines (CIR) and
Michel Rocard's Parti Socialiste unifié (PSU). In July 1969 the SFIO was

eventually dissolved and the PS was formed. In 1971, the CIR joined the party and Mitterrand was elected leader. This marked the beginning of the modern-day PS. In 1974 most of the PSU joined the party and the non-communist left was finally united.

The PS has always been a broad ideological church. In the 1970s, there was fierce competition between the old, Statist and jacobin left, personified by figures such as Jean-Pierre Chevènement, and the new, liberal left, in the form of people like Michel Rocard. However, since the early 1980s the so-called modernizers have been dominant. The contemporary philosophy of the party was summed up very well by Lionel Jospin when he wrote: 'We have to say very clearly to Socialists, to left-wing opinion, to the French, that our objectives are indeed full employment, material well-being, the reduction of income inequalities, and more equitable international economic relations' (Jospin 1991: 255). At the same time, he argued, once these objectives have been declared, 'it is perfectly reasonable and even realistic to explain why we cannot easily reach them, what obstacles we encounter, why we are obliged to use such and such means—sometimes contradictory to the end we are trying to achieve—how it is possible and how long it will take us (prudently) to reach our goals' (ibid. 255–6). In short, the PS closely resembles a modern-day British-style New Labour party. True, some of the Jospin government's policies, such as the 35-hour working week and the State-sponsored youth employment scheme, would be deemed far too radical for the British Labour government. However, both parties stress the prudent management of the economy and promote a regulated free-market system.

In the period 1971–81 support for the PS grew steadily. Indeed, in 1981 the party won 37.5 per cent of the vote at the first round of the legislative election and was by far the largest single party in the system. Thereafter, the party's performance has been uneven, even though it was usually the largest single party in the system at least prior to the advent of the UMP (see below). The PS lost the 1986 election, but regained a majority after the 1988 election. However, at the 1993 election it won just 12.5 per cent of the vote and returned just 67 deputies compared with 282 in the previous parliament. Indeed, tragically, the outgoing Socialist Prime Minister, Pierre Bérégovoy, committed suicide immediately after the defeat, blaming himself for the party's poor performance. By 1997, though, once again the Socialists were the largest force in the political system; but just five years later the party was defeated and now it faces another period of reflection and rebuilding.

A defining organizational feature of the PS has been the presence of *courants*, or factions, within the party (see Table 2.2). Over the years, these factions have been based on both ideological divisions and personality clashes. In the 1970s, the fight was for the ideological soul of the party. In 1990, though, the competition was purely personal. Indeed, that year the PS presented a pathetic picture at the party congress in Rennes when faction fighting between the members of the Mitterrand *courant* tore the party asunder. Since the mid–1990s the situation has stabilized. The Chevènement faction left the PS to form the MDC party (now known as the Republican Pole). Moreover, the Rocard faction effectively disappeared and the rivalry between Jospin and his sworn enemy Laurent Fabius was put to one side. There is always the prospect that the party's most recent defeat will revive internal tensions, but the situation is not likely to be quite as fraught as it was in the early 1990s, especially as Jospin has declared that he is leaving political life. The other main organizational feature of the PS concerns its membership and links with civil society. The PS has never had a mass membership base. In 1999 the party claimed 148,795 members (Mair and van Biezen 2001: 17). Furthermore, it has never had close links with the trade union movement, at least compared with, for example, the British Labour party. That said, over the years the party has developed privileged relations with various new social movements. In the 1970s, it was associated with aspects of the women's movement and in the 1990s it was closely identified with the anti-racist movement. Overall, the party is an elite-centred organization with few internal constraints on the decision-making power of the party leadership.

In terms of strategy, the Socialist party has always faced a difficult electoral dilemma. In order to win, it needs the support of both the non-Socialist left and uncommitted centrist voters. The problem is that if it moves too far to one side, then it risks losing the support of the other. The events surrounding Lionel Jospin's 2002 presidential election campaign illustrate this point very well. The Socialist candidate began his campaign by declaring that he was not proposing a Socialist programme. This was a deliberate attempt to appeal to the centrist vote. However, such declarations only fuelled support for the myriad of left-wing candidates with whom Jospin was competing. As a result, by the time Jospin began to

TABLE 2.2	Figures for factional support within the PS, 1971–1995 (%)[a]					
	Chevènement[b]	Poperen	Mitterrand	Mauroy	Rocard	Mollet
1971	8.5	12.0	15.0	30.0[c]		34.0
1973	21.0	5.5	65.0			8.0
1975	25.4		68.0			3.4[d]
1977	24.0		75.1			
1979	14.4		40.1	13.6	20.4	
1981			single motion[e]			
1983	18.1		77.2		(4.7)[f]	
1985			71.4		28.6	
1987			single motion			
1990	8.5	7.1	28.9/29.0[g]		24.2	
1992	7.4		85.3[h]			
1995	Left to form MDC		Party unity			

[a] At congresses factions propose competing motions. Figures correspond to the support obtained for each motion.
[b] This was known as the CERES faction.
[c] From 1973 to 1979, Mauroy supported the Mitterrand motion, as did Poperen from 1975 and Rocard 1975–9.
[d] The Mollet faction ceased to exist after 1975.
[e] This term indicates that all factions agreed to support one motion at the congress.
[f] This was a dissident *rocardien* list.
[g] Fabius: 28.9%; Jospin/Mauroy: 29.0%.
[h] Poperen/Fabius/Jospin/Rocard.

Sources: Figures for 1971–90 taken from Hubscher (1991: 186–217). Figures thereafter compiled by the author.

radicalize his rhetoric and emphasize his left-wing credentials the damage on the left was done. Moreover, by radicalizing his campaign he only succeeded in alienating, or at least confusing, the centrists. So, while there are many reasons why Jospin failed to get through to the second ballot of the 2002 election, the failure to adopt a coherent strategy is certainly one (see Chapter 1). Indeed, the situation will be no easier for Jospin's successor. The party needs to work with the Greens, the communists, and perhaps even the extreme left. However, such a strategy will only make it all the more difficult to pick up votes in the middle ground.

The Greens

The origins of the French ecology movement can be traced back to March 1971 and the creation of the French branch of the Friends of the Earth movement. Three years later René Dumont stood as the candidate for the ecology movement at the 1974 presidential election and won 1.3 per cent of the vote. Even though the movement performed better at the 1979 European and 1981 presidential elections, the main turning point was the 1983 municipal elections. The introduction of a dose of proportional representation for municipal elections (see Chapter 8) allowed the movement to return over 750 councillors. This success spurred the rather disparate set of ecologist forces to form a party. As a result, the Greens were formed in January 1984. However, the attempt to federate the movement was only a partial success. True to the old adage about French politics that when a new party is formed the first item on the agenda is the split, the ecology movement soon found that it was divided once again. A leading figure in the movement, Brice Lalonde, formed a separate organization, Ecology Generation (Génération écologie, GE). This division hindered the party's development. Indeed, worse was to come. In 1994, the ousted leader of the Greens, Antoine Waechter, left the party and formed his own organization, the Independent Ecology Movement (Mouvement écologiste indépendant, MEI). By 1995, though, the situation had changed. Both GE and MEI failed to win enough signatures to contest the presidential election. Moreover, the Greens established themselves as an integral part of the 'plural left' coalition 1997–2002. While GE and MEI continue to soldier on and while a right-wing ecology candidate, Corinne Lepage, contested the 2002 presidential election, this section focuses solely on the Greens, given their position as the only significant ecology party in the system.

In terms of ideology, not surprisingly the Greens' main focus is on the environment. Indeed, Brice Lalonde held the post of Minister for the Environment in the 1988 Rocard government and Dominique Voynet, the leader of the Greens, held a similar post in the 1997 Jospin government. During her time in office, Voynet was quite outspoken on a number of classic environmental issues. For example, she pressurized the government to reduce its commitment to nuclear power. She also angered the powerful farming and hunting lobbies with her declarations about genetically modified foods and her determination to reduce the length of the hunting season. At the same time, though, the Greens are not a single-issue party. They are concerned with post-material, lifestyle issues in general. They also tend to promote traditional left-wing economic policies. So, for instance, the Greens associate themselves with the anti-globalization movement.

They are suspicious of the EU. They oppose multinational companies. They also enthusiastically supported issues such as the introduction of the 35-hour working week, male/female parity for elections, decentralization, and the PACS legislation. Thus, the party has the potential to gain support from more than just the most committed set of environmentalists.

Over the years, support for the party has varied (see Table 2.3). However, the basic point to note is that when the ecologists have done well, they have tended to do so at less important elections. For example, at the 1989 European election the united ecology list won 10.59 per cent of the vote and returned 8 MEPs. Similarly, at the 1999 European elections the Greens won 9.72 per cent and elected 9 MEPs. However, the Greens performed disappointingly at the 1995 and 2002 presidential elections (3.32 per cent and 5.25 per cent respectively). Moreover, at the 2002 legislative election they won just 4.51 per cent of the vote, even though they elected three deputies. In short, the Greens suffer from the classic problem associated with small parties in the Fifth Republic. Particularly in European and regional elections, small parties can thrive because of the proportional system of election. However, at presidential and legislative elections, the ones which determine where the real power lies in the system, they tend to do badly. The two-ballot majority system that is used for these elections (see Chapters 4 and 5) encourages voters to support larger parties or coalitions of parties at the second ballot. This is the reason why the Greens allied with the Socialists at the 1997 and 2002 legislative elections and it is no coincidence that on these occasions, and these occasions only, the Greens returned deputies to the National Assembly.

The Greens emphasize the importance of internal party democracy. This means that there are various tiers of decision-making and that there is a real sense in which party members are invited to participate in the life of the movement. At times, though, this has created problems. It has encouraged factionalism and it has meant that on occasion the Greens have failed to speak with a coherent voice. Most notably, in a vote of party members in June 2001 Alain Lipietz beat Noël Mamère by 3,528 votes to 3,183 and was selected as the Greens' candidate at the 2002 presidential election. However, Lipietz's campaign was so disastrous that in September 2001 he was obliged to stand down. On 13 October 2001, Mamère stated that his decision not to stand for the presidential election was 'irrevocable' (*Le Monde*, 13 October 2001). The next day, he changed his mind and the party's

TABLE 2.3	Support for the Greens, 1984–2002 (%)			
	Regional	Legislative	Presidential	European
1984				3.4
1985				
1986	3.4	1.2		
1988			3.7	
1989				10.6
1992	6.7			
1993		4.0		
1994				2.9
1995			3.3	
1997		3.6		
1998	5.2			
1999				9.7
2001				
2002		4.5	5.3	

governing committee recommended that he be selected. This decision was then overwhelmingly approved in another vote of the party membership. Even though the party gave Mamère its full support from then on, the damage was done and his election campaign never really recovered. While most of the blame for this episode must lie with Lipietz, the nature of the party's decision-making procedures helped to exacerbate the problem.

As indicated above, the Greens face a recurring problem of political strategy. In the 1980s and early 1990s under the leadership of Antoine Waechter, the party adopted an independent strategy and refused to form an alliance with the Socialists. In so doing, the party's ideological principles remained intact, but its opportunities to influence policy were non-existent. When Voynet took control of the party in 1994, the policy changed and just three years later the Greens were in government and had returned six deputies. As with the communists, though, the experience of office was painful. The Greens were loyal to the end, but party members found it difficult to accept the constraints of office. Moreover, there was little or no electoral reward. The party's performance at the 2002 presidential election was only marginally better than in 1995 and it returned only three deputies at the 2002 legislative elections. Thus, like the PCF, once again the Greens have to determine the most appropriate trade-off between ideology and office. This is a difficult calculation and it is sure to provoke a great deal of debate in the years to come.

The parties of the democratic right

The right in France has always been divided. In a seminal work, one writer (Rémond 1982) has argued that there are three distinct traditions on the French right (bonapartism, *orléanisme*, and what he calls *ultracisme*). The bonapartist tradition dates back to the period 1848–70 and Louis-Napoléon Bonaparte. This tradition promotes a personalized system of politics. While it is fundamentally anti-left, it promotes a populist 'neither-right-nor-left' stance. It is also associated with order and glory, which leads it to promote a decisive role for the State. By contrast, the *orléaniste* tradition has its origins in the period 1830–48 and was originally associated with the desire for the establishment of a modern, constitutional monarchy. The *orléanistes* were inspired by liberalism, promoting political rights, and a free-market. Finally, the *ultraciste* tradition dates back to the period 1815–30. This tradition was explicitly counter-revolutionary. It promoted the concept of the natural order, history, and tradition. It was associated with the family, the Church, and natural hierarchies. Until very recently indeed, these three traditions were still clearly identifiable in the various parties of the right. The bonapartist tradition was maintained by the gaullist RPR; the *orléaniste* tradition manifested itself in the UDF and two of its sometime component parts, the Christian Democrats and Liberal Democracy (Démocratie libérale, DL); and the *ultraciste* tradition could be associated with the extreme right. However, events immediately following the 2002 presidential election have slightly changed this equation. In particular, Chirac's supporters, who were mainly in the RPR, formed a new group, the Union for the presidential Majority (Union pour la majorité présidentielle, UMP), and most of the members of the UDF and DL agreed to join this group in time for the 2002 legislative elections. In November 2002, the UMP changed its name to the Union for a Popular Movement (Union pour un mouvement populaire). Thus, there are still three main groups on the right in France: the UMP, what remains of the UDF, and the extreme right. All the same, these parties no longer correspond quite as neatly as before to the three historical right-wing traditions. The rest of this section examines the UMP and the UDF. The next section looks at the extreme right.

The Union for a Popular Movement

The creation of a single party has the been the Holy Grail of the democratic right for many years. The logic of the French system, though, is that it is only likely to occur in the period immediately before or after a presidential election. This was the case with the UMP. In the run-up to the 2002 election, the supporters of Jacques Chirac decided that they would seriously try to establish a single right-wing party. In November 2000, 364 of the 462 deputies and Senators of the democratic right signed a petition that called for the union of the right.[5] Significantly, the petition was supported by people outside Chirac's party, the RPR, even if the most notable absentee from the list was the leader of the UDF, François Bayrou. In contrast to most initiatives of this sort over the years, this one was followed up. With the President's support, some of Chirac's closest colleagues established the Union in Movement (Union en mouvement, UEM) and in December 2001 the UEM held its first public meeting. Importantly again, the meeting attracted people from the RPR, UDF, and DL, including the future Prime Minister and then DL Senator, Jean-Pierre Raffarin. By the time the presidential campaign was in full swing the faultlines were clear. Only a small proportion of the leading figures in both the UDF and DL actually supported the campaign of their own party leaders, Bayrou and Alain Madelin respectively. It was becoming clear that the party system was going to change. The result of the first round of the election confirmed the situation. Chirac was successful, while Bayrou and especially Madelin performed poorly. Chirac's supporters immediately announced the creation of the UMP. Madelin rallied to the UMP, even though Bayrou and the remnants of the UDF remained apart. The election was a triumph and the UMP emerged with an absolute majority in the National Assembly.

In some respects, it is difficult to identify the ideology of the UMP. This is not merely because it was only formed so recently, but also because it brings together people who have rather different views about the political process. After all, the UMP includes representatives of both the State-centred bonapartist tradition and the free-market *orléaniste* tradition. It is certainly true that in recent years senior gaullists have been increasingly critical of the role of the State. Indeed, the first two waves of privatization in France were spearheaded by senior gaullist figures, such as Édouard Balladur and Alain Juppé (see Chapter 3). However, many of the ex-gaullists within the UMP are still far removed from the ex-DL neo-liberals in the same movement. In the short term, the UMP's ideological agenda, or more accurately its policy priorities, will be set by President Chirac and to a lesser degree by the Prime Minister, Jean-Pierre Raffarin. In his most recent statement of principles, Raffarin proposed what he called 'a new governance' (Raffarin 2002), which was centred around the concept of 'humanism'. It is not entirely clear what the Prime Minister means by the term 'humanism', apart from the fact that it appears to be used to suggest that politicians should listen to the demands of 'ordinary' French people more than they usually do. Of course, in the short term at least, the fact that the meaning of the term is unclear may be an advantage in that it can allow politicians with opposing beliefs to agree upon a common set of policies. Most notably, these include decentralization and tougher law and order measures. In the medium and long term, though, the UMP will have to find a way to manage the ideological divisions that exist within it.

Whatever its ideological ambiguities, at present the UMP is very well placed politically. At the 2002 legislative election, the UMP scored 33.3 per cent of the first-round vote. In comparative terms, this figure is not particularly large. After all, the Conservative party fared scarcely less well when it was whitewashed at the British general election in 2001. In terms of the French right, though, it is huge. Only the gaullists at the very high point of their electoral support in 1968 have exceeded this figure at a legislative election during the Fifth Republic. Moreover, the UMP's position is strong because its main competitor, the UDF, won a paltry 4.85 per cent of the vote. In the not-too-distant future, there is the possibility that the support for the UDF may increase as disillusionment with the UMP sets in or if the divisions within the party become too difficult to manage. There is also the possibility that anti-European right-wing parties may also do well at certain elections. However, for the moment at least the UMP is set fair.

One of the reasons why a single right-wing party was so difficult to establish concerned the problems surrounding the future organization of the party. This was a particularly thorny problem during the negotiations to set up the UMP. Inevitably, the gaullists were going to be the largest element of the new party. As a result, though, the UDF and DL feared that they could always be outvoted in any new organization. This was one of the main reasons why the UDF leadership decided to remain outside the UMP, even though DL agreed to merge. The fact remains that the UMP still faces some very difficult organizational issues. At the 2002 legislative election around 50 per cent of all UMP candidates used to belong to the gaullists, 25 per cent were former UDF members and slightly less than 20 per cent were ex-DL figures. The task of the new UMP leadership will be to ensure that each of these elements feels that it has a voice in the new organization. This is because if any one of them feels that it is being unfairly treated, then its representatives are bound to consider rejoining the UDF or leaving to set up their own party. Moreover, the organizational problems will be particularly acute because political parties are an essential element of a successful presidential campaign. There is already the fear that the UMP is merely the vehicle for Alain Juppé's 2007 presidential ambitions. Consequently, the leadership of the UMP will have to ensure that it devises a way of selecting its presidential candidate that is acceptable to everyone or it will risk experiencing severe internal divisions in a few years time. The former would almost classify as a miracle. The latter is nigh on inevitable.

The UMP is itself the result of a highly audacious political strategy. The democratic right in France has never been so united, at least in terms of the number and relative strength of the individual parties. However, the UMP will face some difficult electoral issues in the coming years. In particular, there will always be the temptation for other right-wing parties to be formed. There is still the space for an anti-European moderate right-wing party in the system. In addition, the UDF has the potential to establish itself as a repository for disgruntled UMP voters. More than that, the UMP must decide how to deal with the extreme right. At the 2002 legislative election, the UMP beat the left, even though the extreme right polled more than 11 per cent of the vote. When the left re-emerges as a serious political force, the UMP will be tempted to try to court the support of extreme right voters. Indeed, the UMP includes people who in the past have been willing to work with the extreme right in the pursuit of their own personal interests. At the second ballot of the 2002 presidential election, Jacques Chirac stood firm against the threat posed by Jean-Marie Le Pen. It is important that the UMP continues this policy and that it finds a way of ensuring that all of its representatives do the same.

The Union for French Democracy

The UDF was originally formed in 1978 as an electoral vehicle for President Giscard d'Estaing (Hanley 1999). Indeed, the party's name was a deliberate

reference to a book that the President had just published at the time
(Giscard d'Estaing 1978). At this point, the UDF was a confederation of
non-gaullist centre-right parties, including the Christian Democrats and
the liberals as well as a number of other very small organizations. Each of
these parties continued to maintain an independent existence, while simultaneously belonging to the UDF. This arrangement worked because there
was strength in numbers. In particular, it meant that the non-gaullist right
could negotiate with the gaullists on equal terms, and this is the main
reason why the UDF continued to exist even when Giscard's own political
ambitions effectively ended in 1981. All the same, the UDF was never a
united organization. It was more a flag of convenience for the representatives of its constituent groups. In the late 1990s matters came to a head. The
liberals, reconstituted in 1997 as DL under the leadership of Alain Madelin,
left the UDF. This was partly because Madelin's own version of Thatcher-
ism with a French face was at odds with the social market beliefs of the
Christian Democrats. It was also because elements mainly within DL were
willing to deal with the FN following an inconclusive set of results at the
1998 regional elections. With DL gone, the UDF reformed as a fully fledged
political party dominated by former Christian Democrats and headed by
François Bayrou. However, divisions within the party soon emerged when
Bayrou announced that he was standing against Chirac at the 2002
presidential election. Those who believed that their interests were best
served by supporting the incumbent President left to join the UMP and the
UDF was left as a rump centre-right party.

One of the UDF's main problems is that its core beliefs are not clear or,
more precisely, it is not clear how its core beliefs differ from those of the
leading figures within the UMP. There are two main elements to the UDF's
ideology. First, the party is unequivocally pro-European. This provides it
with a coherent message to put to the electorate. The problem, though,
is that people within the UMP are equally pro-European. Thus, the party is
not completely distinct from its larger right-wing rival. Secondly, the party
supports a social market economy. This means that its main reference
point is the market, but that it promotes welfare support and a strong
education system so that people from all backgrounds can prosper. Again,
though, while the liberals within the UMP do have a very different vision
of political life, many people within the UDF's main competitor hold the
same belief. Indeed, this overlap is inevitable, given that roughly a quarter

of the UMP's elected representatives came from the UDF. Thus, the UDF has an ideological problem. Unless the UMP changes its core values, the UDF will have tremendous difficulty in asserting a separate ideational identity for itself. It may serve as a refuge for disgruntled right-wing voters, but it is unlikely to be able to carve out a distinctive ideological profile.

The UDF's problems are serious because it now represents only a very small political force. At the 1978 legislative elections, the UDF scored 21.45 per cent of the first-ballot vote, just slightly behind the gaullists who won 22.62 per cent. Indeed, while this was the high point of the party's support, even at the 1999 European election the Bayrou list won 9.28 per cent of the vote. However, at the 2002 presidential election Bayrou scored only 6.83 per cent of the vote, and this was a better-than-expected performance, while at the 2002 legislative election the UDF won just 4.85 per cent of the vote. So, the party would appear to be in almost terminal decline. Correspondingly, the party's membership has suffered as well. As late as 1994, UDF officials claimed that the party had 80,000–100,000 members, even though this was most likely a very generous estimate (Hanley 1999: 188 n. 5). The current figures are not available, but it can be said without fear of contradiction that the membership base will have fallen considerably. In the meantime, the UDF leadership can bask in the glory that for the first time there is little internal dissent within the party. However, this has come at a hefty price. Moreover, experience suggests that it is likely to re-emerge sooner rather than later.

In this context, the issue of political strategy is ever present. In the French system, small parties can maintain an independent existence. They receive State funding as a function of the number of candidates they field at elections and the amount of votes they receive. In addition, the proportional system used primarily for European and regional elections provides the opportunity for voters to support smaller parties, while small parties have an incentive to field a candidate at the first ballot of presidential elections so that they can influence the coalition-building process between the two rounds (see Chapter 4). For these reasons, the UDF can soldier on and hope that disappointed UMP voters and parliamentarians return to the fold. For the most part, though, this is likely to be a vain hope. The UDF is destined to remain a small political force at least until the next realignment of the French right. In the meantime, it will have no option but to negotiate with the UMP and it will do so from a very disadvantageous position.

The parties of the extreme right

The extreme right is not a new phenomenon in France. During the Third Republic, there were groups such as Action française and people such as Charles Maurras who were identified with the extreme right. Similarly, the transfer of powers to Marshal Pétain in 1940 saw the creation of a neo-fascist state in France (see Chapter 1). Needless to say, the extreme right was discredited after the war. However, it re-emerged in 1953 in the form of the UDCA under the leadership of Pierre Poujade. The *poujadiste* movement started life as a collection of small shopkeepers, opposed to the building of supermarkets and to the level of commercial taxes they had to pay. Very soon, though, the UDCA articulated a number of classic extreme right themes. The *poujadistes* were anti-intellectual, anti-parliamentary, anti-communist, anti-Semitic, and xenophobic. In particular, the party opposed France's withdrawal from Indo-China and was in favour of Algeria remaining French. Despite its initial success, the UDCA did not survive the beginning of the Fifth Republic as many of its protest voters rallied to de Gaulle. There was a residual pro-French Algeria vote. More-over, an extreme right candidate, Jean-Louis Tixier-Vignancour, contested the 1965 presidential election. All the same, by the late 1960s the extreme right had disappeared from the political scene. In this context, the National Front (Front national, FN) was formed on 5 October 1972 under the leadership of Jean-Marie Le Pen. For more than a decade the FN was a tiny force. However, it burst on the scene in the early 1980s and has remained a significant political actor ever since. Even so, in 1999 the party split. At this point, the long-standing antagonisms between Le Pen and his main rival, Bruno Mégret, came to a head and Mégret tried to take control of the party. In the end, Le Pen wrested back control of the FN and Mégret established a new party, the National Republican Movement (Mouvement national républicain, MNR). Once again, Le Pen was the undisputed leader of the FN and his performance at the first round of the 2002 presidential election was startling. By contrast, Mégret performed poorly and the MNR is now only a marginal political movement.

The FN is a single-issue party in the sense that immigration is claimed to be the source of most of the country's political ills. For example, the FN wants to end immigration to France and find ways of repatriating immigrants who are resident in the country. The FN sees immigration as a threat to the economy and social order. The party has suggested that unemployment can be reduced by the repatriation of immigrants. It has also proposed that there should be a policy of so-called 'national preference', whereby French citizens (or rather white French citizens) should have prioritized access to welfare benefits. In addition, the party argues that immigrants are responsible for high levels of crime, particularly in inner-city areas. More generally, the FN is opposed to everything which is a threat to what it considers to be traditional French values. So, FN mayors banned from municipal libraries certain books that they deemed to be inappropriate reading matter. The FN also opposes the European Union and globalization because both are said to threaten the established French way of doing things. In short, the FN plays on the fears of the most vulnerable in society and its support now comes disproportionately from the poorer sections of society (Perrineau 1997). While the party's voters are not necessarily racist, its ideology harks back to the fascist groups and movements of the pre-war period.

The continued support for the FN has surprised many observers. At the outset, the party was electorally irrelevant. The FN won only 0.5 per cent at the general election in 1973, while Le Pen himself only won 0.75 per cent at the 1974 presidential election. Indeed, at the 1981 presidential election, Le Pen failed to obtain the 500 sponsors necessary for him even to stand at the election and in the 1981 legislative elections the party won just 0.35 per cent of the vote. Thereafter, though, the party started to win votes. At first, it won support in isolated places. For example, at the March 1983 municipal elections, Le Pen stood as a candidate in the 20th arrondissement in Paris and won 11 per cent of the vote. In September 1983 at a municipal council by-election, the FN candidate won 17 per cent at the first ballot and four councillors were elected at the second ballot after a deal with the other parties of the right. From this point on, the FN won support nationally. At the 1984 European elections the FN won 10.9 per cent, electing 10 MEPs. At the 1986 parliamentary elections it outpolled the communists for the first time and won 9.8 per cent of the vote and, benefiting from the system of proportional representation, returned 35 deputies. Thereafter, the FN's support has fluctuated between the 10–15 per cent mark at most elections.

The FN's low point was in the period immediately after the split with the MNR when it won 5.69 per cent at the 1999 European election. However, at this election the MNR itself won 3.28 per cent so the aggregate vote for the extreme right was still around the lower end of its normal range. Needless to say, the FN's high point was the 2002 presidential election when Le Pen won 16.86 per cent of the vote at the first ballot and 17.79 per cent at the second. For his part, at the first ballot of the same election Mégret scored 2.34 per cent.

The key organizational characteristic of the FN is the top-down approach to decision-making. In short, Le Pen is in full control of the party. More than that, Le Pen has manoeuvred some of his relatives into key positions in the party hierarchy. Indeed, the split within the party was brought about when Le Pen tried to impose his wife as the head of the party list at the expense of Mégret in advance of the 1999 European elections. The party does not have a mass membership. This is partly because there is still a stigma attached to supporting the FN. In most places it is not socially acceptable to be openly associated with the party. However, the 1999 split was disastrous in this regard. At the time, 62 of the party's 96 departmental organizers left to join the MNR. The fact that the MNR failed to establish itself electorally and that most of those who left the party feel that they cannot or do not want to return has meant that the FN has been left with a relatively weak organization for a party with such a large vote. Indeed, the high level of support for Le Pen at the 2002 presidential election was all the more striking because the number of party militants who were involved in routine activities such as putting up campaign posters was relatively small.

There is a body of opinion that suggests the FN will wither away when Le Pen stands down. Whether or not it does so, one day the party will face a key strategic question. Up to now, Le Pen has insisted that the FN should not even try to ally with the democratic right and the party has probably gained support because of this attitude. In the aftermath of the 2002 election, though, the party faces a dilemma. Is it a sufficient return on investment to continue to adopt an independent strategy and win 10–18 per cent of the vote, but to have absolutely no policy influence? Would it not be better, as the MNR believes, to try to do a deal with the moderate right in the hope of forming a coalition and entering government? For Le Pen, the answer is unequivocal. The established parties are corrupt and cannot be dealt with. However, in the post-Le Pen era, the issue is bound to be raised once again and this is the point when the continued existence of the FN will be called into question. That time, though, may still be some way off.

Conclusion

Political parties are the basic actors within the French political system. The competition between their ideas helps to establish the policy agenda. The competition between their representatives is the foundation of electoral life. In France, party competition has certain characteristics. These characteristics are not necessarily unique to France. Indeed, the question of whether or not France is exceptional, be it in this regard or any other, is by definition a comparative issue and can only be addressed properly from a comparative perspective. All the same, what we can say is that political parties establish a particular context in which the institutions of the French political system have operated. Three main characteristics stand out in this regard.

The first is the importance of the left/right divide. Those who can remember the 1970s, never mind the 1930s or before, are acutely aware that the divisions between the left and the right are no longer the same now as they were previously (see Chapter 1). Even so, it still matters whether the left or the right is in power. The outcomes of the political process and the operation of political institutions will at least partly depend upon which side is in power. The most prominent reforms introduced by the left in the period 1997–2002, such as the PACS legislation and the 35-hour working week, are very different from the ones proposed by the Raffarin government immediately following the 2002 election. The second point is that there are multiple divisions within both the left and the right. There is a wide variety of political ideas in the French party system. As with the basic competition between the left and the right, the outcomes of the political process and the operation of political institutions will at least partly depend upon the balance of power within the left and the right at any one time. So, for example, it is tremendously important whether the right is divided between a more or less equal set of forces or whether a single moderate right-wing party is dominant, as is currently the case with the UMP. This is because the internal balance of forces within both the right and the left helps to determine the nature of presidential politics, legislative politics, and indeed many other aspects of the political process (see especially Chapters 4 and 6). The third point is that political institutions themselves help to shape the nature of party politics. For example, the mix of majoritarian and proportional electoral systems in the country helps both to fragment and unite the parties of the left and the right (see Chapters 4, 6, and 8). Similarly, as we have seen, the issue of State financing has helped to strengthen parties that are only moderately successful and that otherwise might have been forced to merge with a bigger organization.

All in all, political parties are both the subjects and the objects of the political process. They are the bearers of long-standing principles and their representatives are the promoters of short-term concerns. They are a source of stability and a motor for change. Thus, by identifying the main characteristics of party competition, it is possible to make some sense of the apparently confusing multi-party system in France. Even so, the ways in which political parties affect the operation of political institutions and are affected by them need to be considered in more detail if we are to appreciate the functioning of the political process more profoundly. As a result, the interaction of parties and institutions is a recurring theme of the chapters that follow.

....

KEY TERMS

- Party system fragmentation
- Left vs. Right
- Left-wing divisions

- Right-wing divisions
- The Extreme right

....

NOTES

1 In 1972 the PCF and the newly formed Socialist party agreed an alliance known as the 'union of the left'. At the centre of this alliance was the so-called Common Programme for Government. For a review of the discourse of the Common Programme, see Derville (1991: 32–3).

2 Except where indicated, all translations are by the author.

3 Details from *Libération*, 6 Apr. 2002.

4 Confusingly, the SFIO's title refers to the Second International in 1889.

5 Published in *Le Figaro*, 24 Nov. 2000.

GUIDE TO FURTHER READING

BELL, D., *Parties and Democracy in France: Parties under Presidentialism* (Aldershot, Ashgate, 2000).

Good introduction to political actors and the impact of presidentialism.

BOY, D., and MAYER, N. (eds.), *The French Voter Decides* (Ann Arbor, The University of Michigan Press, 1993).

Contains a lot of information about the left/right divide in France.

FYSH, P., and WOLFREYS, J., *The Politics of Racism in France* (London, Macmillan, 1998).

A good overview of the National Front.

HANLEY, D., *Party, Society, Government: Republican Democracy in France* (London, Berghahn, 2002).

A good introduction to many aspects of party political life with a historical slant.

LEWIS-BECK, M. (ed.), *How France Votes* (New York, Chatham House, 2000).

Focuses on parties and voters at the 1997 legislative election.

3

....

The State

Overview

This chapter examines the role of the State in France. There are three parts. The chapter begins by outlining the reasons why the French State has long been considered to be so strong. It then demonstrates why the strength of the French State was never quite as great as it was sometimes portrayed. It concludes by identifying the various ways in which the nature of State activity has changed over the course of the last twenty years.

Introduction

Even the author of one of the most influential works on the French State in recent times found it difficult to provide an answer to that most basic of questions, 'what is meant by the term "State"?' (Rosanvallon 1990: 291). At its most basic, the term 'State' is the collective name for a very varied set of political institutions. From the presidency down, the elected representatives and appointed officials who operate within these institutions are the actors who determine the strength of the State and who utilize the strength of the State to help shape the outcomes of the political process. At the same time, the term 'State' also refers to an idea, or more accurately a set of related ideas, about the most appropriate organization of political life. In short, the State is more than just the sum of its institutional parts. In this context, the respective positions of political parties and their representatives are shaped at least in part by long-standing attitudes towards the abstract concept of the 'State'. Equally, over the years the changing context of party politics has helped to shape the understanding of this concept itself. In this context, there is a common perception that the State in France is very strong and there is an assumption that the people who occupy the most important positions within the State are powerful political actors. In fact, the strength of the State was never as great as some of the rhetoric may have suggested and even the most senior political actors were never able simply to change the set of State institutions to suit their own purposes or to rely on the State to implement their political ambitions. In the context of this book, the issue of State capacity is fundamental. The functioning of many French political institutions is intimately associated with the strength of the State. For example, the opportunity for presidential leadership, the role of the judiciary, the position of the administration, and the organization of local government all depend at least in part on the basic role of the State. So, a directly elected president at the head of a cohesive and purposive State is potentially a real force to be reckoned with. However, a directly elected president heading a divided and directionless State will have considerable difficulty in exercising strategic leadership. The evidence suggests that the State in France is moving in the latter direction and that the already fragmented State is becoming smaller and less cohesive.

The strong French State

In France, there is an abiding myth of the strong French State. The notion that change can and should come about by way of the State is long-standing and very widespread. Indeed, this notion has not just been the property of the left, which might be considered naturally sympathetic to such an idea. Over the years, it has also been associated with the right. For example, in his successful presidential election campaign in 1995, Jacques Chirac repeatedly stressed the importance of the 'republican State'. 'The republican State', he argued, 'is an impartial State, one that guarantees national cohesion and solidarity between citizens, between generations, between all parts of the territory' (Chirac 1994: 81). The strength of the French State is based on three elements: a normative belief in the appropriateness of State action; a wide range of State-centred organizations; and considerable evidence of State intervention. Thus, State power in France has both an ideational and an institutional foundation.

The normative element of the strong State is based on the idea that the State represents the common good, the general will, or the national interest. This idea was a central element of the revolutionary doctrine in 1789. The State, it was argued, represented the will of the people. This is because the State was a collective entity. The State did not represent one force, or one set of concerns. Instead, the State was able to transcend individual, factional, and, as we might now put it, party political interests. In this context, the State had a tremendous legitimacy. The State was the incarnation of the will of the people. The sovereignty of the people, or the nation, was expressed through the State. As a result, anything that was done by the State or in the name of the State could be said to have been done in the interests of the people. In this way, the State had a licence to intervene in the affairs of society.

The normative element of the strong State was reinforced by a belief in the efficiency of State action. There has always been a strong positivist tradition in French political life. Indeed, this tradition pre-dates the revolutionary period. This strand of thought, derived from the work of Comte (1798–1857) and Saint-Simon (1760–1825), endorses the idea that there is such a thing as social progress. Societies can advance. They can improve their lot. That said, such progress can only come about if it is properly planned and executed. In other words, it can only come about if it occurs scientifically, if it is based on rational thinking (and not theology or metaphysics). In the context of politics, this idea became linked to the notion that the State is the most appropriate vehicle for bringing about scientific social progress. This is because the State, as we have seen, is deemed to be impartial. As such, it does not contaminate the findings of scientific social advancement, the results of rational thought. Thus, plans for social reform are best conceived within State institutions and reforms are best implemented through State institutions. The net result is the belief not only that the State can legitimately intervene in the affairs of society, but that the State should intervene in the affairs of society because this is the best way of bringing about scientific social progress.

The belief in the legitimacy and the efficacy of State intervention has had a tremendous impact on the normative framework of political life. For example, as we shall see in Chapter 5, the higher civil service has been seen not only as an expression of the public interest, but also as the main motor for social advancement. This is the basis of the idea that France is a technocracy. In addition, the doctrine of 'public service' has been a powerful mobilizing force. In France the term 'public service' is associated with a variety of different meanings and definitions (Denoix de Saint Marc 1996: 13). However, the doctrine is founded on the idea that the public service comprises a set of organizations that respond to a particular set of needs (policing, education, heating, transport, and so on) and that carry out certain social functions (ibid. 49). This latter aspect is especially important because it relates to one of the fundamental principles of the Revolution, namely equality. In practical terms, it means that a citizen living in, say, a mountainous region has an equal right to electricity, water, telecommunications, and so forth to a citizen living in a major city. In other words, it means that even if the cost of providing public services to the former is much greater than to the latter, nonetheless the State has a basic responsibility to do so. More generally, in the post-war period the belief in the legitimacy and the efficacy of State intervention resulted in strong support for *dirigisme*, or State control of the economy. Indeed, the importance of *dirigisme* was that it was seen not only as a means of managing the domestic economy, but also as a way of maximizing France's influence as an economic actor on the world stage. In this latter regard, *dirigisme* was an instrument of foreign policy as well as domestic policy.

All told, the idea of State intervention is deeply embedded in French political life. It is associated with the Republic, hence the uncontested political organization of the regime. It is also associated with a conception of the 'good life', hence the basic aspiration of the citizens of the Republic. This is one of the main reasons why historically the parties of the right, especially the gaullists, have championed the State. Indeed, the gaullist idea that a strong State was necessary for the reconstruction of national grandeur was fundamental to the development of the political system in the early years of the Fifth Republic. So, for example, referring to France in 1958, de Gaulle wrote: 'After the terrible decline which she had suffered for more than a hundred years she must use the respite which chance had accorded her to re-establish her power, her wealth and her influence in tune with the spirit of modern times. Failing this, a catastrophe on the scale of the century might one day crush her for ever. The means of this renewal were the State, progress and independence' (de Gaulle 1971: 36).[1] In this context, when Chirac refers to the State (see above), he is trying to associate himself not just with the General, but also with some of the most fundamental and cherished values of French political life, values that transcend the parties of the right and that are embedded in the most basic beliefs of the people as a whole.

The normative element of the strong State model is important not just because it forms a core set of values and beliefs but also because it has resulted in the creation of an almost bewildering range of State-centred organizations. In fact, so vast is the number and so great is the variety of State institutions and services that it is almost impossible, and certainly impractical, to provide a comprehensive list of them. All the same, there are various indicators of the vast range of State-centred organizations in France.

The strength of the State in France can be gauged by the number and organization of government departments. In August 2002 there were fifteen full Ministers and a further twenty-three junior Ministers (see Table 3.1). Indeed, these figures are actually smaller than for some of the governments in the late 1980s and early 1990s. For example, in 1988 the Rocard government included no fewer than thirty-one Ministers and seventeen junior Ministers. That said, the range of State activity in this regard is best measured by the areas covered by the activity of government departments, rather than by the number of departments alone. In this regard, it is scarcely an exaggeration to say that there is no element of French life that is not shadowed by a government department. To put it another way and perhaps more accurately, the State has the potential to intervene in every aspect of public and private life and government departments are organized accordingly. So, as in most other countries, there are Ministries relating to Finance, Defence, Employment, Sport, and so forth. In addition, the State is constantly trying to find new ways of responding to issues as they arise. For example, in the late 1980s a Minister for Towns was established to find a global response to the particular problems faced in urban areas. Indeed, on occasions the creativity of the State in this regard seems to know no bounds. For example, in 2001 only the Minister himself, Guy Hascoët, seemed to know precisely what his department, the Secretariat of State for the Solidarity Economy, actually stood for and was trying to achieve. The basic point is that one indicator of the tremendous range of State-centred organizations in France is the number and nomenclature of government departments.

A further indicator of the range of State-centred institutions can be

TABLE 3.1	Ministries and junior Ministries in the Raffarin government, 2002

Ministry (in order of protocol)	Associated junior Ministries: delegated Ministers and Secretaries of State
Prime Minister	Secretary of State for Parliamentary Affairs
Minister of the Interior, Internal Security, and Local Freedoms	Delegated Minister for Local Freedoms
Minister of Social Affairs, Employment, and Solidarity	Delegated Minister for Cities and Urban Renewal
	Delegated Minister for Parity and Professional Equality
	Secretary of State for the Fight against Social Exclusion
	Secretary of State for the Elderly
Minister of Justice	Secretary of State for Building Programmes for Justice
Minister of Foreign Affairs	Delegated Minister for European Affairs
	Delegated Minister for Cooperation and Francophone Countries
	Secretary of State for Foreign Affairs
Minister of Defence	Secretary of State for Veteran Affairs
Minister of Education	Delegated Minister for Teaching
	Delegated Minister for Research and New Technologies
Minister of the Economy, Finance, and Industry	Delegated Minister for the Budget and Budgetary Reform
	Delegated Minister for Industry
	Delegated Minister for Foreign Trade
	Secretary of State for Small and Medium-Sized Firms, Trade, Crafts, Liberal Professions, and Consumption
Minister of Infrastructure, Transport and Housing, Tourism, and the Sea	Secretary of State for Transport and the Sea
	Secretary of State for Tourism
Minister of the Ecology and Sustainable Development	Secretary of State for Sustainable Development
Minister of Health, the Family, and the Handicapped	Delegated Minister for the Family
	Secretary of State for the Handicapped
Minister of Agriculture, Fishing, and Rural Affairs	
Minister of Culture and Communication	
Minister of the Public Service, State Reform, and Territorial Development	Secretary of State for State Reform
Minister of Overseas Departments and Territories	
Minister of Sport	

found in the various forms of public enterprises that exist in France. There is a long history of public-sector companies in France. Indeed, even before the Revolution there were State-owned mining companies as well as a variety of other State-controlled commercial and industrial activities. That said, the majority of the most familiar examples of State intervention were established somewhat later. For example, in 1889 the State telephone monopoly was established, while in 1923 the State broadcasting monopoly was created. Thereafter, the range of State-centred public enterprises was extended further on two main occasions (see Table 3.2). The first occurred from 1944–6. During this period, the Liberation governments (headed initially at least by General de Gaulle) nationalized a wide range of private companies. As a result, from this point on most utilities were under State control as was a large proportion of the banking and insurance industries. The second occasion occurred in 1982. The newly elected Socialist government passed a bill which nationalized a range of private industrial companies as well as the remaining banks and insurance companies (see Chapter 1). By this time, therefore, the number of public-sector enterprises was very large indeed as was their range of economic and industrial activity.

In fact, though, the breadth of State intervention in this domain extends far beyond public utilities and nationalized companies. For example, the public-sector includes hospitals, universities, and schools. These are common to all countries and France is no exception. In contrast, though,

TABLE 3.2	The dates of the main nationalizations in France
Date	Company/area of activity
1937	Railways
1944–6	Coal
1945	Renault (cars), Air France (airline)
1946	Electricity, gas
	The Bank of France and four commercial banks (inc. Société Générale and Crédit lyonnais), plus the main insurance companies
1982	Thomson-Brandt (electronics), CII Honeywell-Bull (computers), Pechiney-Ugine-Kuhlman (aluminium and chemicals), Dassault-Breguet (defence), Matra (aeronautics), Saint-Gobain (glass), Rhône-Poulenc (textiles and chemicals)
	Steel
	The remaining banks and insurance companies

France supports cultural projects perhaps more than in most other countries. For example, there are cultural organizations such as museums,
libraries, and national theatres, including the Comédie-Française. Moreover, the French continue to spend considerable sums on promoting the
use of the French language throughout the world. In addition, there is a
wide range of economic development organizations, such as the Planning
Commission, which was established in 1946, and the Regional Development and Action Authority (DATAR), which was set up in 1963 to oversee
the process of regional regeneration (see Chapter 8). Indeed, in the economic domain the level of State intervention goes far beyond these sorts of
organizations and includes a myriad of specific initiatives and policy
instruments. For example, in the 1960s and 1970s the State was associated
with certain high-profile programmes or *grands projets* (Berger 1981).
These included the development of Concorde, Airbus, the high-speed
train, and support for the French computer industry. More recently, State
intervention was a fundamental component of the French contribution to
the Channel Tunnel (in contrast to the British attitude towards the project). Indeed, the French State continues to play an active role in the European space programme as well as various other international high-tech
research projects. Also in the 1960s and 1970s the State was willing to
provide financial support for lame ducks (ibid.). This was reflected not just
in support for particular firms that were threatened with bankruptcy, but
also in laws that restricted the activity of supermarkets and defended the
position of small shopkeepers. All told, the French have long used the State
as a vehicle for promoting economic, social, and cultural development
both domestically and abroad. As a result, there is an almost incredible
variety of institutions through which the State's activity has been
channelled over the years.

Against this background, the activity of the State can be measured in a
number of ways. For example, even though the Court of Accounts was
unable to identify the precise number of people employed by the State (see
Chapter 7), one official report estimated that in 1992–3 a total of 6,460,000
people were engaged in State-sector activities (Picq 1995: 147). This figure is
reflected in the extent to which State-controlled companies are responsible
for delivering public services (see Table 3.3). France has a higher level of
public-service delivery than the UK, but a lower level than a country like
the Netherlands. The level of State activity can also be shown by the use of

the country's gross domestic product (GDP) (see Table 3.4). Government consumption in France is higher than the European average and much higher than in the USA, even though it is still less than in the UK and Scandinavian countries, like Sweden, where there is a well-developed welfare state. The almost inevitable consequence of a relatively high level of government consumption in France is a similarly high level of tax as a percentage of GDP (see Table 3.5). In France, the overall tax burden is much higher than in the USA and is also higher than in the UK and Europe generally, even though it remains lower than in Sweden. The bottom line is that France is not exceptional. The various measurements of activity suggest that the State's presence is greater in certain other countries than in France. All the same, there is no doubt that the French State has been extremely active over time and that this activity can be seen in a variety of different indicators.

The myth of the strong French State

There is no doubt that in France the State has been the subject of a powerful mobilizing discourse, that it has been associated with a myriad of public-sector institutions, and that its presence can be indicated in a variety of different ways. All the same, the myth of the strong French State

TABLE 3.3	The percentage of the population receiving services from public-sector organizations, 1992		
Sector	France	The Netherlands	UK
Water	25	100	12
Cleaning	60	100	17
Household waste	20	82	70
Heat	20	100	—
Electricity	100	100	10
Gas	100	100	10
Cable	20	—	0
Urban transport	30	100	—

Source: Adapted from Les Cahiers français, *L'État en question*, no. 271, Paris, La Documentation française (1995: 62).

TABLE 3.4	The use of GDP in France and elsewhere, 1992 (%)					
Country	Private con- sumption	Government con- sumption	Gross fixed capital formation	Change in stocks	Balance of exports and imports	GDP at market prices
France	60.5	18.6	20.0	0.3	1.2	100.0
USA	67.1	17.7	15.7	0.1	−0.7	100.0
UK	64.0	22.3	15.6	0.4	1.6	100.0
Sweden	54.2	27.0	18.9	−1.7	1.6	100.0
EC average	62.7	16.4	20.3	0.0	0.0	99.4

Source: Adapted from Edye and Lintner (1996: 420).

TABLE 3.5	The tax structure in France and elsewhere, 1991 (% of GDP)					
	Tax	Income tax	Business tax	Social ins.	Goods/ services	Others
France	43.7	11.8	5.4	40.6	28.2	14.1
USA	29.9	35.8	7.3	28.2	16.5	12.2
UK	36.7	28.4	11.0	16.6	30.4	13.6
Sweden	56.9	37.9	3.1	25.4	24.6	9.0
EC average	40.8	25.9	7.6	25.9	31.9	8.7

Source: Adapted from Les Cahiers français, L'État en question, no. 271, Paris, La Documentation française (1995: 15).

is just that: a myth. So, while there is no doubt that people have looked to the State to solve their economic and social problems and that the State has devised a tremendous number of ways in which it has tried to respond to this demand, all the same the State has never been quite as purposeful and cohesive as some of the more exaggerated rhetoric has suggested. More than that, the State has very often worked with private actors in order to expedite its affairs. In short, two of the basic assumptions on which the myth of the strong French State is based are false. The State has never been a cohesive unit and the State has always operated in association with social forces. This section addresses both of these issues.

In France, the State is often assumed to be a unitary actor. That is to say, reference is made to the term 'State' in the singular and the State as a unitary actor is deemed to be a coherent and cohesive force. This way of viewing the French State is misleading. The State has never been a unitary actor. It has always been divided. In fact, the term 'State' is best understood as referring to a collection of ideas, institutions, and policy instruments. In this context, coherent and cohesive State action is almost a contradiction in terms. Individual elements of the State may have been able to act successfully. Moreover, under certain conditions the State as a whole was able to act relatively coherently. As Vincent Wright noted, when the State 'mobilised around simple objectives (immediate post-war reconstruction) or when it operated in propitious conditions, this machine could provide the sense of direction which elicited the admiration of foreign observers and provided the basis for myth-making' (Wright 1997: 151). However, in general terms the State as a collective entity has always had considerable difficulty in acting purposefully. Thus, there is no doubt a real sense in which the individual elements of the State have been important actors in French political life. Moreover, there is also no doubt that collectively the various components of the State have played an important role in the economic, social, and political life of the country. However, the French State has always been internally divided and these divisions have often rendered purposive State action very difficult.

The divided nature of the French State can been seen in a variety of different ways. For example, the government is a conglomeration of competing Ministries (see Table 3.1). Undoubtedly these Ministries share a basic collective loyalty. After all, the government stands or falls together. However, there are basic and unavoidable conflicts within the government. For example, there is a basic tension between the Finance Ministry, which seeks to balance the government's budgetary books, and all the other Ministries, which need to spend money to pay for their projects. This tension is reflected in the often tense discussions that take place each year during the preparation of the budget. More than that, there is intense competition between the spending Ministries. After all, there is a finite amount of money at the government's disposal and each Ministry wants as much of the share of the budgetary pie as possible for itself. Thus, the very nature of the budgetary process means that the collective loyalty of the government is always severely tested. More than that, the government is divided between vertical Ministries and horizontal Ministries. The former concern themselves with a discrete aspect of government activity. Examples include the Defence Ministry or the Education Ministry. The latter range over various policy areas. They include the Finance Ministry as well as others, including the Ministry for Towns. Horizontal Ministries are in a difficult position. They can only act with the cooperation of other Ministries. These same Ministries, though, are often reluctant to facilitate such cooperation. They have a particular policy turf to defend and they have little incentive to allow another Ministry to trespass upon it. The result is trench warfare and an absence of joined-up government. In this context, cohesive State action is the exception rather than the rule.

Similar divisions can be seen across the range of public-sector organizations more generally. For example, there are various categories of public-sector companies in France. There are public enterprises of an administrative nature (*établissements publics à caractère administratif*). These include museums and schools. There are public enterprises of an industrial and commercial nature (*établissements publics à caractère industriel et commercial*). This category includes companies like EDF, GDF, the SNCF (since 1982), and the RATP. There are mixed economy companies. As their name suggests, the capital of these companies is held at least in part by private investors. Examples include France Télécom (since 1996). There are also private companies with public capital. These are companies that operate in the manner of private-sector businesses, but where the State is the sole shareholder. The best-known examples include the public-sector broadcasting company, France Télévision. The differences between these organizations relate amongst other things to the type of legal regime to which they are subject (public or private), the status of their employees (civil servants or otherwise), and the extent to which the State controls their activities (including appointments to the board of management). The net effect, though, is a very varied set of institutions that operate under an almost equally varied set of legal, economic, and political conditions. In this context, the opportunity to mobilize these organizations in the pursuit of collective interests is very small indeed. More than that, some of the aforementioned institutions themselves are conglomerations of deeply entrenched interests and concerns. Thus, not only is it difficult to exercise strategic State-centred leadership through these institutions as a whole, it may be almost equally difficult to exercise leadership in one particular domain. For example, in

1995 the government's plans to change the pension structure of railway workers in the SNCF met with huge resistance and had to be abandoned in the most humiliating manner. Whether or not the reform plans were justified is immaterial. The important point is that the government has always had difficulty in exercising strategic direction over State institutions both individually and collectively. Thus, the notion of cohesive State-centred leadership is largely a myth.

By the same token, the idea that the State has operated separately from civil society is also a myth. In this regard, there is a natural tendency to see the State and society as two opposed and antagonistic forces. Indeed, this is the logic of the traditional rhetoric of the republican State. The individual elements of society are necessarily self-interested, so the argument goes, whereas the State is the expression of the national interest, or general will (see above). If the State and society are separate, it makes sense to talk about 'State power' and the extent to which the State intervenes in the affairs of civil society. In fact, though, experience has shown that in France the State and society are not two mutually exclusive entities. The relationship between them has not been zero-sum, whereby more power for one has necessarily meant less power for the other. On the contrary, there has been a long tradition of mutually beneficial cooperation. This is what Jack Hayward famously called the mobilization of private interests in the service of public ambitions (Hayward 1982). Indeed, Hayward identified this feature as the key characteristic of what he called the 'dual French policy style' (ibid.). In this context, it is something of a misnomer to talk about purposive State-centred leadership. This is because in many of the areas where the State has intervened in economic and social activity, it has done so with the cooperation and participation of social actors. In other words, State actors and private actors have worked together. There are plenty of examples to illustrate this point.

The first example of State/society cooperation can be found in the long-standing experience of public–private partnerships (PPPs) in France. A PPP is the situation where the responsibility for delivering a public service is transferred to a private organization. In France, PPPs take two main forms (Ribault 2001). The first, known as a *concession*, is where the public authorities choose a contractor who will finance and operate a particular service for a limited, but nonetheless usually substantial, period of time. The State saves the costs of setting up and maintaining the service, while the contractor is able to charge for the service and make a profit. After a fixed period, often up to seventy years, the responsibility for the service returns to the State. The second, known as an *affermage*, is where the public authorities finance the project, but the private actor operates the service on a day-to-day basis. In France, PPPs have a long history (ibid. 50–1). They were used to facilitate the development of the railway network in the 1870s. They became common in the 1930s when the electricity, gas, and water network was being constructed. They were also utilized in the 1950s and 1960s when the country's road network was extended. In the 1940s, some of the existing PPPs were taken over by the State as part of the government's programme of nationalization. However, in a number of areas PPPs continued to operate very successfully. Perhaps the best-known example in this regard concerns the provision of water supplies (see Table 3.6). Indeed, the long-standing French expertise in this domain was one of the main reasons why French water companies were given a number of the contracts to supply water in the UK when the system was privatized in the early 1990s.

Another example of State/society cooperation concerns the presence of sectoral corporatism. Corporatism is defined as 'a system of representation in which the constituent units are organized into a limited number of singular, compulsory, non-competitive hierarchically ordered and functionally differentiated categories, recognized or licensed (if not created) by the state and granted a deliberate representational monopoly within their respective categories in exchange for observing certain controls on their selections of leaders and articulation of demands and supports' (Schmitter

TABLE 3.6	The private delivery of water services in France
Year	% of total population served by private water companies
1938	25
1956	37
1970	48
1983	57
1995	75

Source: Ribault (2001: 51).

1974: 93–4). In the French context, this sort of arrangement has tended to work on a sector-by-sector basis (Jobert and Muller 1987). This is to say that in certain policy areas the State has developed privileged relations with key interest groups, while in other areas the relationship is more fluid. The most commonly cited examples of sectoral corporatism have been the relationship between the Agriculture Ministry and the main farmers' union, the Fédération nationale des syndicats d'exploitants agricoles (FNSEA), and the Education Ministry and the main teachers' union, the ex-Fédération de l'éducation nationale (FEN). In terms of the former, the relationship has been particularly strong under right-wing governments. Indeed, in 1986 a former head of the FNSEA was appointed as Minister for Agriculture by Jacques Chirac. In terms of the latter, the relationship used to be stronger under left-wing governments, although in recent times internal problems within the FEN and within the teaching profession more generally have made matters more difficult. The basic point, though, is that in these areas and others State actors and societal actors have often worked together to the mutual benefit of both parties.

Another good example of the interrelationship of State and society can be seen in the form of mutualism, or the management of policy areas by social partners in conjuction with the government. One good example of mutualism is the country's social security funds. The contemporary French system of social security was established in the period immediately after the Second World War. The central element of this system was the institutionalization of a set of social security funds. These funds are separate from the ordinary State budget and are run by special boards. In this context, the key point is that the social security system has been managed by a mixture of both State and societal actors. For example, the government (or, more specifically, the legislature, according to the wording of Article 34 of the 1958 Constitution) maintains the right to change the 'fundamental principles' of the system by way of ordinary legislation. Indeed, major reforms were passed in 1960, 1967, 1982, and 1996. Moreover, each year the government sets the basic level of insurance payments and establishes the different types of benefits to which subscribers are entitled. Thus, the government has been responsible for the overall functioning of the system. At the same time, the funds have been run on a day-to-day basis by boards mainly comprising representatives of trade unions and employers' organizations. In addition, these organizations have been responsible for collecting the contributions from the members of the fund and distributing the benefits to them. Over time, the relationship between the government and the boards has varied. For example, in 1967 a law was passed that reduced the representation of the unions on the boards, only for it to be increased again in 1982 when the newly elected Socialist government took office. Over and above such changes, the basic point is that in a key area, which includes pensions, health insurance, and unemployment benefits, the policy process has been managed jointly by the State and social actors.

The bottom line is that the State has never been quite as powerful as it may sometimes have appeared. Without doubt, there is a clear sense in which the State has always had a great deal of legitimacy. As a result, the rhetoric of State-led change sits well with some of the most basic traditions of French political competition. There is also no doubt that the State has had the capacity to shape the everyday life of its citizens. For example, and it may come as a surprise to British or American readers, in France the State has long since stipulated that parents cannot give their children 'inappropriate' first names and has approved the names that parents have selected. That said, the State has never been all-powerful. It has always been extremely divided, making it difficult to mobilize in support of a particular plan. Moreover, the State has always relied upon the support of private actors. The success of a particular policy has often been at least partly the result of cooperation between State and social actors, while attempts by the State to bring about change without the support of private actors have usually ended in humiliation. In this context, the strong French State, as it is commonly understood, is a myth. Indeed, this point is all the more important in the context of the ways in which the role of the French State has been reassessed over the course of the last ten years or so. This is the issue to which we shall now turn.

The changing architecture of the French State

In recent times, the State has faced a number of challenges and has responded to them by offloading some of its responsibilities, reorganizing its activities, and reimagining its basic ethos. In short, the French State has become less authoritative, less expansive, more responsive, and more multi-level.

The State has become less authoritative in the sense that its fundamental legitimacy has been challenged. In particular, the notion that citizens need to be protected from the State has become more prevalent. The idea that the State only imperfectly incarnates and guarantees the rights of man has become more widespread. This change has come about for a number of reasons. For example, in the 1960s and 1970s there were claims that the right was systematically appointing its supporters to key positions of influence within the public sector. In the 1980s the same charge was made against the left. The net result, though, was that the supposedly impartial State was considered to have been colonized by partisan interests. In a similar way, the State was seen to be acting increasingly arbitrarily. In the 1970s laws were passed by the right that increased the powers of the police to stop and search citizens. Equally, in the 1980s the left passed a number of symbolic reforms, such as the abolition of the death penalty, but was still willing to use the State for its own political interests, including illegal telephone tapping and the sinking of the Greenpeace ship the *Rainbow Warrior*, which was protesting against French nuclear tests in the South Pacific. More generally, the growth of the State in the 1950s and 1960s meant that there was an increase in rules, regulations, and basic State activity. In this context, there were more opportunities for public servants to make mistakes. There were more opportunities for the relationship between the citizen and the State to be contested. Against this general background, there was an increasing desire to control the State. The State needed to be checked in order to ensure that it worked effectively. Paradoxically, but probably unavoidably, most of these controls have been carried out by organizations situated within the State sector broadly understood. All the same, over time many of these organizations have proved to be able to carry out their tasks quite effectively.

One such institution is the so-called Mediator of the Republic, the French equivalent of the British- or Swedish-style ombudsman. The office of the Mediator was set up in 1973. The basic role of the Mediator is twofold. First, the Mediator investigates claims that citizens have been unfairly treated by public servants. In this context, it should be noted that the Mediator is not part of the judiciary. The office does not consider cases from a legal perspective. Indeed, the Mediator only issues recommendations, not judgments, and these recommendations have to be acted upon by the institution concerned. All the same, if a person believes that the administration, a local authority, a public enterprise, or any institution with a public-service mission has acted unfairly, then the matter can be referred to the Mediator via a deputy or Senator. Secondly, the Mediator can make proposals for change. Again, these proposals have to be taken up by others. Nonetheless, the Mediator has the opportunity to suggest ways in which the administration can operate better. At the outset, the fact that the Mediator was appointed by the President of the Republic in the Council of Ministers was criticized. There was a fear that partisan appointments might be made. In fact, this has not occurred. The current Mediator, Bernard Stasi, was a former centre-right Minister. However, he, like his predecessors, has maintained the independence of the office. More than that, a range of institutional features ensured that the post would be as far removed from partisan politics as possible. For example, the Mediator serves for a six-year, non-renewable term. Moreover, during this time, the incumbent cannot be removed from office. Perhaps most importantly of all, in law the Mediator is officially classed as an 'independent authority' and one which 'receives instructions from no other authority' (**www.mediateur-de-la-republique.fr**—accessed 11 March 2002). In this context, the impact of the office can be gauged by the increasing number of cases that have been referred to it over the years (ibid.). In 1973 1,773 cases were taken to the Mediator. In 1999, the figure had increased to 51,189. Overall, there is little doubt that the Mediator has had a direct effect on the lives of individual citizens, particularly regarding matters of immigration and consumer rights, and has helped to improve the relations between the consumers of public services and the State.

Another set of institutions that can be included in this category are the so-called independent administrative authorities (*autorités administratives indépendantes*, AAIs).[2] These are agencies that regulate State and private-sector activity in specified areas (see Table 3.7). In general terms, they regulate certain economic activities (e.g. the Commission for the Regulation of Electricity); they protect the citizen against the bureaucracy (e.g. the National Commission for Data Protection and Freedoms); and they have a particularly important role to play in the domain of public opinion, political campaigning, and communications (e.g. High Council for Broadcasting). As their name suggests, these institutions remain part of the

TABLE 3.7	Examples of independent administrative authorities

Year created	Name/area
1967	Commission for the Operation of the Stock Exchange
1977	Opinion Poll Commission
1978	National Commission on Data Protection and Freedoms
1978	Commission for the Access to Administrative Documents
1983	Commission for Consumer Protection
1984	National Commission for the Control of Election Campaigns Relating to the Presidential Election
1988	High Council for Broadcasting
1989	Insurance Control Commission
1989	Competition Council
1990	National Commission for Campaign Accounts and Political Financing
1996	Telecommunications Regulatory Authority
1999	Authority for the Control of Airport Disturbances
2000	The Children's Ombudsman
2000	Commission for the Regulation of Electricity

administration broadly understood. All the same, they are not part of any hierarchical chain of administrative command. In this sense, they operate independently. So, while there is no doubt that some institutions have been less independent than some might have wanted (most notably, the predecessors to the High Council for Broadcasting—the High Authority, established by the Socialists in 1982, and the National Commission for Communication and Freedoms, set up by the right in 1986), AAIs have become an increasingly common feature of the French administrative landscape. They are significant for two reasons. First, because they are a further sign of the belief that the State needs to be prevented from acting arbitrarily. They have the power to issue rules in certain areas. For example, the High Council for Broadcasting (Conseil supérieur de l'audiovisuel—CSA) ensures that all parties or presidential candidates receive a fair amount of radio and television airtime at elections. They also have the power to penalize both State and private actors if they fail to meet their responsibilities. For example, in July 1999 the Telecommunications Regulatory Authority threatened to fine France Télécom and withdraw its operating licence if it failed to change its policies. Secondly, they are also significant because they ensure that the State is only indirectly involved in the regulation of private-sector activity. Rather than civil servants or government Ministers directly intervening in the affairs of private companies, this responsibility is incumbent on a quasi-independent agency. Thus, in 1995 the CSA temporarily shut down a popular radio station, Skyrock, because of the controversial remarks of one of its presenters.[3] This decision was extremely unpopular in some quarters. However, the fact that it was carried out by an AAI meant that the government could not be accused of censorship. Overall, there is no doubt that AAIs mark a major break with the French republican tradition and that they are likely to be an increasingly common feature of the French political landscape.

The State has become less expansive in the sense that it has offloaded a number of its responsibilities onto the private sector. In 1982, the newly elected Socialist government embarked upon a major programme of nationalizations (see above). This policy, though, was a failure and for two reasons. It was a failure because the cost of the programme was excessive, not just because of the one-off amount that had to be paid to reimburse private shareholders, but also because of the ongoing charges associated with running often uncompetitive and loss-making concerns. It was also a failure because the government gave no impression that there was a strategic reason for the nationalizations, even after the programme was complete. In short, it seemed like a costly and merely symbolic reform. Against this background, and in the context of wider European, particularly British, developments, in the early 1980s the right was converted to a programme of privatization that it promoted in both the periods 1986–8 and 1993–7. Perhaps more significantly still, even though in 1988 Mitterrand was re-elected on the basis of a so-called 'ni-ni' policy (neither privatization, nor nationalization), in fact the government went ahead and introduced private capital into the public sector over the course of the next five years. More than that, in the period 1997–2002 the left-wing coalition approved a number of high-profile privatizations, even though the communists were part of the so-called plural majority. Indeed, there is good reason to believe that the receipts from privatization were greater under the left-wing government 1997–2002 than under the right-wing government 1993–7 (*Le Monde*, 8 April 2002). The net result is that since 1986 there has been a sporadic, but nonetheless fairly consistent process of privatization (see Box 3.1). Moreover, this process is all the more noteworthy because it has resulted in the privatization not only of most of the companies nationalized in 1982, but also of many of the public-sector companies that were taken under State control in the period 1944–6. True, it may well have been the case that nationalized companies never acted as a coherent industrial or economic bloc either prior to 1982 or after. In this sense, they never rendered the State a strategic actor. All the same, the fact that many of these companies have now returned to the private sector means that the State no longer has any opportunity to manipulate them for its own ends. This is the sense in which the State has become less expansive.

The State has become more responsive in the sense that it now has to pay much more attention to the demands of its citizens than was previously the case. In one sense, institutions such as the Mediator are an illustration of this point. In addition, though, the responsiveness of the State is seen across a much broader range of areas as well. In this regard, the French State has introduced a limited, but nonetheless important, set

BOX 3.1		The main full and part privatizations in France
The right	1986	Saint-Gobain (industrial)
	1987	Paribas (finance), Crédit commercial de France (credit), Agence Havas (publicity), TF1 (television station), Société générale (bank), Suez (bank), and others
	1988	Matra (defence)
	1993	Banque nationale de Paris (bank), Rhône-Poulenc (chemicals)
	1994	Elf-Aquitaine (petrol), UAP (insurance)
	1995	SEITA (tobacco), Usinor-Sacilor (steel), Pechiney (aluminium, packaging)
	1996	AGF (insurance), Renault (cars), and others
	1997	Bull (computers)
The left	1991	Crédit local de France (credit)
	1992	Total (petrol)
	1997	France Télécom (telecommunications)
	1998	Thomson CSF (high-tech industrial), GAN (insurance), France Télécom, Radio Monte Carlo
	1999	Air France (airline), Aérospatiale-Matra (aerospace), Crédit lyonnais (bank)
	2000	Thomson multimédia (media)
	2001	Banque Hervet (bank), Société française de Production (media)
	2002	Renault, Thomson multimédia, Autoroutes du sud de la France (roads)

of new public management (NPM) reforms (see Chapter 5). Derived from UK and American experience and based on the notion that the citizen is a consumer of public services and that these services need to be provided as efficiently and effectively as possible, NPM reforms privilege ideas such as internal competition for service delivery within the public sector, the evaluation of public services in terms of their cost-effectiveness, and the flexibility of public-sector institutions so that they can react to the changing demands of consumers more rapidly. More broadly, there has been an increase in competition in sectors that previously were under monopoly public-sector control. Here, the main impetus for change has come from the European Union. In a number of areas, France has dragged its feet compared with its European counterparts. Even so, there have been changes. Indeed, the usual pattern is for French governments to oppose European reforms in a very vocal and public way and then for the reforms to be introduced, albeit in a rather piecemeal manner and with less speed than in other European countries. So, for example, there is now more competition than ever before in telecommunications. Equally, prior to the Barcelona summit in March 2002 both Chirac and Jospin announced that they were not going to abandon the French way of delivering public services in the electricity and gas sectors. In effect, this meant maintaining a public-sector monopoly. In the end, France and Europe agreed a compromise. In relation to the supply of energy to businesses, the degree of competition would be increased. However, this reform would not extend to individual consumers. This allowed the President and Prime Minister to save face, while a row with France's European partners was avoided. Overall, the degree of liberalization in France has been smaller than in certain other countries, including Britain. All the same, pressure from Europe has meant that the French State has started to change in this regard. What is more, even this limited degree of change has challenged the foundations of some of the traditional French attitudes towards the public service, notably in terms of the uniformity of service provision across the national territory (see above and Chapter 8).

Finally, the State has become more multi-level in the sense that decision-making is no longer a purely Parisian affair. For a long time, the highly centralized system of local government meant that the policy-making process was centred on the capital (see Chapter 8). In this context, it made more sense to talk about the local administration of centralized policy decisions, rather than local self-government or local democracy. However, this situation has changed. As we shall see later in the book, the 1982 decentralization reforms reinvigorated local authorities. In particular, they permitted increasing policy differentiation at the sub-national level. Again, this change challenged the long-standing principle of the supposedly one and indivisible French Republic. However, it also meant that, more and more, public-sector policies could be tailored to meet the demands of specific local circumstances. By the same token, as we have already seen in the case of market liberalization, European integration has meant that policy decisions are increasingly taken at the supranational level. The best examples in this regard are agriculture policy, competition policy, and monetary policy. Indeed, in some cases the change in political practice has been spectacular. For example, in the post-war period French governments became used to manipulating the interest rate to suit the economic needs of the economy as a whole as well as the political needs of the government of the day. However, when France agreed to participate in Economic and Monetary Union, it also agreed to give up this power and transfer it to the European Central Bank. This marked a major change not just in the process of policy-making but also in attitudes towards policy-making. Governments were willing to divest themselves of important policy-making instruments so as to pursue the policy of European integration. Overall, the basic point is that decision-makers in Paris are less in control of their own destiny than was previously the case. In short, the domestic, centralized State is now merely one part of a more complex system of multi-level governance.

Conclusion

The notion of the strong French State was always more a myth than a reality. The State was always highly compartmentalized, riven with internal tensions, and reliant on the support of actors in the private sector. In this way, the State was never quite the cohesive and purposive unit that it sometimes appeared to be. Even so, the State was a significant force. Indeed, this point applied to individual elements of the State as well as to the State collectively. As a result, the people who occupied the key positions in the State had the potential to benefit from its authority and power. In practice, this applied to decision-makers in Paris and, in particular, to the

President, the Prime Minister, government Ministers, and those who worked at the highest levels of the public administration. True, the nature of the State was such that the power of these actors was always contested and their ability to deliver coherent policy outcomes could never be guaranteed. All the same, there were legitimate popular and political expectations that these people, or at least some of them and especially the President, could make a real difference to the policy process and, hence, to the everyday lives of individuals in the country. Now, the situation is different. The State is a much more contested and even less coherent actor than was previously the case. It is true that the party political competition for the presidency remains intense (see Chapters 1 and 4). However, there is little doubt that the successful candidate is now less well placed than ever before to be able to make good on the promises that were made during the electoral campaign. So, while the State remains a key component in the French system of governance, the opportunity for the State-centred leadership is now even less great than it ever was. As we shall see throughout the course of the book, this change has had a considerable impact on the political institutions of contemporary France and the French way of politics in general.

KEY TERMS

- Public ownership
- Administration
- Compartmentalisation
- European integration
- New public management

NOTES

1 Cited in translation.

2 In France, certain institutions which in other countries are usually classed as regulatory agencies do not have the status of an AAI. For example, the French Agency for Food Safety, which was created in 1999, is officially classed as a public enterprise of an administrative nature rather than an AAI.

3 The presenter was alleged to have said: 'a cop's dead, that's good news'.

GUIDE TO FURTHER READING

GUYOMARCH, A., MACHIN, H., and RITCHIE E., *France in the European Union* (London, Macmillan, 1998).

Good overview of the impact of Europe on France.

HALL, P., *Governing the Economy: The Politics of State Intervention in Britain and France* (Cambridge, Polity Press, 1986).

A path-breaking book on institutions from a comparative perspective.

LEVY, J., *Tocqueville's Revenge: State, Society, and Economy in Contemporary France* (Cambridge, Mass., Harvard University Press, 1999).

The best of the most recent books on the changing French State.

Modern and Contemporary France, 5/2 (1997).

Special edition on the changing French State with contributions from leading authors.

SCHMIDT, V., *From State to Market? The Transformation of French Business and Government* (Cambridge, Cambridge University Press, 1996).

Good overview of reform in the 1980s and 1990s.

4

The Dual Executive

Overview

This chapter focuses on the relationship between the President and Prime Minister. It has three main sections. The first section identifies the key constitutional and administrative powers of Presidents and Prime Ministers. The second section considers the importance of the direct election of the presidency. The third section accounts for the variations in presidential power by focusing on the role of political parties.

Introduction

The political system of the Fifth Republic is presidentialized, but the Fifth Republic does not have a presidential system of government. The political system is presidentialized in the sense that there is the expectation that the President will exercise leadership. Even so, the Fifth Republic has a semi-presidential system of government. This is a system where a popularly elected fixed-term President exists alongside a Prime Minister and Cabinet who are responsible to parliament (Elgie 1999a: 13). The important point about semi-presidential regimes is that the President is not the only key person within the executive. Instead, there is a dual executive in which a President and Prime Minister exist alongside each other. This type of system is associated with a fundamental problem. In semi-presidential regimes there is the potential for conflict between the President and Prime Minister. In some countries, conflict is avoided because the President is merely a figurehead and the Prime Minister is the dominant political figure. In France, the situation is different. The presidentialized nature of the political system means that the President is the only person who has the potential to exercise leadership over the political system as a whole. However, the constraints of the dual executive mean that the President is obliged to interact on an ongoing basis with the Prime Minister. Moreover, the capacity for presidential leadership is contingent upon the particular configuration of party politics at any given time. On occasions, the configuration of party support has allowed the Prime Minister to emerge as the main force within the dual executive. This is known as 'cohabitation'.

Presidents and Prime Ministers: constitutional and administrative resources

Constitutional powers

The 1958 Constitution indicates a range of areas in which the President and Prime Minister each has the right to act unilaterally. These can be called the discretionary powers of the President and Prime Minister. In addition, the Constitution also indicates a range of areas where powers are shared between the President and Prime Minister.[1] Overall, the Constitution creates a situation where there is the potential for conflict between the President and the Prime Minister especially during periods of cohabitation— the situation where the President comes from one political party and the Prime Minister comes from an opposing party (see below). (For a list of Presidents and Prime Ministers since 1959, see Table 1.2.) As a result, the constitutional balance of power is sometimes an uneasy one.

The discretionary powers of the President and Prime Minister

In contrast to the popular perception that France has a presidentialized system of government, the discretionary powers of the head of State are in fact relatively restricted. Indeed, Article 19 of the 1958 Constitution outlines just eight areas where the President can act independently.[2] In this respect, the President's most important powers include the appointment, but not the dismissal, of the Prime Minister (Article 8); the ability to dissolve the National Assembly, although not more than once in any twelve-month period (Article 12); the freedom to resign and, hence, to provoke a presidential election at which the President may stand again (implicit in Article

7); the right to chair the Council of Ministers, the French equivalent of the British Cabinet (Article 9); the right to have a message read out in the National Assembly and the Senate (Article 18); the power to ask the Constitutional Council to scrutinize a piece of legislation (Article 61); the opportunity to appoint three of the nine members of the Constitutional Council (including its President), albeit usually at certain predetermined times (Article 56); and the right to assume emergency powers, but only when there is a serious and immediate threat to the system (Article 16). In addition, mention should be made of Article 5 which states that the President 'endeavours to ensure respect for the Constitution' and that 'he provides, by his arbitration, for the regular functioning of the public authorities and the continuity of the State'.

Although limited in range and, in the case of Article 5, rather nebulous in meaning, there is no doubt that these powers may be very significant. For example, the use of Article 16 has been especially controversial. In April 1961, there was an attempted coup in Algeria by officers opposed to the process of decolonization there. In response, de Gaulle invoked Article 16 and assumed emergency powers for a full five-month period until 29 September, even though the rebellion in Algeria was quashed within a few days. While de Gaulle's use of his unilateral decree-making powers was actually quite limited during this time, the experience showed that Article 16 was an extremely important presidential prerogative. Another example concerns Article 56 and appointments to the Constitutional Council. Over the years, Presidents have taken full advantage of their powers in this regard to shape the partisan composition of the Council (see Chapter 7). For example, in February 1995, just three months before the end of his second term of office, Mitterrand appointed the staunch *mitterrandiste* and former Minister for Foreign Affairs, Roland Dumas, as President of the Council. Then, in March 2000, following Dumas's resignation on account of allegations about his part in a highly embarrassing corruption scandal, Chirac appointed a former colleague and loyal gaullist, Yves Guéna, as head of the Council. To the extent that the Council has the capacity to influence the political process, then the President is in a position to shape the content of the Council's decisions. Finally, Presidents have been quick to use both Article 12 and Article 8 to underpin their political authority (see below). So, in 1981 and 1988, Mitterrand invoked Article 12 and dissolved the National Assembly, allowing a pro-presidential majority to be returned.[3] Equally, successive Presidents have been able to use Article 8 to appoint loyal and indeed sometimes deferential Prime Ministers. Notable examples in this regard include de Gaulle's appointment of Pompidou and Couve de Murville, Pompidou's appointment of Messmer, Mitterrand's appointment of Cresson and Bérégovoy, and Chirac's appointment of Juppé and Raffarin.

These examples are telling. They indicate that the President is a significant actor in constitutional terms. However, the important point to note about the President's constitutional powers is that, with the main exception of the right to chair the Council of Ministers and to send a bill to the Constitutional Council, they are either one-off powers (the right to resign) or ones that can only be exercised either at pre-programmed intervals (appointments to the Constitutional Council), in exceptional circumstances (emergency powers), or with the support of either public opinion (the dissolution of the National Assembly) or a loyal parliamentary majority (the appointment of a subservient Prime Minister). Thus, the Constitution does not guarantee that the President will be directly involved in the day-to-day running of the country. Instead, it indicates that, while the head of State is undoubtedly an integral part of the political process, the President is only an independent and autonomous actor of either the first instance or the last resort.

In some respects, the Prime Minister is in a similar position. For example, like the President, the head of government has the power to send a bill to the Constitutional Council (Article 61). Similarly, the Prime Minister chairs the Council of Ministers should the President be absent (Article 21).[4] More importantly, though, and in stark contrast to the role of the President, the 1958 Constitution establishes the Prime Minister as the key day-to-day policy-making actor within the executive. In this respect, the head of government enjoys two general powers. First, the Prime Minister leads the government (Article 21), while the government is officially charged with determining and conducting the nation's policies and has the administration at its disposal (Article 20). Secondly, the Prime Minister is responsible for the government's dealings with parliament (implicit or explicit in most of Articles 34–50).

In constitutional terms, Articles 20 and 21 clearly indicate that the Prime Minister enjoys a privileged position *vis-à-vis* government Ministers. One very regular manifestation of this pre-eminence can be seen during the annual budgetary process. Here, the head of government is responsible for arbitrating between the conflicting demands of the spending Ministers, and, exceptional circumstances aside, the Prime Minister's decision is final (Carcassonne 1997: 400). Less frequently, Prime Ministers have taken it upon themselves to provide a lead in specific policy areas. For example, in 1989 Rocard issued a circular in which he outlined the government's policy with regard to the changing nature of the French public sector. Indeed, so influential was this document that it remained the main point of reference in this area for a number of years thereafter. However, perhaps the best indication of the Prime Minister's influence over the governmental decision-making process can be seen in the head of government's decree-making power. The Constitution gives the Prime Minister the power to pass the equivalent of secondary legislation in the areas that are outside the so-called 'domain of the law' (the combination of Articles 21, 34, and 37—see Chapter 4). As a result, whereas parliament passes around 70 laws each year, the Prime Minister issues around 8,000–9,000 interministerial decrees or orders (*règlements*) that have the force of law (Ardant 1991: 110). Although the decrees are prepared in conjunction with Ministers and the government's administrative services, the head of government's so-called *pouvoir règlementaire* means that the Prime Minister is intimately associated with the day-to-day business of governing.

In addition, Articles 34–50 endow the Prime Minister with a special constitutional position *vis-à-vis* parliament. Here, there is a major difference between the respective roles of the President and the Prime Minister. The President is not even allowed to set foot in the parliamentary chambers. Instead, as noted above, the President can merely request that a message be read out in the two houses (Article 18). By contrast, the Prime Minister plays a full role in the parliamentary process. The government is responsible to parliament (Articles 20, 49, and 50) and as head of government the Prime Minister assumes the role as the administration's main spokesperson, most notably during the weekly session of questions to the government in the National Assembly (see Chapter 6). In addition, the Prime Minister is closely involved in setting the parliamentary timetable (Article 48). More generally, the head of government is explicitly given the right to initiate legislation (Article 39).

The Prime Minister, then, bears personal responsibility in parliament for the government's record. This is, of course, a poisoned chalice. Some

Prime Ministers have established a reputation for being skilled parliamentarians. Examples include Pompidou during the de Gaulle presidency, Chaban-Delmas under the Pompidou presidency, and Mauroy during Mitterrand's first term in office. Others, though, have been less successful. The best example in this regard is Edith Cresson, whose spell in power at least made it clear to future generations how not to behave as Prime Minister. Whether they have been ultimately successful or not, the point remains that the Prime Minister rather than the President operates within the parliamentary domain.

Powers shared by the President and Prime Minister

In addition to the discretionary powers of the President and Prime Minister, both institutions possess two sets of shared constitutional powers. The first set comprises three policy areas (defence, foreign policy, and the independence of the judiciary) in which there are joint responsibilities but where ordinarily the President is the most important political figure.[5] So, the 1958 Constitution establishes the President as the commander-in-chief of the armed forces (Article 15) and as the guarantor of national independence and the integrity of the national territory (Article 5). It also states that the President negotiates and ratifies treaties (Article 52) and is then responsible for ensuring that treaties are respected (Article 5). Finally, the Constitution indicates that the President guarantees the independence of the judiciary (Article 64) and heads the Higher Council of the Magistrature, the body which oversees the judiciary (Article 65) (see Chapter 7). At the same time, however, the Constitution states that the Prime Minister is responsible for national defence (Article 21). It also implies that the government is involved in the process of drawing up certain forms of treaties (Article 52). Moreover, the Minister of Justice is designated as the Vice-President of the Higher Council of the Magistrature (Article 65), while various judicial decisions have to be countersigned by the Prime Minister.

In these three areas, therefore, the President, the Prime Minister, and other members of the government share certain constitutional powers. As a result, there is the potential for conflict between the various elements of the executive. Indeed, during cohabitation low-level skirmishes between the President and Prime Minister have been relatively commonplace (see below). Outside cohabitation, though, examples of conflict have been rare. For example, there was a problem in December 1984 when President

Mitterrand invited the Polish leader and head of the communist-supported *de facto* military government, Wojciech Jaruzelski, to an official meeting in Paris (Favier and Martin-Roland 1990: 361–71). Speaking in the National Assembly, the Prime Minister, Laurent Fabius, announced that he was 'troubled' by the President's decision and implied that he did not support the logic behind it. However, while Fabius's declaration undoubtedly caused a media stir, it did not provoke a change of policy or process. The visit went ahead as scheduled and the President continued to take decisions in the same way as before, namely without reference to the head of government.

In fact, this example simply confirms the point that in practice the President has been the pre-eminent political figure in each of these three areas. Indeed, together they comprise what is commonly known as the President's 'reserved domain', meaning that the head of State is responsible for setting the aims and objectives of policies, whereas the government is responsible for implementing decisions once they have been taken (Vedel 1993: 40). In the realm of defence the President's supremacy has been particularly notable. In part, this is because the President's constitutional powers are reinforced by a number of key legal prerogatives. For instance, the 1962 decree that restructured the organization of French defence policy-making indicates that the President is responsible for the 'conduct of operations' in the event of war (Howorth 1993: 152). Thus, when the Gulf War broke out in August 1990 the President told the Prime Minister not to bother coming back from holiday to attend the first meeting of the war crisis group (du Roy 2000: 121). In foreign affairs Presidents have been no less influential. Each President has been keen to speak as the voice of France. As a result, the history of the Fifth Republic is replete with presidential initiatives, or at least rhetoric. In this regard, the de Gaulle presidency was especially noteworthy. For example, the General's famous statement, 'Vive le Québec libre', was received euphorically in Montreal, even if it temporarily soured French relations with Ottawa. Similarly, the so-called Fouchet Plan, which was designed to institutionalize foreign policy cooperation between EC leaders, caused a great stir, but eventually failed. Mitterrand too was very active in this domain. His speech to the German Bundestag in January 1983 was particularly significant. In calling for short-range US nuclear missiles to be stationed in Germany and Belgium, Mitterrand clearly signalled his Atlanticist credentials. Moreover, he also laid the foundations for the subsequent deepening of Franco-German relations that occurred over the course of the next decade. Indeed, the only major difficulty between the two countries during this time came with Mitterrand's reaction to the fall of the Berlin Wall. Mitterrand's caution put him at odds with Chancellor Kohl's desire for a speedy unification of the two Germanys. Whatever the precise details of the situation, these examples all demonstrate that in defence and foreign affairs the President is without doubt the most important political player in the system. For the most part, Foreign and Defence Ministers merely articulate the official presidential line, while the Prime Minister, as the Jaruzelski example demonstrated, plays merely a bit part in the whole proceedings.

The second set of shared powers covers three more general types of situation. Here, experience suggests that the President and Prime Minister sometimes work together rather more closely. The first type of situation comprises the cases where the decision-making initiative lies with the Prime Minister, but where the President must formally approve the decision in question. For example, the President appoints and dismisses government Ministers on the proposal of the Prime Minister (Article 8); the President can call a referendum on certain issues on the basis of a proposal by the government or following a joint resolution by the two chambers of parliament (Article 11); the President also has the right to propose a constitutional amendment, but again only on the proposal of the Prime Minister or members of parliament (Article 89). The second type of situation involves decisions which are taken by the President but which then have to be countersigned by the Prime Minister and/or by other members of the government. This category includes the President's right to make certain administrative and State-sector appointments (Articles 13 and 21). The third type of situation consists of the instances where prime ministerial decisions have to be discussed in the Council of Ministers. This category includes government bills, all of which have to be approved in the Council of Ministers before they can go to parliament. In this case, the President, as the chair of the Council of Ministers, is at least party to the decision-making process (Article 9). It also includes the occasions when the government decides to make a bill a matter of confidence (Article 49).

The net effect of this second set of shared powers is to tie in many of the President's decisions with the approval, or at least the acknowledgement, of the Prime Minister and vice versa. For example, while the Prime

Minister proposes the names of government Ministers to the President, on occasions Presidents have imposed their own particular favourites on the head of government. Thus, during the Mitterrand era a number of presidential advisers, such as Pierre Bérégovoy and Jean-Louis Bianco, moved directly from the President's personal staff into governmental posts. At the same time, though, the fact that the powers of the President and Prime Minister are so closely intertwined in the aforementioned set of areas means that inevitably they are also contingent upon the political circumstances of the day (see below). For example, outside cohabitation the President can be reasonably sure that the Prime Minister will propose a referendum should the President wish one to be held. As a result, to date there have been in effect six *de facto* 'presidential' referendums (see Table 4.1).[6] During cohabitation, though, the Prime Minister has in effect a veto over any such proposal. Thus, in 2000 the referendum on the five-year presidential term was only held when the President and the Prime Minister could both finally agree to it. Overall, the picture that emerges is one where both the President and the Prime Minister are important constitutional actors. At the same time, as we shall see, in practice the relationship between the President and the Prime Minister is very much a function of the political circumstances of the day.

TABLE 4.1	Referendums in the Fifth Republic		
Date	Topic	Result (%)	Turnout (%)
8 Jan. 1960	Algerian self-determination	Passed 75.0	73.8
8 Apr. 1962	Algerian settlement	Passed 90.8	75.3
28 Oct. 1962	Direct election of the President	Passed 62.2	77.0
27 Apr. 1969	Reform of Senate and regions	Failed 47.6	80.1
23 Apr. 1972	EEC enlargement	Passed 68.3	60.2
6 Nov. 1988	New Caledonia agreement	Passed 80.0	36.9
20 Sept. 1992	Maastricht Treaty	Passed 51.0	69.8
24 Sept. 2000	Five-year presidential term	Passed 73.2	30.6

Administrative resources

Personal staffs

The President and Prime Minister are assisted by a set of hand-picked personal advisers when they come to office. The President's advisers are collectively known as the General Secretariat of the Presidency (GSP), whereas the Prime Minister and Ministers are supported by a personal staff known as a *cabinet*.[7] (For more information about *cabinets*, see Chapter 5.)

The President can call upon the help of the General Secretariat of the Presidency.[8] The GSP is a group of around 25–30 policy advisers. The GSP is headed by the General Secretary of the Presidency who is the President's closest personal adviser and whose influence can at times be decisive. For example, Chirac's General Secretary 1995–2002, Dominique Galouzeau de Villepin, played a key role in the ultimately disastrous decision to dissolve the National Assembly in 1997 (Colombani 1998: 135–6). In addition, the GSP generally includes a small number of experienced political advisers who are primarily concerned with issues of electoral strategy. Thus, Chirac has worked closely with Alain Devaquet, a former Minister and colleague from Chirac's days as mayor of Paris. However, the bulk of the GSP comprises policy advisers. In this respect, Chirac has tended to organize the GSP into three distinct sections. There is a diplomatic section, including people responsible for African affairs, Europe, and strategic defence issues; an economics and society section, covering the range of domestic policy issues and comprising about eight people; and a communication section headed by the President's daughter Claude Chirac. The basic role of the GSP is to support all aspects of the President's work. Its members are the President's 'eyes and ears' in the round of policy-making meetings (see Box 4.1). They also look after the President's political interests, keeping a close watch on party and parliamentary matters. In short, they are intimately involved in the most central aspects of the political process. In this way, while they can make mistakes (as the de Villepin example clearly showed), they are an indispensable source of support for the President.

By virtue of their role, members of the GSP often work closely with the Prime Minister's *cabinet*. Indeed, as a general rule, the relationship between the President and Prime Minister is usually reflected in the dealings between their respective sets of advisers. Thus, at times, the relationship has been particularly harmonious. Perhaps most notably, as a former

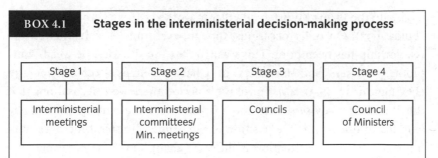

BOX 4.1   Stages in the interministerial decision-making process

Stage 1	Stage 2	Stage 3	Stage 4
Interministerial meetings	Interministerial committees/ Min. meetings	Councils	Council of Ministers

- Interministerial meetings usually bring together ministerial *cabinet* members, a representative of the GSG, one or more members of the Prime Minister's *cabinet* (including one as chair of the meeting), and, outside cohabitation, the GSP. These are ad hoc meetings. There were 1,669 meetings in 1994 and 1,295 in 1995 (an election year).
- Interministerial committees usually comprise the Prime Minister (as chair), Ministers, ministerial *cabinet* members, a representative of the GSG, one or more members of the Prime Minister's *cabinet*, and, outside cohabitation, the GSP. The composition of individual committees and their tasks are established by decree. There were 14 interministerial committees in 1994.
- Ministerial meetings usually include the same people as interministerial committees. The difference between the two types of meetings is that ministerial meetings are ad hoc. There were 109 ministerial meetings in 1994.
- Interministerial councils (*conseils restreints*) usually include the President (as chair), the Prime Minister, Ministers, a representative of the GSG, one or more senior members of the Prime Minister's *cabinet*, and the GSP. These are ad hoc meetings. Only a small number are held each year.
- The Council of Ministers is the equivalent of the British Cabinet. It consists of the President (as chair), the Prime Minister, all full government Ministers and some junior Ministers (*ministres délégués*), the General Secretary of the Government, and the General Secretary of the Presidency. Meetings are held weekly except in August. There are three parts to the meeting. Part A approves all bills and decrees. There is little discussion as decisions have been taken prior to the meeting. Part B deals with appointments. Again, there is no discussion. Part C comprises ministerial communications (including a weekly presentation by the Minister for Foreign Affairs). These may provoke comment.

adviser to the Prime Minister, de Villepin worked closely with Juppé 1995–7 (Fulda 1997). On other occasions, though, even outside cohabitation the relationship has been poor. This was true for the situation between Pompidou's advisers and members of Chaban-Delmas's *cabinet* 1969–72 (Decaumont 1979: 137–44). During this period there were accusations that the President's advisers were too intrusive and that they were actually working to undermine the position of the Prime Minister. Moreover, during cohabitation the situation is different again. On these occasions, the only point of contact between the two camps is between the General Secretary of the Presidency and the director of the Prime Minister's *cabinet*. All other contacts are forbidden (Favier and Martin-Roland 1991: 486–7). While the President's advisers must keep themselves apprised of policy developments, they no longer attend policy-making meetings (see below). The policy process is centred firmly and squarely on the prime ministership.

In organizational terms, there are very clear parallels between the Prime Minister's *cabinet* and the GSP. The *cabinet* comprises around fifty people and is headed by a director who is the Prime Minister's closest political adviser. There are also a number of senior advisers who have a strategic view of the political process. Thus, the *cabinet* is organized hierarchically with a clear chain of command. At the same time, the *cabinet* is subdivided into five basic policy-related sections (*cellules*). There is a social affairs section, dealing with issues such as unemployment and social security; a small international section, which works closely with the Foreign Affairs Ministry; an economic and finance section, which has particular responsibilities for budgetary policy-making; a parliamentary section, whose role is to ensure the smooth passage of legislation; and a press office.

The *cabinet* is charged with upholding the Prime Minister's interests in much the same way as the GSP supports the President. At the same time, though, *cabinet* members are more involved in the coordination of government business than their counterparts at the Élysée. In this capacity, they work very closely with government Ministers and ministerial *cabinet* members. There is, in effect, one prime ministerial *cabinet* member for each government Minister. The former 'shadow' the latter. However, this situation can lead to tension between the Prime Minister and the various Ministries. Indeed, just as the President's advisers have been accused of interfering in the business of the Prime Minister's work, so members of the

Prime Minister's *cabinet* have faced the same charge with regard to ministerial matters (Thuillier 1982: 90–100). In fact, tension is almost unavoidable. One of the main tasks of the Prime Minister's *cabinet* is to pilot the decision-making process to a satisfactory conclusion. In this capacity, senior *cabinet* members help to arbitrate between the conflicting demands of government Ministers. In the last resort, the Prime Minister will step in personally and decide a particular matter. Most issues, though, are resolved by members of the Prime Minister's *cabinet* without the need for the head of government to intervene personally. As a result, the Prime Minister's advisers are bound to make enemies. Inevitably, they will be accused of interference and high-handedness.

Administrative organizations

In terms of personal staffs the President and the Prime Minister have approximately equal resources. The same point does not apply, however, to the situation with regard to the various administrative organizations within the State system. Here, the President has very few formal responsibilities. By contrast, the Prime Minister is at the head of a large number of committees, commissions, delegations, councils, and so forth. At the same time, though, the President is still able to influence the work of some of these organizations, most notably those concerned with defence and European issues. Thus, the President is not as powerless in this domain as it might at first appear.

The President is charged with very few formal responsibilities. For example, somewhat bizarrely, the President still holds the official title of co-Prince of Andorra.[9] As recently as 1981 this position has meant that the President has been associated with controversial decisions relating to the domestic politics of the independent principality. In practice, though, this is a purely ceremonial title. In fact, the main institution with which the President is associated is the Higher Council of the Judiciary (see Chapter 7). However, the President does not take part in the work of the Council when it meets to carry out its more routine tasks relating to promotions, disciplinary matters, and the like. Thus, consistent with the general logic of the President's constitutional powers, the fact that the head of State chairs the Higher Council of the Judiciary does not mean that the President is implicated in the day-to-day work of the judiciary.

The situation is very different with regard to the Prime Minister. The head of government is officially responsible for a wide range of administrative organizations (see Box 4.2). Indeed, in 1979 a grand total of around 5,000 people were associated with these organizations (Massot 1979: 175). That said, the Prime Minister's relationship with many of these organizations is rather more complex than it might at first appear. In most cases, the Prime Minister is only the titular head of these organizations. In practice, their day-to-day work is carried out by Ministers and officials. Moreover, in other cases, the President has in effect usurped the position of the Prime Minister. Against this background, three institutions are worth singling out for attention: the General Secretariat of the Government (GSG); the General Secretariat for National Defence (GSND); and the General Secretariat of the Interministerial Committee for Questions Relating to European Economic Cooperation (usually known by its French acronym, the SGCI). The Prime Minister is closely associated with the work of the GSG, whereas the President has come to control both the GSND and the SGCI.

The General Secretariat of the Government is the equivalent of the British Cabinet Office and provides administrative support to the government as a whole (Py 1985). That said, it is closely linked to the Prime Minister. Most notably the head of the organization, the General Secretary of the Government, occupies an office close to the Prime Minister at the Hôtel Matignon and there is daily, almost hourly, contact between the two. The General Secretary is a civil servant and part of the permanent administration. As a result, the General Secretary usually remains in post when a new government comes to power. Indeed, there have been only six incumbents of the office in the period since 1958. The current General Secretary, Jean-Marc Sauvé, was appointed in May 1995.

The GSG totals around thirty senior officials. Their function is fourfold: to give legal advice to Ministers preparing legislation; to facilitate the circulation of government documents and to ensure the implementation of government decisions; to oversee the administrative organizations under the authority of the Prime Minister; and to assist in the formation of a new government. In this context, one of the GSG's main tasks is to prepare and take the minutes at the weekly meetings of the Council of Ministers. In this capacity, the General Secretary is in regular contact with the General Secretary of the Presidency and, indeed, the President personally. In addition, the members of the GSG represent the government

| BOX 4.2 | The Prime Minister's services |

1.Organizations under the direct authority of the Prime Minister
  (i)   The *cabinet*
  (ii) Interministerial coordination units:
        The General Secretariat of the Government
        The General Secretariat of the Interministerial Committee for Questions
            Relating to European Economic Cooperation
        The General Secretariat for National Defence
        Government Information Service
  (iii) Support unit:
        Direction for Administrative and Financial Services
  (iv) General information:
        The *Official Journal*
        Publishing house (La Documentation française)
        Interministerial centres for administrative intelligence
  (v)   Sectoral policy coordination:
        Interministerial Delegation for Road Safety
        The General Secretariat of the Interministerial Committee for Nuclear
            Safety
        Government Commissioner to the National Commission for Data
            Protection
        The Higher Commission for Codification
        The General Secretariat of the Sea
        The Interministerial Commission of Technical Support for the
            Development of Information Technology and Communication in the
            Administration
        The Commission for Administrative Simplification
  (vi) Research, advice, training:
        The General Planning Commission
        The National Council for the Evaluation of Public Policy
        The Centre for Prospective Studies and International Information
        The Council for Employment, Incomes, and Social Cohesion
        The National Council of Associative Life
        The National Committee for the Publication of the Preparatory Work on
            the Institutions of the Fifth Republic
        The Higher Council for Integration
        The National Council for Social Integration through Economic Activity
        The General Secretariat of the High Committee for Housing for the
            Disadvantaged
        The Central Committee of the Inquiry about the Cost and the Output of
            the Public Services
        The Observatory for Male/Female Parity
        The Centre for the Advanced Study of Africa and Modern Asia
        The Interministerial Mission for the Fight against Sects
        The Study Mission on Despoilment of the Possessions Belonging to Jews
            Resident in France during the Occupation
        The Council for Economic Analysis

BOX 4.2 *continued*

2. Organizations under the authority of a Minister
   The *cabinet* of the Minister for the Public Service, State Reform, and
      Decentralization
   The *cabinet* of the Minister for Relations with Parliament
   The General Direction of the Administration and the Public Service
   The Interministerial Delegation on State Reform
   The Delegation for Territorial Development and Regional Action
   The Direction for the Development of the Media
   The Interministerial Mission for the Fight against Drugs and Drug Addiction
   The Interministerial Delegation on the Liberal Professions
   The Interministerial Mission on the Greenhouse Effect
   The High Council for International Cooperation

3. Independent Organizations funded from the Prime Minister's budget
   The Ombudsman
   The Commission for the Access to Administrative Documents
   The National Consultative Commission on the Rights of Man
   The Higher Council of Broadcasting
   The National Commission for the Control of Data Transfers
   The Consultative Commission for National Defence Secrets

4. Public enterprises
   The École nationale d'administration
   The International Institute for Public Administration
   The regional institutes for the administration of Bastia, Lille, Lyon, Metz, and
      Nantes
   The Institute for the Advanced Study of National Defence (under the control
      of the General Secretariat for National Defence)

5. Sponsored Organizations
   The Research Centre for the Study and Observation of Living Quality
   The Centre for the Study of Mathematical Economic Forecasting Applied to
      Planning
   The Institute for Economic and Social Research
   The Franco-British Council (French section)
   The French Institute for International Relations
   The Centre for European Studies in Strasbourg

6. Organizations supported by the Prime Minister's services
   The Delegation for the Repatriated
   The High Council of the French-Speaking World
   The Centre for European Studies in Strasbourg

7. Ministerial organizations under the authority of the Prime Minister's services
   The Financial Controller
   The National Archives Mission

when bills are being discussed by both the Council of State and the Constitutional Council (see Chapter 7). All told, even though the GSG is part of the permanent administration (unlike its Élysée counterpart, the GSP), the work of the organization is very closely linked to the government's political programme. As a result, although the organization provides the government with legal advice, its members may also find that they are being asked to offer policy advice and, indeed, political advice as well.

Like the GSG, the General Secretariat for National Defence is an institution designed to facilitate interministerial policy coordination. Unlike the GSG, though, the GSND is only concerned with one area of policy coordination. The GSND is responsible for preparing meetings of the defence council (*conseil de défense*), which are chaired by the President. The GSDN also has particular responsibilities for issues concerning the export of arms, as well as the protection of information systems and defence secrets. In contrast to the GSG, the GSND contains around 240 people in total. However, only about thirty people are engaged in coordination functions in the strict sense of the term. The rest are more concerned with matters of strategic reflection and policy-planning. The nature of the organization's role means that officials in the GSND work in close collaboration with officials in various Ministries, most notably Defence, Finance, Foreign Affairs, and the Ministry of the Interior. More importantly, however, even though the GSND reports to the Prime Minister,[10] its members also work very closely with the President and members of the GSP. Indeed, the 1978 decree that established the current basic structure of the GSND indicated that the President was empowered to issue it with instructions. Thus, the ambiguities inherent in the Constitution (see above) are reflected in the Janus-like nature of the GSND, with the organization having one head turned to the Prime Minister and another to the President.

In many respects, the same point also applies to the General Secretariat of the Interministerial Committee for Questions Relating to European Economic Cooperation. The SGCI is responsible for organizing France's European policy (see Chapter 5). It liaises with French and other officials in Brussels and it also ensures the interministerial coordination and implementation of European policy at the domestic level. The SGCI is under the authority of the Prime Minister. However, the desire of successive

Presidents to influence European affairs has meant that the President has paid close attention to the organization and work of the SGCI. Indeed, on occasions the head of the SGCI has been a personal friend and collaborator of the President, perhaps most notably Elisabeth Guigou 1985–90 (Lequesne 1993: 104). As with the GSND, therefore, Presidents have compensated for the lack of *de jure* authority over administrative organizations by exercising *de facto* control.

The direct election of the President

At the start of this chapter it was asserted that the Fifth Republic has a presidentialized system of government. So far, though, while plenty of examples of the presidentialized nature of the political process have been provided, no explanation of this phenomenon has been presented. This is because constitutional and administrative resources merely indicate the institutional context within which the political system operates. They do not explain why the President has been so strong. Indeed, if we were to go by the Constitution alone, then we would be forced to conclude that the Prime Minister is at least as important as the President, if not more so. In fact, the main reason for the presidentialization of the political system is the 1962 constitutional reform that established the direct election of the President by the people of France (see Table 4.1). This reform marked the beginning of the semi-presidential system of government in France (see above) and brought about a turning point in the history of the regime (see Chapter 1). Presidential elections are now the defining moments of the political system and for two reasons. First, while candidates are always associated with particular political parties and ideological families, successful candidates are the ones who are best able to transcend their own party political space. Secondly, even though support for candidates is at least partly a function of their personal qualities, electoral success depends at least in part on the presentation of a programme for government. In this way, presidential elections set the political agenda and put the President's policy proposals at the heart of the political debate.

In the original version of the 1958 Constitution, the President of the Republic was elected by an electoral college consisting mainly of parliamentarians and representatives of local government. In the Fifth

Republic's first presidential election on 21 December 1958, Charles de Gaulle defeated the Communist party candidate and the candidate of the non-communist left. However, in 1962 this system was changed. From this point on, the President has been directly elected by way of a two-ballot majority system.[11] Under this system, there can be two ballots. At each ballot, voters can cast just one vote. In order to be elected at the first ballot, a candidate must win more than 50 per cent of the valid votes cast. If no candidate does so, then a second ballot is held two weeks later. At the second ballot, only the top two candidates at the first ballot are allowed to stand again. This time, the candidate with the most votes is elected. In 1965, at the first election under the new rules, de Gaulle was re-elected, winning more than 13 million votes at the second ballot.

The mechanics of the electoral system help to explain the transcendent nature of the presidency. In France, no single party has ever won more than 50 per cent of the votes cast at any legislative election and no party is ever likely to do so at least in the foreseeable future (see Chapter 2). As a result, presidential candidates know that in order to be elected they have to win support from beyond the confines of their loyal party identifiers. In short, they have to build coalitions. This process begins even before the first ballot, but it continues with a vengeance between the two ballots. The need to construct a coalition means that Presidents naturally court the support of voters from ideologically like-minded parties. For example, socialist candidates look to the communists and the Greens. At the same time, though, candidates also appeal to the independent and politically unattached voter. Indeed, more than that, they seek to appeal to the common person, the plain people of France, *la France profonde*. The narrowness of the result means that the support of floating voters is likely to be crucial to success or failure at the election. At the same time, an appeal to the people of France more generally helps to create what has been called the presidential myth, or the symbolic construction of a presidentialized political profile (Braud 1992; Milne 1997). The net result is that while the President has a party political affiliation, an association with a wider left- or right-wing political family, and the temporary support of a certain number of floating voters, at the same time he or she can also claim to be the representative of the people, speaking to the nation directly as the voice of France.

In this way, the direct election of the President acts as a critical link between the institutional position of the presidency and the political manifestation of presidential power. Paradoxically, the fact that the Constitution provides the President with very few discretionary powers actually reinforces the myth of the presidency. As noted above, in constitutional terms the President is primarily responsible for ensuring the Constitution is respected, for guaranteeing the continuity of the State, for negotiating treaties with foreign powers, and for defending the national territory. This is the realm of high politics. Indeed, it is the realm of high politics in terms of both domestic and international affairs. With regard to the system of direct election, presidential candidates have to enlarge their electoral domain. They have to appeal to the people as a whole. They have to portray themselves as the nation incarnate. Here, too, they enter the realm of high politics. In this case, it is the realm of high electoral politics. This mixture of constitutional and electoral factors is a powerful one. The President gains the right to be treated as the foremost person in the State in both institutional and electoral terms. This situation guarantees the President an authority and legitimacy which ordinarily no other political actor can come anywhere near to matching.

This point can be underscored by comparing the presidency with the Prime Ministership. The Prime Minister comes to office by virtue of being appointed by the President. Moreover, the Prime Minister remains in office only by virtue of retaining the support of the National Assembly and (outside cohabitation) the President as well. As a result, though, the Prime Minister operates in a very different institutional and political context from the President. Unlike the President, the Prime Minister is intimately associated with the everyday business of government, with managing the policy-making process, and with defending the government's record in parliament. What is more, also unlike the President, the position of the Prime Minister is constantly at risk. Even Prime Ministers whose parliamentary support has been rock solid have sometimes fallen foul of the President. Pompidou's dismissal of Chaban-Delmas in 1972 is a case in point. On this occasion, the Prime Minister had just won a parliamentary vote of confidence by an overwhelming majority. Still, the President dismissed him. All told, whereas direct election helps the President to transcend the mundane, the Prime Minister cannot help but be captured by it. While direct election means that the President can claim to speak as the voice of the nation, the Prime Minister is merely the spokesperson for the government of the day. Thus, while the Constitution might appear to make the Prime Minister the central figure within the executive, in fact the Prime Minister is very much subordinate to the President. This is not to say that the Prime Minister lacks authority. On the contrary, the Prime Minister has a great deal of authority when it comes to day-to-day affairs and dealings with Ministers. It is simply to say that the Prime Minister can never match the President in this regard.

The direct election further strengthens the President's authority by allowing the successful candidate to set the political agenda. As mentioned earlier, presidential elections are the centre-piece of the political system. Naturally, they are highly mediatized affairs, providing ample opportunity for sound-bites and photo-opportunities. Moreover, they encourage personality-based competition. In 1995 at least part of Chirac's first-ballot success was due to the fact that his main right-wing rival, Édouard Balladur, appeared stiff and formal on television. That said, presidential elections are not simply political beauty contests. Elections are won and lost on past records and future promises. In this latter regard, each candidate campaigns on a personal programme. For example, in 1981 Mitterrand announced his so-called '110 Proposals for France', comprising a long list of policy promises. By contrast, in 1988 he wrote what he called a 'Letter to the French People', which in comparison with the 1981 manifesto was a much more discursive affair, containing few concrete policies but guaranteeing stability. In 1995 Chirac published a book called *La France pour tous* which served as his campaign slogan and his policy manifesto. In 2002, Jospin published a book in which he set out his reason for standing and the basic principles that he stood for (Jospin 2002).

In this way, the direct election of the President is a particularly effective device for establishing a dominant policy discourse. While legislative elections are pivotal (see below), there is still a sense in which they are simply the outcome of 577 local elections. Moreover, to the extent that parties are conglomerations of people with varying interests and ideas, then legislative elections cannot create the same sense of focus as presidential elections. At presidential elections, candidates can articulate a vision. Of course, they often do so badly and incoherently. In this case, they usually lose. At the same time, if they do it well and succeed, they can set the terms of the political debate for a number of years to come. Moreover, presidential elections are doubly important because they indicate the policies that are associated with the political debate. This is particularly important in terms of presidential/prime ministerial relations. Immediately following an election, Presidents tend to appoint a Prime Minister whose task is to implement the President's electoral programme. This was very clearly the case when Mitterrand appointed Mauroy in 1981 and when Chirac appointed Juppé in 1995 and Raffarin in 2002. In so doing, however, Presidents limit the Prime Minister's decision-making freedom. The Prime Minister is put in charge of the policy-making process and is responsible for seeing the process of legislation through to completion. This is exactly what the Constitution indicates. At the same time, though, the policies for which the Prime Minister is responsible have been determined by the President in advance. And yet, this would not be apparent from a literal reading of the Constitution.

Accounting for variations in presidential power

The direct election of the President ensures that the head of State is the pre-eminent political figure within the system. The 1962 constitutional reform served to presidentialize the whole of the political system. At the same time, over the years the power of the President has varied. There have been periods of very strong presidential government under the presidencies of de Gaulle, Pompidou, and Mitterrand (1981–6 and 1988–93). There have been times when the President's authority has been contested, notably during the latter part of the Giscard presidency (1976–81). There have also been times when the Prime Minister has dominated the decision-making process. This has occurred during the three periods of cohabitation under the Mitterrand presidency (1986–8 and 1993–5) and during Chirac's first term (1997–2002) (see Elgie 1997). The question that needs to be asked, therefore, is why does the President's power vary so much? The answer is simple. It varies as a function of the particular configuration of party politics at any given time.

The *de facto* founder of the Fifth Republic, Charles de Gaulle, was profoundly mistrustful of political parties. To him, they were necessarily self-interested creatures. They defended their own turf and they were incapable of promoting the national interest. As a result, in the early years of the Fifth

Republic the role of political parties was downplayed. There was little mention of parties in the Constitution of the new regime. Ministers were appointed from the higher levels of the civil service. Most importantly of all, the 1965 constitutional amendment was designed to bypass parties and provide the President with a direct link to the people. And yet, parties have remained as central to the working of the system as they ever were. As we have seen, parties are the basic building block of a successful presidential election campaign, providing a reservoir of voters and organizational back-up. More than that, parties are crucial for the ongoing exercise of presidential power. In this regard, there is one key variable: whether the President is supported by a parliamentary majority. However, account must also be taken of whether the majority takes the form of a single-party government or a coalition, whether the coalition is uneven or balanced, and whether the governing party is/parties are cohesive or factionalized.

Presidential and prime ministerial majorities

The Fifth Republic has constructed a presidentialized system of government. However, the foundations of this system are built on shifting sand. The President is only in a position to exercise leadership with the support of a loyal parliamentary majority. When the majority opposes the President, the President must appoint a Prime Minister who has the support of parliament. In this case, the Prime Minister will also oppose the President and the executive will be split. This is known as cohabitation. During cohabitation power shifts to the Prime Minister. Backed by the support of a parliamentary majority the Prime Minister is responsible not just for managing the day-to-day business of government and parliament, but also for the initiation of policy reforms. To date, there have been three periods of cohabitation: 1986–8, 1993–5, and 1997–2002. On each occasion, cohabitation began part-way though a President's term of office (after five years in 1986 and 1993, but after only two years in 1997). On the first two occasions it occurred as a result of the incumbent party/coalition being defeated at a scheduled set of legislative elections. In 1997 it was brought about when Chirac dissolved the National Assembly prematurely, so bringing defeat upon himself.

The circumstances in which cohabitation occurs mean that the President is relatively powerless. This is because cohabitation undermines the President's electoral resources. First, the President's link with the people is broken, or at least weakened. Defeat for the President's party at the election is taken as a sign that the President has been personally disavowed. Whether or not this is actually true is immaterial. What matters is that the myth of the presidency is exposed. The emperor is seen to have no clothes. Secondly, the policy agenda is set by the incoming party/coalition and, in particular, by the Prime Minister. As a result, the President is on the defensive. The head of State has to respond to a programme that has been put forward successfully by an opposing political force. By contrast, the Prime Minister is liberated. The Prime Minister is now the main source of policy leadership. This is not to say that during cohabitation the Prime Minister ever enjoys the authority and legitimacy that is associated with an extremely popular, newly elected President. The Prime Minister can make no real claim to being the nation incarnate and is still primarily seen as the spokesperson for the government of the day. It is simply to say that during cohabitation the Prime Minister acts and the President reacts. This point is particularly true with regard to the conduct of domestic policy, although in foreign and defence matters the President does maintain a certain degree of influence.

In terms of domestic policy, there is no doubt that Prime Ministers have exercised policy leadership during cohabitation. For example, they have decided which elements of the government's programme should be introduced and in what order. So, in 1993 one of Balladur's main priorities was to improve the economy. To this end, he quickly promoted a government-sponsored savings scheme (*l'emprunt Balladur*), which was a considerable success and which was used to reduce the budget deficit and increase spending in key areas. Similarly, in 1997 Jospin moved swiftly to tackle the problem of unemployment by introducing an ambitious State-directed job creation scheme to reduce youth unemployment (see Chapter 1). At the same time, cohabitation Prime Ministers have also been responsible for key policy arbitrations at the most sensitive stages of the policy-making process. So, in 1986 the government decided to privatize one of the country's State-controlled television channels. Following a fierce debate between rival Ministers, it was finally Chirac who personally decided that TF1 was the most appropriate channel to be sold off (Elgie 1993b). Equally, on more than one occasion after 1997 Jospin was obliged to choose between the competing demands of his socially minded Minister for Employment and Solidarity, Martine Aubry, and his more business-friendly Minister for the

Economy, Finance, and Industry, Dominique Strauss-Kahn, at least until the latter's resignation in November 1999.

In stark contrast, Presidents have been relatively powerless in domestic affairs. Generally speaking, they have been able only to delay the introduction of certain reforms. For example, in 1986 President Mitterrand refused to allow the government to legislate by decree (*ordonnance*), which blocked some of the more controversial aspects of the government's reform programme for a few weeks or months. Similarly, in 1993 Mitterrand refused to allow the bill on the financing of private schools to be debated in a special session of parliament. This meant that the bill, which would have been introduced in June of that year, had to be put back until the autumn. Furthermore, in February 2001 during the third period of cohabitation Chirac initially refused to allow the government's bill on the future of Corsica to be placed on the agenda of the Council of Ministers. In effect, though, he delayed the discussion of the bill by only a week.[12] That said, Chirac did effectively veto the Jospin government's proposed constitutional amendment regarding the Higher Council of the Magistrature, thus stifling plans for a major reform of the judiciary.

All told, in terms of domestic policy Presidents have been able to establish themselves as the main opposition to the Prime Minister, which in political terms can be extremely important especially when the President intends to stand again at the next presidential election. This was the case with Mitterrand in the period 1986–8 and Chirac 1997–2002. All the same, only very rarely have Presidents been able to shape the policy-making process in any meaningful way. They cannot propose. They can only oppose and then sometimes only for a short period.

In terms of defence and foreign policy, however, Presidents have enjoyed somewhat greater latitude. So, in 1986 President Mitterrand successfully insisted that France's short-range nuclear arms were not 'tactical', battlefield weapons, but were part of a wider, 'strategic' whole (Howorth 1993: 158). Also in 1986 defence was the only budget to be decided in a meeting chaired by the President. All the others were decided by the Prime Minister and the Finance Minister in the absence of the President and his advisers (Elgie 1993b). Similarly, throughout the whole of the second period of cohabitation Mitterrand managed to maintain France's moratorium on nuclear weapons testing, despite the opposition of the Prime Minister (Favier and Martin-Roland 1999: 453–62). Moreover, during this time

Mitterrand also used his position as head of State to insist that he was the main representative of France at G7 meetings. As a result, Prime Minister Balladur refused to attend at all rather than be seen as subordinate to the President in this respect (Balladur 1995: 81–3). Indeed, this situation is typical. During cohabitation when Prime Ministers have attempted to assert themselves in this domain they have failed. This is because of the President's authority and because they are so closely associated with domestic affairs. So, for example, when Jospin visited Brazil in April 2001 the newspapers back home paid scant attention to the speeches he made about the effects of globalization and concentrated instead on the political aftermath of municipal elections that had just taken place in France.[13] The net result is that during cohabitation in contrast to domestic policy the President does maintain a degree of influence in foreign and defence policy. Nonetheless, all things considered the President is a much less influential political actor.

Presidential and prime ministerial majorities: variations on the party theme

It is clear, therefore, that the main variable which determines the respective powers of the President and Prime Minister is the majority in parliament. When the majority supports the President, the head of State is best placed to exercise policy influence. When the majority opposes the President, the Prime Minister is responsible for domestic affairs. Whatever the situation, though, three other party-related factors are also important in determining the extent of presidential and prime ministerial powers: whether there is a single-party or a coalition government; whether the relationship between coalition parties is uneven or balanced; and whether the governing party is (or governing parties are) cohesive or factionalized (see Figure 4.1).

Presidential and prime ministerial powers are affected by whether there is a single-party or a coalition government in power. All other things being equal, single-party governments make it easier to exercise leadership than coalition governments. This is because in single-party governments Presidents and Prime Ministers can dispense with the need to manage inter-party relations. Moreover, in France coalition governments usually come to power on the basis of an agreed, albeit often short and ambiguous, policy document (Thiébault 2000: 512–14). This results in a situation where the

FIGURE 4.1 Fifth Republic majorities and party competition, 1959–2002

	Presidential majority 1959–86[a], 1988–93[b], 1995–7, 2002–			Prime ministerial majority 1986–8, 1993–5, 1997–2002		
	Single-party 1984–6, 1988–93, 2002–	Coalition 1959–84, 1995–7		Single-party None	Coalition 1986–8, 1993–5, 1997–2002	
		Balanced 1959–62, 1978–81, 1995–7	Imbalanced 1962–78[c], 1981–4[d]		Balanced 1986–8, 1993–5	Imbalanced 1997–2002
Faction-alized	1988–93, 2002–?	1959–62, 1995–7	1969–78	n/a	1993–5	None
Cohesive	1984–6	1978–81	1962–9, 1981–4	n/a	1986–8	1997–2002

[a] Duverger (1996: 574–87) classifies the period 1959–62 as one where there was neither a presidential nor a prime ministerial majority.

[b] There was a minority government 1988–93. However, the government supported the President and was able to survive for the full length of the parliamentary term. Thus, for the purposes of this exercise it is classed as a *de facto* majority government. (For an overview of this period, see Elgie and Maor 1992.)

[c] From 1968 to 1973 the gaullist party was supported by an absolute majority in parliament. However, the government remained a coalition out of respect for pre-electoral agreements.

[d] From 1981 to 1984 the Socialist party enjoyed the support of an absolute majority in parliament. Like the period 1968–73, though, the Socialists formed a coalition government with the communists because of pre-electoral agreements.

Source: Thiébault (2000: 499–500).

government's policy agenda has been at least partly determined in advance. Indeed, for coalition governments formed after a legislative election such a document has the potential to restrict the decision-making freedom of the Prime Minister. That said, even when no formal policy document has been agreed, relations between coalition parties can still be problematic, especially if the personal ambitions of party leaders collide or if the policy priorities of the coalition parties differ significantly.

Against this background, what is clear from Figure 4.1 is that there have been very few single-party governments in the Fifth Republic. Indeed, given that the 1988–93 administration failed to enjoy majority support in parliament and had to construct a majority on an ad hoc basis, then the only periods of true single-party majority government were 1984–6 and the period after the 2002 legislative elections. During these periods the decision-making process has been presidentialized and there is no doubt that the existence of a single-party government is one factor that contributed to this situation. For the most part, though, Fifth Republic governments have been coalition governments. Accordingly, on occasion the position of the President and Prime Minister has been weakened. This was particularly the case during the period 1978–81 when competition between the RPR and the UDF was at its height. At this time, the President, Giscard, and his loyal Prime Minister, Barre, were determined to follow a particular set of economic and social policies. However, there was opposition to these policies from the RPR. The result was persistent low-level political skirmishing between the coalition 'partners' in the government and especially the parliamentary arena (see Chapter 6). There is no doubt that Giscard's authority as President was undermined by this situation. Indeed, so too was his 1981 presidential election campaign.

In addition to the simple presence or absence of a coalition government, presidential and prime ministerial powers are affected by the nature of the coalition government in power. In this regard, a distinction can be made between balanced and imbalanced coalitions. A balanced coalition is one where the coalition parties are of relatively equal size. An imbalanced coalition is the situation where one of the parties in government is much larger than any other. Again, all other things being equal, an imbalanced coalition increases the likelihood of presidential leadership on condition that the larger party supports the President. The reason for this is that the problems associated with inter-party rivalries are likely to be greater if the coalition comprises, say, two parties of equal weight than if the President's party dominates its coalition partner.

In the main, the Fifth Republic has experienced imbalanced coalitions. Moreover, the nature of most of these coalitions has helped presidentialize the system. From 1968 to 1973 the gaullists enjoyed an absolute majority of support in parliament and dominated the governing coalition. This was a period of extreme presidentialization (Decaumont 1979), as Pompidou's dismissal of Chaban-Delmas as Prime Minister clearly demonstrated. The same situation occurred 1981–4 when the Socialists overwhelmed the communists in government. This, too, was a period of presidentialization. As Prime Minister, Mauroy was integral to the policy-making process. However, as President, Mitterrand assumed final responsibility for all key decisions (Pfister 1985). On both occasions, the relative absence of inter-party problems meant that one potential obstacle to governing was removed. On other occasions, though, some coalitions have reduced the capacity for effective leadership. This was particularly the case during the first two periods of cohabitation. On these occasions the potential for prime ministerial leadership was reduced by virtue of the intense competition between the two main coalition partners. In both cases, each party had its own preferred candidate for the forthcoming presidential election.[14] This meant that long-standing ideological tensions between, for example, certain State-centred gaullists and free-market liberals were complicated by the presence of personal rivalries and ambitions. True, on both occasions each party had more to lose from wrecking the government than from working within it. Thus, the coalition held together. However, the nature of the rivalries was such that the decision-making process was sometimes very difficult indeed as each grouping demanded what it saw as its rightful share of the governmental pie.

Finally, presidential and prime ministerial powers are also at least in part determined by whether the parties they head, or with which they are associated, are either internally factionalized or cohesive. Once more, all other things being equal, the opportunity for leadership is greater under a government with a cohesive party than a factionalized party. The reason is that a factionalized party is, in effect, a coalition of people with different ideological and/or personal interests. In such a case, one of the main tasks of the leader is to manage intra-party tensions. In so doing, however, the

President or Prime Minister's policy agenda may be compromised as the political agenda is set elsewhere.

For the most part, governing parties in the Fifth Republic have been fairly cohesive. This is not to say that on these occasions parties have been submissive and purely leader-oriented. It is simply to say that the level of intra-party dissent has not seriously threatened the functioning of government. Thus, from 1962 to 1968 the gaullist party can be classed as a cohesive party, despite the fact that during this period there were party 'barons' whose influence could not be ignored (Charlot 1971). The same is true of the Socialist party 1981–6, when its so-called 'elephants' undoubtedly shaped policy but not in such a way as to threaten the integrity of the President's programme overall. Generally speaking, on these occasions Presidents have benefited from the backing of a loyal party and this has helped to presidentialize the system. Indeed, it is no coincidence that two of the most highly presidentialized periods of the Fifth Republic (1962–8 under de Gaulle and 1981–6 under Mitterrand) are associated with parties that were especially loyal to the President of the day. On other occasions, though, parties have been more factionalized. This was most notably the case in the period 1988–93 when the Socialist party was split into competing 'courants', the divisions between most of which were purely personal rather than policy-oriented (see Chapter 2). Accordingly, during this period the authority of the President and Prime Ministers was weakened. This was particularly true in terms of domestic and especially budgetary policies where factional in-fighting was at its most intense (Elgie 1993*b*: 89–98). Similarly, the impact of internal party divisions was also evident in the period 1995–7. During this time, the RPR was on the verge of splitting between pro- and anti-European camps. Moreover, there were residual rivalries between Chirac's and Balladur's supporters following the presidential election campaign. What is more, the situation within the centre-right was also difficult as the UDF was divided over matters of both policy and strategy. The result was an extremely fractious government and one that rapidly lost the support of the public. The hope for the current UMP government is that these internal tensions will not be revived.

All told, the factor that most affects the relative influence of the President and the Prime Minister is party politics. In the period immediately following a presidential election if the President is supported by a cohesive, single-party majority, then the chances are that the President will be the centre of political attention and will exercise leadership within the executive accordingly. By contrast, towards the end of a President's term if there is a coalition government where the governing parties are relatively evenly balanced, competing, and internally divided, then the likelihood is that the business of government will be difficult to manage. Over the years, the Fifth Republic has experienced many different types of party activity and the degree of presidentialization has varied accordingly. There have been times of extreme presidentialization, periods of prime ministerial government, and occasions when the sometimes almost regal appearance of presidentialism has masked a much more messy reality.

Conclusion

The experience of the French dual executive tells us much about semi-presidential regimes in general and the operation of the French political system in particular. In recent years, there has been a great deal of debate about the relative merits of presidential, semi-presidential, and parliamentary regimes (see, for example, Shugart and Carey 1992). The main criticism of semi-presidentialism is that the dual executive creates the opportunity for tension between the President and Prime Minister that can lead to political gridlock or worse. The evidence suggests that this criticism is valid when both actors have significant constitutional powers and when the party system enables the President and the Prime Minister to establish themselves as major political figures. In Ireland and Austria the President has neither constitutional nor political authority, which makes the Prime Minister the undisputed political leader and avoids any tensions within the dual executive.[15] In other countries, though, the situation is different and France is one of those countries. As we have seen, in France both the President and the Prime Minister have constitutional powers and administrative resources. The system is presidentialized because of the direct election of the President. However, the nature of party politics means that the Prime Minister has been able to assume decision-making power on several occasions and, in any case, the head of government is always a senior political figure with whom the President has to work very closely. Thus, France is a good example of the problem inherent in a semi-presidential regime. In the French case, the experience of cohabitation was traumatic. It did not lead to a more consensual political system. The President and Prime Minister did have to cooperate on certain issues. However, the basic situation was one in which two competing leaders were engaged in an ongoing competition for power (see Elgie 2002). The constitutional amendment that reduced the President's term of office from seven to five years was a deliberate attempt to address this problem. As a result, the likelihood of future periods of cohabitation is greatly reduced. In 2002, the President and the National Assembly were elected within a few weeks of each other and there is little doubt that the momentum of Chirac's presidential victory led to the UMP's overwhelming legislative majority.

The experience of the French dual executive also tells us much about the nature of institutional politics in the Fifth Republic. In some respects, there has been a great deal of institutional stability in this area over the years. Since 1958, and particularly since the 1962 constitutional reform, France has had a presidentialized system of government. What is more, the reduction of the President's term of office in 2000 was an attempt to safeguard this situation and maximize the opportunity for presidential leadership in the future. In other respects, though, there has been institutional change. The 1962 and 2000 reforms were important institutional reforms in their own right. More generally, even within the basic constitutional and administrative framework of the dual executive, variations in party politics have led to very different types of relationships between the President and Prime Minister. This is an important lesson. Evidence from the French dual executive emphasizes the importance of the interaction between institutions and political actors (see Introduction). To understand how institutions operate, we need to examine the politics of the actors who operate within them. This point was seen very clearly in this chapter. It is also evident in many of the chapters that follow.

KEY TERMS

- President
- Prime Minister
- Cohabitation
- Elections
- Party system

NOTES

1 This section draws heavily on Massot (1997: 95–138).

2 These are the areas where the President can dispense with the need for the Prime Minister's counter-signature.

3 It should be remembered, though, that in 1997 Chirac took advantage of this power, but with disastrous results.

4 So, for example, on 22 April 1964 Pompidou stepped into the breach while de Gaulle was recovering from surgery.

5 Massot (1997: 108) acknowledges that it is slightly unusual to include justice in this class of powers.

6 The exceptions are the 1988 and 2000 referendums. In 1988 the Prime Minister was intimately associated with the negotiations surrounding the New Caledonian agreement. Moreover, on this occasion the decision to hold a referendum was part of the deal agreed between the French 'unionists' and the New Caledonian 'secessionists'. Thus, it is misleading to label this example as a 'presidential' referendum. For an account, see Huchon (1993: 87–94).

7 In this book, the term *cabinet* is used to apply to personal advisers, whereas Council of Ministers is used to refer to the British and US equivalents of the Cabinet.

8 In fact, the President is supported by a number of institutions. For example, the President's *cabinet* is a small group of people who are primarily concerned with management issues (arranging presidential visits and so forth). The *État-major particulier* is an equally small group of people who provide the President with technical assistance in his or her role as commander-in-chief of the armed forces with responsibility for France's nuclear weapons. However, in political terms the GSP is the most important institution. For an overview of the President's office, see Elgie (2000).

9 See Massot (1986: 35–47) for the history of this title and certain other rather baroque presidential prerogatives.

10 From 1969 to 1973 the GSDN was under the authority of the Defence Minister.

11 This system is similar but still slightly different from the one used for elections to the National Assembly (see Chapter 6).

12 The President refused to discuss the bill the first time it was due to be presented, but agreed the second time, a week later.

13 On the plane back to France Jospin was so incensed about the coverage his trip had received that he was verbally abusive to a number of reporters. He was subsequently obliged to apologize for his outburst (see *Le Monde*, 17 Apr. 2001).

14 In 1988 the RPR supported Chirac, while the UDF supported Barre. In 1995, both organizations were much more factionalized (see Figure 4.1), but generally speaking the RPR once again supported Chirac, while most of the UDF supported Balladur.

15 For an overview, see the country studies in Elgie (1999b).

GUIDE TO FURTHER READING

BELL, D., *Presidential Power in Fifth Republic France* (Oxford, Berg, 2000).
Chronological account of Presidents since 1958.

COLE, A., *François Mitterrand: A Study in Political Leadership* (London, Routledge 1994).
Plenty of information about Mitterrand's presidency.

ELGIE, R., *The Role of the Prime Minister in France, 1981–1991* (London, Macmillan, 1993).
Modesty almost forbids, but this is still the only book on the French Prime Minister.

GAFFNEY, J., and MILNE, L. (eds.), *French Presidentialism and the Election of 1995* (Aldershot, Ashgate, 1997).
The 1995 election in detail and from the perspective of presidentialism.

HAYWARD, J. (ed.), *De Gaulle to Mitterrand: Presidential Power in France* (London, Hurst, 1993).
Good introduction to all aspects of the presidency.

5

....

The Bureaucracy

Overview

This chapter examines the role of the bureaucracy. There are three main sections. The first section identifies the position of civil servants and examines the structure of the bureaucracy. The second section focuses on the issue of civil service reform. The third section examines the role of the higher civil servants in the system and explores the idea that France is a technocracy. It outlines the normative distinction between politics and the administration in the French system and suggests that in practice this distinction is not quite as clear cut as it might at first appear.

Introduction

Over the years, the strength of the State in France has sometimes been exaggerated (see Chapter 3). The State was never quite as purposive and coherent as some people suggested. Moreover, in recent years the State has been reformed. As a result, the potential for State-centred policy leadership has been reduced. All the same, the State has always been and remains a key component in the French system of governance. The State is still a basic normative reference point and comprises an extensive set of institutions. The institutions of the State are staffed by bureaucrats, although this label fails to capture the full range of public servants, public agents, functionaries, and other types of public-sector actors that can be found in the French system. Rather like some of the views of the State as a whole, on occasion the influence of the bureaucracy in France has been overstated. It is certainly true that the various elements of the civil service defend their rights and privileges with a passion. At the same time, the bureaucracy does not operate as a unitary and cohesive actor. On the contrary, the bureaucracy is riven with special interests, the main aim of each of which is to protect and promote their own particular concerns. As a result, the system is both difficult to reform and difficult to manage. The opportunity for political actors to impose a coherent policy on the bureaucracy as a whole is very slim. This point applies to all levels of the civil service. At times, the higher civil service in France has been accused of exercising considerable power. However, France is not a technocracy. The system is not governed by a small set of people who have attended the most prestigious administrative training schools and who belong to the so-called *grands corps* (see below). All the same, in a fundamentally State-centred system, like the one in France, the behaviour of higher-level bureaucrats helps to shape political events. Overall, there is no doubt that bureaucrats are key political actors and that the organization of the system in which they operate helps to determine political outcomes.

The structure of the bureaucracy

As we saw in Chapter 3, the bureaucracy in France is extremely large. The true number of civil servants in the French system is extremely difficult to establish (see Chapter 7). All the same, at the end of 1998 official figures indicated that no fewer than 4,887,400 people were employed in the three statutory elements of the bureaucracy, or *fonctions publiques* (**www.fonc-tion-publique.gouv.fr/fp/statistiques/stats**—accessed 6 June 2002).[1] This figure comprised 2,523,100 State bureaucrats in the strict sense of the term (*la fonction publique de l'État*), a further 1,507,300 civil servants working for local government institutions (*la fonction publique territoriale*—see Chapter 8), and 857,000 people employed in the hospital sector (*la fonction publique hospitalière*). The 2,523,100 people in the *fonction publique de l'État* comprised 1,861,000 civil servants in government departments, 409,100 military personnel, and 253,000 people employed in public-sector enterprises (including institutions such as museums, but excluding organizations like the State electricity company—EDF). It should be noted, though, that the figure for the people in government Ministries included more than 100,000 members of the police force, as well as nearly one million teachers and people in the university sector. What this means is that the number of people engaged in routine administrative functions in government Ministries is smaller than the headline figures might suggest. Even so, there is no doubt that bureaucrats occupy an important position in the system of governance as a whole. The rest of this section identifies the position of civil servants and examines the structure of the bureaucracy. The main aims of the section are to highlight the highly regimented set of rules that govern the operation of the civil service and the fragmented nature of the bureaucratic system.

The position of civil servants

The bureaucracy in France is governed by a very formalized system of rules. The basic framework of the system was established in 1946 with the passage of the so-called General Statute of the Public Service. This was the result of a historic agreement between the trade unions and the Liberation government (communists, Socialists, Christian Democrats, and gaullists — see Chapter 1). Even though the 1946 General Statute has been amended over the years, it established the basic organization of the contemporary civil service system. Moreover, it did so in a very detailed way concerning matters of recruitment, promotion, pay, rights and duties, and so forth. However, by interlinking many of these issues and by doing so in such a complicated way, it also made the system very difficult to overhaul. In short, the General Statute helped to institutionalize an extremely complex and highly regimented system that is difficult to reform.

Entry to the civil service and promotion within it are by competitive exam (*concours*). True, at the highest levels of the system, appointments are made in the Council of Ministers (see Chapter 4). Even so, the civil service as a whole has the characteristics of a meritocracy rather than a spoils system. Each year, the examinations for the different departments are widely advertised and the figures for the number of places available and the number of people who apply are a matter of public record. There are two basic types of examinations: internal exams for people who are already working in the bureaucracy and who want promotion and external exams for people who wish to join. There are different categories of civil servants (see below). People who have a university qualification or the equivalent are eligible to take the exam for a Category A post; people who have a *baccalauréat* (the basic secondary school qualification) are eligible to take the exam for a Category B post; and people without any qualification can apply for a Category C post. In the past, ways have certainly been found to circumvent these rules. Most notably, people have been recruited on one-year contracts that do not require an examination, only for them to be made permanent once the initial contract has expired. For the most part, though, entry to the system is based on a very rigid set of rules. The same point is true for the dismissal of civil servants. It is certainly the case that civil servants who break the law will be removed. The system of administrative courts is a very effective way of punishing corrupt behaviour (see Chapter 8). However, in practice it is very difficult to dismiss bureaucrats for most other work-related matters. Indeed, this is one of the main reasons why there has always been such a demand to enter the bureaucracy. In effect, employment in the civil service has constituted a job for life and, while there have been plans for redundancies in recent years, this point still applies for the majority of bureaucrats.

As noted above, there are three basic categories of civil servants. Category A civil servants constitute the managerial class. Category B civil servants are the people who carry out routine administrative tasks and secretarial duties. Category C civil servants are engaged in manual work and similar tasks. In addition, within each category civil servants belong to particular *corps*. The untranslatable term 'corps' refers to a group of officials who enjoy the same conditions of service and who carry out the same tasks within the administration. Every civil servant is a member of a *corps* and there are over 1,500 different *corps* within the administration, each of which is governed by its own particular set of rules. For example, there is a *corps* of tax inspectors in Category A of the civil service, as well as a *corps* of police officers in Category B. Within each *corps* there are different grades of civil servants; within each grade there are different classes of civil servants; and within each class there are different echelons of civil servants. Finally, it should be noted that various types of public-sector employees are employed according to distinct sets of rules, or regimes. For example, this applies to the highest civil servants in some of the so-called *grands corps* (see below) as well as some of the workers in various public-sector enterprises. The result is a very fragmented, extremely regimented, and very hierarchical system. In this system, each person is acutely aware of his or her own position within the system as a whole. Each person is also very aware of his or her position relative to everyone else.

In this context, it is hardly surprising that the rules governing the pay of French civil servants are also extremely complex. Pay is calculated as a function of the salary associated with the particular grade of each civil servant plus an amount based on the various benefits and indemnities to which she or he is entitled, less the deductions to which she or he is subject. For example, there is a basic annual pay level for every civil servant. In 2002, it was 5,212.84 euro. This figure is then multiplied by another figure corresponding to the *corps* and grade of the civil servant in question. In 2002, the multiplier ranged from a figure of 261 to 820. In turn, the resulting figure is divided by 100 to determine an annual salary. So, an average Category B civil servant who occupies a post that is associated with a multiplier of, say, 300 would earn an average monthly wage of 5,212.84 multiplied by 300, with this figure being divided by 100, and with the resulting figure being divided by 12, making a total of 1,303.21 euro per month. This figure would then be supplemented by the bonuses and indemnities to which she or he is entitled, the details of which are again established by a very complicated set of rules. Finally, various deductions would be made in relation to pensions and taxes. What emerges is a system in which there is a very formalized set of pay differentials across the system as a whole. This makes the system extremely difficult to reform. Global reforms are difficult because of the range of issues that need to be addressed. Piecemeal reforms are equally difficult because of the desire of each group to maintain its position relative to all the others.

Whatever their rank and whatever their pay, bureaucrats are bound by a number of duties, and they also enjoy certain rights. In terms of duties, civil servants are obliged to keep matters secret that relate to the individuals they deal with; wherever possible they have a responsibility to provide members of the public with information requested; they have a duty to obey the instructions that are passed down by their superiors; and, last but not least, senior civil servants must not use their position to comment publicly on government policy or the work of their departments generally. In terms of rights, civil servants have the right to join a union; they have the right to strike, even though a day's income is lost for each day of the strike; they have the right to be represented on internal decision-making bodies; they have the right to stand for election and, if unsuccessful, they have the right to return to their post. The existence of a set of duties is necessary to establish the neutrality of the civil service. They ensure that bureaucrats operate in a strictly professional and impartial manner. By the same token, the existence of a set of rights is an acknowledgement that civil servants are not just agents of the State, they are also citizens. Thus, they have the right to enjoy the same sorts of privileges as all other citizens.

This combination of public service and private motivation in the context of a highly regimented system of workplace rules is key to understanding the functioning of the French civil service. On the one hand, the bureaucracy is a relatively popular institution. In a recent opinion poll, 63 per cent of people said that they had confidence in civil servants. This compared with an equivalent figure of 99 per cent for firefighters, 76 per cent for the police, 52 per cent for business people, and only 18 per cent for politicians (**www.sofres.com/etudes/pol/120701_chron_r.htm**—accessed 6 June 2002). The popularity of the civil service ties in with the ongoing desire to protect the system of public services in France (see Chapter 3). In a country where the State is seen as the embodiment of the national interest, civil servants, or the agents of the State, are seen as true public servants. Indeed, this partly accounts for the negative perception of politicians, who are seen as party political and, therefore, necessarily self-interested actors. On the other hand, the various elements of the bureaucracy are themselves highly politicized and undeniably self-interested. For example, the level of public-sector unionization remains high at least relative to the figure for private-sector organizations. Moreover, civil servants have not been slow to exercise their right to strike. So, while the level of strike activity varies from year to year, recent experience has shown that concerted public-sector opposition can result in reforms being abandoned. Most notably, this happened in the case of the proposed reorganization of the Finance Ministry in March 2000 (Bert 2000; Séréni and Villeneuve 2002) and the reform of the education system around the same time.

In recent years, though, what has been perhaps most notable about these strikes and others like them is that they have often involved particular groups of public servants using their organizational strength to defend their own sets of rights and privileges. The bureaucracy has rarely been united in a struggle against the government or the system as a whole. Instead, individual elements of the bureaucracy have frequently engaged in quarrels with Ministers over specific matters relating to pay, pensions, and conditions of work. In this context, there has been constant temptation for the government to give in to such demands because in each case the budgetary cost of finding an agreement may be relatively small, whereas the political cost of a protracted dispute may potentially be high. The result is a bureaucracy which has been extremely difficult to reform, even though the country's most senior political actors have enjoyed an extensive set of constitutional, administrative, and political powers (see Chapter 4). This is not to say that reform has been impossible. As we shall see below, various changes have been made in recent years. It is simply to say that reform is difficult. As a result, while there has been a degree of new public management reform in France, these reforms have perhaps been less extensive in France than in other equivalent countries (Pollitt and Bouckaert 2000: 231).

The internal organization of the bureaucracy

The organization of the bureaucracy in France is characterized by a set of highly entrenched divisions (see Rouban 1995: 42–7). These divisions reinforce the difficulties involved in reforming the civil service. This is because they entrench rigid sets of professional and personal differentials. In other words, reforming one element of the system, which may be possible, often means reforming many other elements as well, which may not. At the same time, these divisions also mean that the civil service cannot behave as a unitary actor. The bureaucracy does not have a cohesive set of interests or a common vision of its role. This means that it does not act as a bloc that challenges the power and/or legitimacy of elected representatives. Equally, it also means that it can be difficult for political actors to impose their will upon the system. The system is too fragmented to be manipulated coherently.

The divisions between the different elements of the bureaucracy can be seen in various ways. For example, the French system is marked by a profound set of intraministerial rivalries. The internal organization of French Ministries is very different from their British counterparts. In France, there is no equivalent of the British permanent secretary (the Sir Humphrey character from the programme *Yes Minister*) (see Figure 5.1). Instead, ministries are split on a functional basis into divisions

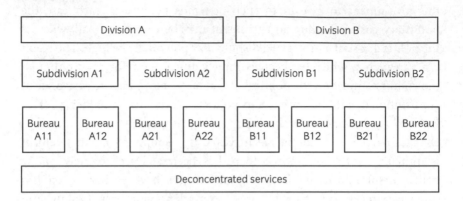

FIGURE 5.1   The internal organization of French Ministries

(*directions*), each of which has responsibility for a particular area of the Ministry's work and which is headed by a director. For example, in 2002 the Ministry for Civil Engineering, Transport, Housing, Tourism, and the Sea comprised thirteen separate divisions, such as the Roads Division and the Air Transport Division, as well as the ministerial information service which had the equivalent status to a division. Divisions are then split on a functional basis into subdivisions (*sous-directions*), each of which in turn has responsibility for a separate aspect of the division's work and which is headed by a sub-director. For example, in the Roads Division of the Ministry for Civil Engineering there were four subdivisions, including the Subdivision for Motorways and Toll Roads and the Subdivision for Road-Building Investment. These subdivisions are further split on a functional basis into bureaux, each of which itself has responsibility for a restricted element of the subdivision's work and which is headed by a bureau chief. For example, the Subdivision for Road-Building Investment was sub-divided into four bureaux, including the unit responsible for road-building in the greater Paris region. Over and above these units, Ministries invariably include other organizations. For example, the Ministry for Civil Engineering had overall responsibility for the State railway company as well as the organization that managed the transport system in Paris. Finally, at the local level French departments have a well-developed range of deconcentrated services (or field services as they used to be known) that work closely with civil servants at the local level (see Chapter 8). For example, in 2002 the Ministry for Civil Engineering included 22 Regional

Civil Engineering Divisions (*directions régionales de l'équipement*) and 101 Departmental Civil Engineering Divisions (*directions départementales de l'équipement*).

The internal fragmentation of French Ministries means that there is competition for resources between divisions within each Ministry, between subdivisions within each division, and between bureaux within each subdivision. This competition can be seen most clearly in the annual round of budgetary negotiations. As a general rule, the ministerial budget is the amalgamation of the budget for each division in the Ministry. In turn, the budget for each division is the amalgamation of the budget for each subdivision in the division. Likewise, the budget for each subdivision is the amalgamation of the budget for each bureau in the subdivision. Thus, within a Ministry, divisions will be in competition with each other for scarce resources; within a division, subdivisions will be in competition with each other; and within a subdivision, bureaux will be in competition with each other. Moreover, the potential for intraministerial conflict is further increased by the divisions that can occur between a Ministry's deconcentrated services in the periphery and its central offices in Paris. The former often believe that the latter are too remote, too technocratic (see below), and too removed from the 'everyday' lives of 'real' people. For their part, the latter often think that the former are too parochial and that they fail to take sufficient account of the national interest. The net result is that Ministries can be very difficult to manage. Certainly, it can be very difficult for the Minister to impose a coherent direction on the organization as a whole.

A further element of fragmentation concerns the rivalries that exist between the various civil service *corps*. These rivalries cut across the divisions that already exist both between and within Ministries. They can be seen most clearly at the most senior levels of the administration with the competition between the extremely prestigious so-called *grands corps*, but they also occur throughout the system as a whole. 'Grands corps' is the name given to the highest-ranking *corps* within the bureaucracy. They include the diplomatic *corps* and the prefectural *corps* (see Chapter 8). However, the three most renowned administrative *corps* are the Finance Inspectorate (Inspection des finances) for public-sector tax inspectors; the Court of Accounts (Cour des comptes) for public-sector auditors; and the Council of State (Conseil d'État) for constitutional and administrative lawyers (see Chapter 7). In addition, there are two technical *corps*, the Mines, and the Bridges and Highways *corps* (the *corps des Mines* and the *corps des Ponts et Chaussées* respectively), for public-sector engineers. The *grands corps* occupy such a prestigious position because they belong to institutions that control the operation of the civil service. The Finance Inspectorate is responsible for exercising financial control over the public sector as a whole; the Court of Accounts is the supreme auditing authority for all public-sector institutions; and the Council of State is the highest administrative court in the country (see Chapter 7). In this way, the members of these institutions have the responsibility for judging or at least watching over the activity of their peers. Thus, inevitably they occupy a more elevated position than their counterparts in government Ministries and other public-sector institutions. For their part, the technical *corps* occupy an equally prestigious position by virtue of the fact that they can claim to have an unrivalled scientific understanding of particular issues. As a result, when it comes to planning infrastructure projects they have a virtual monopoly of advice.

The importance of the *grands corps* lies not just in their exalted status, but also in the extent to which they have colonized particular parts of the administration and jealously defend what they deem to be their own fiefdoms. This is particularly the case between the two technical *corps*. For example, within the Ministry for Civil Engineering members of the Bridges and Highways *corps* have a virtual monopoly over the most senior positions within the Roads Division of the Ministry. Elsewhere, members of the Finance Inspectorate have considerable influence over many of the most important posts in the Ministry of Finance. By the same token, members of the Council of State occupy many of the top positions within the General Secretariat of the Government, the French equivalent of the British Cabinet Office (see Chapter 4). More generally, even if whole Ministries or divisions are not within the purview of a *corps*, it may be the case that specific positions within individual Ministries are seen to 'belong' to particular *corps*. This is not to say that *corps* can always successfully defend their 'own' positions. It is merely an indication of the fact that the French bureaucracy is riddled with rivalries and divisions. For example, the director of the Archives Division of the Culture and Communication Ministry was traditionally someone with a specialized professional background in history and archival research. However, in 1998 for the first time a member of the Council of State was appointed to head the Archives Division. At the time, the reason why the change at the Archives Division caused such a stir was not simply because the archivists appeared to have lost one of their traditional posts, but also because the Council of State was thought to have 'colonized' another position within the administration and because there was the feeling that it would be reluctant to relinquish control of the position at a future date. Indeed, it might be noted that in 2001 the next director of the Archives Division was also a member of the Council of State. The initial fears of the archivists seemed to have been well founded. Overall, these rivalries, and others like them, ensure that it is difficult to manage in a purposive and coherent way. As a result, the issue of civil service reform is politically salient and has been for a considerable period of time.

Reform of the civil service

The issue of civil service reform has never been absent from the political agenda in France and it would be incorrect to think that the desire to reform the civil service suddenly became salient at any given time. All the same, a number of matters relating to civil service reform began to emerge in the 1970s and since this time these issues have remained fundamentally unchanged. This was the period when France began to be affected by chronic economic problems, when there were societal demands for a different mode of governance and when international and particularly European pressures increased. As a result, since this time the issue of civil service reform has been dominated by three concerns: the cost and efficiency of the bureaucracy, the responsiveness of the administration, and the question of technocracy. This section examines the first two concerns, the next section looks at the issue of technocracy.

Since the 1970s, France has experienced three dilemmas.[2] The first dilemma was economic. The post-war period was marked by three decades of almost continuous economic growth. The so-called 'trente glorieuses' resulted in the transformation of the French economy. There was a big decline in the agricultural sector and a concomitant increase in industrial production, notably in high-tech industries with tremendous growth potential. However, the world economic crisis of the mid–1970s was felt particularly severely in France. The country was heavily dependent on imported raw materials. As the price of these commodities rose, the level of inflation increased rapidly. In turn, there were severe balance of payments difficulties, the value of the currency declined, and economic growth was stifled. Moreover, the country's financial situation worsened and the budget deficit increased. The left attempted to spend its way out of the crisis in 1981, but was soon obliged to do an economic U-turn and follow the path of fiscal rectitude (see Chapter 1).

This situation helped to focus attention on the cost of France's public services. In particular, it led to pressures to reduce the number of civil servants, to reform the complex and costly system of service-wide pay differentials, and to reconsider the pension rights of civil servants. The fact that the majority of proposals to these ends have been postponed or defeated is testimony to the difficulties involved in reforming the bureaucracy (see above). Indeed, in the period 1994–8 the number of people employed in the public service actually increased (see Table 5.1). Moreover, the increases occurred under both left- and right-wing governments. At the same time, the increasing cost of the civil service also led to a desire for more efficient, or cost-effective, government. In this area, reforms have been somewhat more successful. There has been a move to ensure value for money in the delivery of public services and to promote goal-oriented government. One example concerns the evaluation of public policy. In contrast to other countries, in France for a considerable period of time the process of policy evaluation remained somewhat underdeveloped. Even so, by the late 1980s a number of reports into the efficiency of particular areas, including the university sector, had been carried out. Moreover, in 1998 this policy was reinforced with the creation of the National Council for Evaluation. As a result, the number of value-for-money studies has increased.

TABLE 5.1	The total number of civil servants in France, 1994–1998			
	31 Dec. 1994	31 Dec. 1996	31 Dec. 1997	31 Dec. 1998
The official number of civil servants	2,410,138	2,466,640	2,488,187	2,523,130

Source: www.fonction-publique.gouv.fr/fp/statistiques/effectifs/effectifs_index.htm

More importantly, there has been a change of mentality within the French public services. The principle of cost-effectiveness has been internalized to a much greater extent than before.

The second dilemma was social. In this area, so great was the degree of change that one writer (Mendras 1994) has argued that there was, in effect, a second French revolution in the 1960s and 1970s. He pointed out that the period 1944–65 was marked by economic growth, a rising population, the decline of the peasantry and rural life in general, and the rise of the salariat. After 1965 the birth rate fell, immigration and unemployment rose, the Catholic Church modernized, and there was an Americanization of French cultural life. These changes brought about a profound desire for social change. The first manifestation of this desire was the student and worker unrest in 1968 (see Chapter 1). After this time, the various elements of the movement continued to promote their own very varied agendas. The unifying aspect of these very different movements was a concern for lifestyle issues. Rather than, or at least in addition to, material issues, people became increasingly preoccupied with matters relating to representation, identity, and self-expression.

This change of attitudes had an impact on a wide range of political issues. In relation to the public sector it was one of the prime motivations for the decentralization of the system in the early 1980s (see Chapter 8). More specifically, in the context of the civil service it can also be associated with the policy of deconcentration, or the transfer of public-sector employees from the Paris region to the provinces (see also Chapter 8). In some cases, this policy has proved extremely controversial. Most notably, members of the elite public administration training school, the École nationale d'administration (ENA), objected to being relocated in Strasbourg. The government backed down and as a result students at ENA still spend most of their time in Paris as before (Gaillard 1995: 191–4). In most cases, though, the policy of deconcentration has been welcomed. Indeed, in the period 1991–2001 a total of 22,214 posts had already been transferred from Paris to the regions with a further 5,750 under way (*Le Monde*, 20 February 2002). More generally, the increasing importance of lifestyle politics has affected issues such as freedom of information, the availability of administrative information on-line, and the simplification of administrative activity. The latter has been a particular focus of activity in recent years. In 1998, the Jospin government established the Commission for the

Simplification of Administrative Formalities. This body has overall responsibility for demystifying the administrative process. It has been able to abolish certain bureaucratic forms altogether and has worked hard on trying to make the language of the administration more accessible to the ordinary citizen. Those who have ever had any dealings with the authorities in France will know that there is still some way to go in this regard. All the same, there have been steps in the right direction.

The third dilemma was international and related to issues of globalization and the development of the European Union (EU). For example, in terms of globalization the spectre of Americanization has haunted the French scene for a very long time. While there was tremendous solidarity with the USA in the immediate aftermath of the 11 September attacks (in fact, Chirac was the first foreign leader to visit the USA), over the years American cultural hegemony has consistently been viewed as a threat to the French language (*le bulldozer*), French cuisine (*le fast-food*), French music (*l'exception culturelle*), and many other aspects of the country's way of life. So, even though the French have firmly defended their own way of doing things, there is no question that international pressures have had a profound effect on the conduct of French politics in recent times. Indeed, what is true of globalization generally is equally true of Europeanization more specifically. As with all member states France has been obliged to conform. Sometimes it has done so willingly. For example, France was at the forefront of European monetary integration. Moreover, as a net beneficiary, France has always championed the Common Agricultural Policy. At other times, France's attitude has been more ambiguous. Most notably, de Gaulle's so-called 'empty chair' policy stalled the process of European integration in the mid–1960s. In addition, the French courts were slow to recognize fully the supremacy of European over domestic law (see Chapter 7). Whatever the attitude, there is no doubt that the French political system has been irrevocably altered by the impact of events at the European level.

In terms of the bureaucracy, the twin processes of globalization and Europeanization have had both a general and a specific effect. In general terms, the very concept of new public management (NPM) can be seen as something which has been imported to France from outside. The idea that the citizen is a consumer of public services and that these services need to be provided as efficiently and effectively as possible has its contemporary origins in the USA. Moreover, in a national context, NPM reforms have been implemented most passionately in Australia, New Zealand, and the UK. So, while the cross-national application of NPM reforms has undoubtedly been uneven, the fundamental principle underlying the process of NPM reforms has been international and most certainly European. Indeed, this is the context in which we need to place the aforementioned civil service reforms in France. These reforms are not a domestic reaction to a peculiarly French problem. They are merely the French expression of an international response to a general problem. In more specific terms, the organization of the administration has been affected by the ongoing process of European integration. In particular, Europeanization has increased the need to improve the procedures for policy coordination or, to use the language of NPM, joined-up government. In this regard, the main change has been the increased importance of the SGCI in the decision-making process (see Chapter 4). The basic task of the SGCI is 'to provide negotiating briefs for France's permanent representation in Brussels or for Ministers at different meetings of the [European] Council' (Guyomarch, Machin, and Ritchie 1998: 59). To this end, the SGCI 'has to persuade the ministries and ministers to come to agreement and to do so in time for Brussels negotiations' (ibid.). However, given the number and intensity of interministerial and intraministerial rivalries in the French system (see above), very often this is no easy task. Indeed, in 1992 on average there were around five conflict-resolution meetings a day at the SGCI (ibid.). This is testimony to the difficulties involved in coordinating the work of the French administration. In turn, though, the fact that France has consistently been a significant player at the European level is a sign that the SGCI has performed its task as well as might be expected.

Technocracy

In France, the republican tradition requires that a clear distinction be made between politicians and bureaucrats. The former, in their capacity as representatives of the people, have the legitimacy to make decisions on behalf of the people. The latter, as the set of functionaries who implement the decisions made by politicians, do not have any such legitimacy. The net result is that bureaucrats should play a merely neutral role, whereas the real decision-making power should lie with the political class. This distinction has been enshrined in the fundamental texts of the French political system for more than 200 years. Article 3 of the 1789 Declaration of the Rights of Man, which is officially part of the Fifth Republic's constitutional block (see Chapter 7), states that 'sovereignty rests with the nation', meaning the people of France, and that 'no organization or individual may exercise sovereignty without having expressly been granted the right to do so by the nation'. Similarly, Article 20 of the 1958 Constitution states that 'the government directs and determines the nation's policies' and that in so doing 'it has the administration at its disposal'. Thus, the normative distinction between politicians and bureaucrats is very clearly and formally established in the founding texts of the Fifth Republic.

In practice, though, this distinction is less clear than the constitutional situation would appear to indicate (Suleiman 1984: 108). In France, there is a long-standing argument that France is a technocracy, meaning that the country is ruled by a set of people who have undergone a common process of training at the elite civil service schools and who belong to the most prestigious of the *grands corps*. These people, it is observed, occupy not simply senior posts within the administration, they have also entered politics and hold the most important political positions in the system. Thus, there is a blurring of the division between the administration and politics. Indeed, it is observed that people from this background have also colonized many of the most important posts in the business community through the process of *pantouflage* (civil servants moving to other public- and private-sector jobs) (Piastra 2000). The net result is said to be a cohesive power bloc that shapes the economic, social, and political direction of the country not simply because its representatives hold all the main positions of power within the system, but also because there is an intellectual similarity between the various members of the technocratic elite as a result of their common educational background and professional training.

The accusation that France is ruled by technocrats has a very long history. However, as with the more general arguments for civil service reform that were outlined in the previous section, the notion that France is a technocracy has been put forward consistently since the 1970s. For example, one writer explained from an academic perspective why members of the *grands corps* were so influential: '[They] are drawn from a few administrative training schools [*grandes écoles*]: the Polytechnique and

ENA. From this perspective, the basic link that maintains the existence of these castes is the link with the past. They construct a network of friends and acquaintances, acquired by young intelligent people in privileged places of education that provide them with a common intellectual and emotional past, a way of reasoning and shared memories' (Thoenig 1973: 274). More humorously, one leading gaullist politician, Philippe Séguin, provided a particularly vitriolic but nonetheless amusing account of technocrats. Civil servants, he argued, 'can be divided, as everyone knows, into two main categories: on the one hand, those who serve no purpose whatsoever and who are by far and away the most numerous; on the other hand, those who want to run the whole show and whose appetite for power explains the omnipresence of the State. The latter are the more targeted; we might be able to get along with bureaucrats, but as for technocrats, no quarter! If you ever need to get a lacklustre or sleepy audience going at a public meeting, all you have to do is to denounce the psychopaths who think they are serving the State but who really are only looking to serve themselves' (Séguin 1985: 100). In recent times, the argument about technocracy has taken a very particular turn as some people have tried to link it to the process of Europeanization. For example, in 1992 Séguin, the *de facto* leader of the 'no' campaign at the time of the referendum on the Maastricht Treaty, consistently argued that one of the reasons for rejecting the Treaty was that Economic and Monetary Union would lead to government by technocrats. 'My European battle', he argued, 'is not a matter of partisan cleavages or tactical considerations. It is a battle for the values in which I believe, a battle for the Republic. By defending the idea of a political Europe against a technocratic Europe, of a solidaristic Europe against a monetaristic Europe, of an organized Europe against a Europe which is open to all points of the compass, *I firmly believe that I am being faithful to the inspiration of the founding fathers of the Community*' (Séguin 1994: 28).[3] In short, the stakes in the argument about technocracy are very high. They concern the very legitimacy of the republican system of government. Is the country governed by the representatives of the people, or is it run by a coterie of highly trained intellectuals who cannot be removed from power because they have colonized the most important positions within both the public and private sectors?

There is plenty of superficial evidence to support the idea that France is a technocracy and that the distinction between politicians and bureaucrats is blurred. First, there is no doubt that the French system creates an elite set of highly trained administrators. The two basic pillars of this system are the two main administrative training schools (or *grandes écoles*), the École polytechnique and the École nationale d'administration (ENA), and the system of *grands corps* (see above). The École polytechnique was founded in 1794. It provides technical training for public-sector scientists and engineers. The École nationale d'administration was set up in 1945. It provides a more general training background for non-specialist civil servants. Each of these two schools only has an intake of around 80–100 people per year and entry to them is by way of a competitive public exam. The number of people wanting to enter the schools is large, so there is fierce competition. Typically, having completed a first degree, these candidates prepare for the entrance exam by attending a year of special preparatory classes which are put on by certain institutions, most notably the Institut d'Études Politiques in Paris, entrance to which is itself determined by a competitive public exam. Once at the schools, the training period usually lasts for just over two years. Taking ENA as the example, the first year is spent on an internship, usually in a public-sector organization such as a prefecture (see Chapter 8). The second year is devoted to classroom study in Strasbourg from January to July and Paris from September to February. On the basis of the marks they receive in all of their subjects, the students are graded and a rank-order is generated. The person who is ranked first has the opportunity to select the most prestigious of the very limited number of administrative positions that the government has placed on offer that year. In practice, the highest-ranked students invariably choose to enter one of the *grands corps*. For students graduating from ENA in April 2002 the government created six vacancies in the Council of State, five in the Court of Accounts, and five in the Finance Inspectorate. The remaining students could choose from lesser-ranking (but nonetheless still prestigious) positions within the administration generally (*JO* 226, 29 September 2001: 15367). The net result is that the specialized training procedure for higher civil servants creates not just a highly trained administrative elite, but an elite within that elite. Moreover, it creates an elite that is bound by a number of commonalties—the special classes that prepare candidates for the entrance exam to the *grande école*, the curriculum and social life at the schools themselves, and the sense of belonging to the most prestigious *corps* within the administrative system.

Secondly, there is also no doubt that many of the country's most senior politicians have a background in the civil service and, in particular, the higher civil service. So, for example, both Lionel Jospin and Jacques Chirac were trained at ENA. Indeed, on graduation Chirac joined the Court of Accounts. In fact, since 1959 no less than nine of the country's sixteen different Prime Ministers have been members of one of the so-called *grands corps*.[4] For their part, Mitterrand and de Gaulle are the only Presidents who have not belonged to one of the *grands corps*.[5] The same point applies to Ministers. In the Fifth Republic, an average of around 50 per cent of all Ministers have had a background in the civil service. Indeed, in the 1988 Rocard government the figure was as high as 70 per cent (Bigaut 1997: 35). Furthermore, in the 1997–2002 legislature, thirty-five deputies were members of the *grands corps* and an additional forty deputies were lesser-ranking members of the bureaucracy (source: **www.assemblee-nationale. fr/qui/statistiques.asp**—accessed 30 May 2002).[6] In general, throughout the history of the Fifth Republic around 15 per cent of deputies have had a civil service background (Rouban 1998: 66). All told, in the sense that many elected representatives are drawn directly from the ranks of the civil service, and in particular from the ranks of the higher civil service, the constitutional distinction between the political class and bureaucratic class is less clear that it might at first appear. Moreover, it is clear that the politicians from this background often hold some of the highest positions of responsibility in the land.

The distinction between politicians and bureaucrats is further blurred by the existence of ministerial *cabinets*. Since the Third Republic, it has become the established practice for every Minister, as well as the President and the Prime Minister (see Chapter 4), to appoint a set of loyal personal advisers. Ministers generally appoint around ten people to their *cabinet*. At one time in the early 1990s there was a total of no less than 861 *cabinet* members in the government as a whole, although the average figure in the period 1984–96 was around 500 (Rouban 1997: 17).[7] The role of *cabinet* members is unequivocally political. They give policy advice (both political and technical); they provide political counsel (including speech-writing and opinion-polling); and they supply logistical support (diary management and matters of protocol). Moreover, *cabinet* members are appointed when the Minister assumes office and can be dismissed at any time and for any reason during the Minister's time in office. In this sense, the *cabinet* is not part of the permanent administration and *cabinet* members do not have the same official status as civil servants, even if their remuneration is similar. All the same, one of the main tasks of *cabinet* members is to liaise with their former colleagues in the administration. Furthermore, typically up to 70 per cent of all ministerial *cabinet* members are recruited directly from the civil service (Rouban 1997: 19). They are seconded to the *cabinet* by the government department or administrative institution in which they normally work and, after serving in the *cabinet*, they return to their original position at the same level as before, if not a higher one. In these ways, the *cabinet* system further confuses the distinction between politicians and bureaucrats. Moreover, a considerable proportion of these civil servants are drawn from the highest ranks of the administration. In the period 1981–93 one study showed that 41 per cent of *cabinet* members were ENA graduates (Mathiot and Sawicki 1999: 16). Moreover, in the same period 13.8 per cent of *cabinet* members belonged to the *grands corps* (ibid.). What is interesting is not just the fact that these figures show the over-representation of these groups compared with the population as a whole, but also the fact the authors of the study conclude from the figures that the system was not as 'technocratized' as people usually consider it to be (ibid.). Whatever the conclusion, the bottom line is that highly trained people with a background in the higher levels of the administration hold many of the most important positions within the French system of government. This is the foundation of the claim that France is a technocracy.

The problem with this claim is that the foundation on which it is based is very shallow. There is no doubt that highly trained people with a background in the administration hold important positions of political responsibility. There is also no doubt that there is a certain solidarity and, quite literally, a shared *esprit de corps* between the individual elements of this elite set of people. The example of the supposed 'colonization' of the head of the Archives Division by the Council of State (see above) can be treated as a case in point. At the same time, though, the weakness of the claim that France is a technocracy lies in the implication that these people act, purposefully or otherwise, as a cohesive unit (Wright 1974: 52–5). They do not. As we saw earlier in the chapter, the administration in France is racked with divisions. These divisions manifest themselves not just at the lower levels of the civil service but at the higher levels of the bureaucracy as well. There are differences between the people who are trained at ENA and the people who graduate from the École polytechnique in terms of their education, their contacts, and their career trajectories. Moreover, as we have already seen, there are differences between the members of the *grands corps*. People may have a loyalty to their own *corps*, but they have little, if any, loyalty to any other *corps*. Furthermore, there are political differences between this set of people. The claim that France is a technocracy is based on the idea that technocrats can be found on both the left and the right and that, as a result, whichever party or coalition is in power, technocrats with a shared mentality and common network of contacts will continue to govern the country. This is absurd. There is no question that there are many people on both the left and right who have been to ENA, who belong to one of the *grands corps*, and who hold a position of political influence. But however similar or different the policies of the left and the right may now be, the fact people have chosen to support the left or the right is a sign that they differ in their basic attitudes towards the organization of economic, social, and political life, not that they hold common values or mind-sets.

Overall, the operation of the administration in France and the relationship between the administration and politics is very complex. There is no doubt that there are complicities between members of the administration. There are networks. There are solidarities. However, these link small groups of people. At best, they unite the members of individual *corps*. They do not extend to the system as a whole. There may be a desire for individual *corps* to maximize their own influence within the system, but there is no technocratic power bloc. Moreover, there is also a clear sense in which increasingly political actors on both the left and the right, many of whom have a background in the higher levels of the administration, have pursued the same sorts of policies. As we saw in Chapter 2, while there remain basic ideological differences between the left and the right, there is no doubt that over the last twenty years these differences have narrowed. All the same, the fact that both left- and right-wing governments have pursued similar policies has nothing to do with the *grandes écoles* or the prevalence of members of the *grands corps* in the most powerful positions of political authority in the State. The increasing ideological similarity between the left and the right is a European, indeed a world-wide, phenomenon. It is not unique to France. What is more, in France it is not caused by the highly specialized system of administrative training for elite civil servants. It is a much more widespread occurrence that manifests itself in the context not just of the administration but of political life more generally.

Conclusion

Over the last twenty years there has been a considerable amount of ideational change in relation to the French bureaucracy. There is an increasing belief that citizens are consumers, that public services should be cost-effective, that the administration should be more flexible, and that technocrats should not exercise too much influence. At the same time, some of the more established ideas still have considerable force. There is the belief that bureaucrats are public servants, that they should continue to enjoy certain rights and privileges, and that the French system needs to be protected from international and European forces. The result is a difficult mixture of the old and the new. There is a belief that the bureaucracy needs to change, but a fear that change will not necessarily lead to a better situation. These very conflicting preferences are very clearly present within the political class. Left- and right-wing governments have both argued that the system needs to be reformed and both have taken steps to bring about such reforms. At the same time, the degree of reform has been somewhat modest. Moreover, when reforms have been opposed, governments have often backed down. The institutional result is equally mixed. The extremely fragmented nature of the bureaucracy means that institutional reform in this domain is very difficult to bring about. The organization of the bureaucracy in France is still based on the principles and structures that were established nearly sixty years ago. All the same, within this general framework, some reforms have been implemented. In a comparative perspective, the extent of the change is relatively small. In the French context, though, the fact that there has been any change at all is significant. The bureaucracy remains popular, but its position has been challenged. The most senior elements of the bureaucracy, the technocrats, remain powerful, but their legitimacy has been contested. Thus, there has been change in this area. However, there is plenty of room for further developments.

KEY TERMS

- Public service statute
- Rigidity
- Reform

- Technocracy
- Internal divisions

NOTES

1 This figure does not include the 455,000 employees of the postal service and France Télécom. It also excludes 147,700 private-sector teachers whose salaries are paid by the State.

2 The term 'dilemma' is used here to mean the situation where a new idea stands in opposition to existing beliefs or practices and so forces a reconsideration of the existing beliefs and associated tradition (Bevir, Rhodes, and Weller 2002).

3 Italics in the original.

4 The exceptions are Couve de Murville, Messmer, Barre, Mauroy, Cresson, Bérégovoy, and Raffarin.

5 Even then, of course, the General was part of the elite military establishment.

6 Indeed, a further group of deputies were previously employed in public-sector companies or were retired civil servants.

7 This figure includes a large number of 'unofficial' *cabinet* members (see Schrameck 1995: 27).

GUIDE TO FURTHER READING

CROZIER, M., *The Bureaucratic Phenomenon* (Chicago, University of Chicago Press, 1967).
Still widely quoted, this book explores the inertia in the French bureaucratic system.

MEYNAUD, J., *Technocracy* (London, Faber & Faber, 1968).
A classic text about the supposed powers of technocrats in France.

ROUBAN, L., *The French Civil Service* (Paris, La Documentation française, 1998).
Good introduction by a leading author on the French administration.

SULEIMAN, E., *Politics, Power and Bureaucracy in France* (Princeton, Princeton University Press, 1974).
Another frequently cited book with a clear message.

6

The Legislature

Overview

The aim of this chapter is to explore the role of the French parliament. The first part outlines the constitutional and legal framework within which the Senate and the National Assembly operate. The second part examines the nature of party politics and reflects on the weakness of parliamentary politics in a highly competitive political system.

Introduction

In a classic study, Philip Williams once stated that with the onset of the Fifth Republic 'the parliament of France, once among the most powerful in the world, became one of the weakest' (Williams 1968: 21). In one sense, this conclusion is as true today as it was over thirty years ago. It is not totally misleading to describe the French legislature as a talking-shop, to deride deputies as government lobby-fodder, and to suggest that substantial reforms are needed in order to allow the parliamentary system to operate more efficiently.[1] In another sense, though, the politics of the parliamentary process are more complex than these simple formulations would suggest and, moreover, they always have been. In short, the role of the parliament cannot be understood simply in terms of the constitutional relationship between the executive and legislative branches of government. Instead, as Huber notes, we need to view parliament 'as the place where representatives from political parties must cooperate . . . while competing for legislative success' (Huber 1996: 179). This means that we should see parliament not merely 'as an agent in conflict with the government' (ibid.), but as an arena in which one element of a wider political game is played out. To be sure, the Constitution helps to establish the rules of the game, but at bottom the game is a party political one in which the prize is electoral victory and political power generally. In this context, there is no doubt that for the most part parliament does indeed do little more than rubber stamp the government's proposals. However, this is primarily because of party politics, not constitutional rules.

The institutional framework: the Senate and the National Assembly

There are two chambers to the French parliament. The upper chamber, the Senate, is indirectly elected and has an in-built conservative majority. Mainly because of the guaranteed right-wing majority, in 1998 the then Prime Minister, Lionel Jospin, called the Senate an 'anomaly' among democratic systems. Luckily for Jospin, a Socialist, the Senate also has very few powers. While it can obstruct certain reforms, it has very little capacity for systemic leadership. In contrast to the Senate, the lower chamber, the National Assembly, is directly elected for a five-year term. Like the Senate, though, it too has only limited constitutional powers. This section examines the Senate and the National Assembly in turn.

The Senate

There are 321 Senators. They are elected for a nine-year term with one-third of all Senate seats being contested every three years. Senators are not elected by the people, but by an electoral college. The members of the electoral college comprise deputies and local councillors (regional, departmental, and municipal). The college totals around 150,000 people, most of whom (around 95 per cent) are municipal councillors.[2] The electoral system is quite complex and has been reformed on two occasions, most recently in July 2000. (Box 6.1 summarizes this system.)

The composition of the electoral college has given the Senate an in-built right-wing majority. This is mainly because of the large numbers of municipal councillors who are included in the college. It must be remembered that there are more than 36,000 communes in France, over 32,000 of which

---

BOX 6.1   **The electoral system for the French Senate**

- There are 321 Senate seats.

  304 Senators are elected at the departmental level. The number of Senators per department varies according to population. So, for example, the Ariège department has only one Senator and the Jura has two, whereas the Nord has 11 and Paris has 12. In addition, 5 Senators are drawn from overseas areas, such as New Caledonia, while 12 Senators represent French people who are resident outside France.

- There is a mixed-member electoral system.

  Since 2000, there has been a two-ballot majority-plurality system for departments that elect either one or two Senators. To be elected at the first ballot, a candidate must receive more than 50 per cent of the valid votes cast (a majority) provided that more than 25 per cent of registered electoral college members have voted. When there is a second ballot, the candidate who receives the most votes (a plurality) is elected. In two-seat departments, the top two candidates are elected in this event.

  In departments that elect more than 2 Senators a proportional quota/highest average list system is used. For example, assume that 5 Senators are to be elected, that 1,500 electoral college members cast their vote, that three parties contest the election, and that party A receives 1,080 votes, party B receives 220 votes, and party C receives 200 votes. In the first stage, the quota system is used. The quota is calculated by dividing the number of valid votes cast by the number of seats to be won. So, in this case the quota is 300 (1,500 ÷ 5). The entitlement to seats is then determined by dividing the number of votes cast for a party list by the quota. In this case, the first three candidates on party A's list will be automatically elected (1,080 ÷ 300 = 3.6), while party B (0.73) and party C (0.66) will not elect a candidate at all. In the second stage, the highest average system is used. The average is calculated by taking the number of votes cast for each party and dividing it by the number of seats already won, plus one. In the above case, party A's average is 270 (1,080 ÷ (3 + 1)), party B's average is 220 (220 ÷ (0 + 1)), and party C's average is 200 (200 ÷ (0 + 1)). In this case, party A has the highest average and gains another seat. However, in the next iteration party B now has a higher average (220) than party A (216 = 1,080 ÷ (4 + 1)) and so gains the final seat.

- Under the proportional element of the system, there is male/female parity.

  Since 2000, in departments where the proportional system is used, party lists must alternate male and female candidates. So, if candidate number one on a party list is male, then candidate number two must be female and so on. In the above example, party A will have elected two men and two women.

have fewer than 2,000 inhabitants and over 27,000 of which have fewer than 1,000 residents (see Chapter 8). As a result, the electoral college over-represents very small towns, villages, and hamlets. Given that many of these communes are found in rural areas and that the population of these areas tends to be conservative, then the electoral college has a distinctly right-wing flavour. In addition, the right-wing bias has also been a function of the Senate's electoral system. In departments where Senators are elected by the two-ballot majority system, the electoral importance of rural and small-town councillors is exaggerated. In effect, their votes outweigh those from people representing larger population centres that are likely to be more left-leaning. Indeed, prior to the July 2000 reform, only departments that were entitled to elect five Senators did so on a proportional basis.[3] This amounted to around one-third of all Senate seats.

So, by virtue of both the electoral college and the electoral system, the Senate has always been unrepresentative in a party political sense. From 1958 to 1981, when the right had a majority in the National Assembly, this feature was less striking. In fact, for various reasons the Senate sometimes acted as the most effective parliamentary check on the government during this period (see below). Since 1981, though, institutional and/or electoral reform of the Senate has increasingly become the subject of political debate. The reason for this is not simply because the composition of the Senate has sometimes been out of step with the National Assembly, but because alternating left–right majorities in the lower chamber have under-scored the guaranteed right-wing majority in the upper house. In practice, the left has stood no chance of winning power in the Senate however well it has done in the lower chamber. True, the 2000 reform did give some small hope to the left in this regard, but the 2001 senatorial election confirmed that for the foreseeable future at least the right maintains an in-built advantage (see Table 6.1). For this reason, calls for reform are likely to continue.

Another important feature of the composition of the Senate concerns the number of Senators who also hold elected office at the local level. The so-called *cumul des mandats* (or multiple office-holding) is one of the most long-standing and paradoxical features of French political life. Over the years, the French State has been highly centralized, and yet local interests have always been strongly represented in the main institutions of government (see Chapter 8). In relation to the Senate, multiple office-holding is

TABLE 6.1	The party political composition of the Senate, December 2002	

Party group	Seats
Communist, Republican, and Citizen Group	23
European Democratic and Social Rally Group (non-gaullist right)	17
Union for a Popular Movement Group	166
Socialists (inc. Greens)	82
Centrists (mainly Christian Democrats)	27
Total left	105
Total right	210
No group	5
Vacant	1
Total	321

Note: As at 7 Aug. 2002.

Source: www.senat.fr (accessed 31 December 2002).

common mainly for two reasons. First, the Senate has a local bias. It should be noted that Article 24-3 of the 1958 Constitution officially states that the Senate 'ensures the representation of the local authorities' in the parliamentary system. In this context, it is unsurprising that Senators seek out election at the local level. Secondly, the Senate is sometimes seen as a home for people who are coming towards the end of their political careers. Given that multiple office-holding is common in the political system as a whole, Senators often hold elected office at the local level prior to their election to the upper house. In this case, they simply hold on to their previous position. Whatever the reason, the net result is that after the 2001 elections over 130 Senators held elected office at the municipal level; a similar number of Senators held elected office at the departmental level; and nearly 40 Senators held elected office at the regional level. In fact, only 60 Senators (18.75 per cent) failed to hold any sort of elected office at the local level. While this may allow Senators to claim that they are in touch with the local areas they represent, the high incidence of multiple office-holding also means that the upper chamber, like its National Assembly counterpart (see below), has a peculiarly parochial perspective to some of its decision-making.

Whatever the composition of the Senate, the upper chamber and its representatives enjoy relatively few constitutional and legal powers. True, the President of the Senate is the second highest-ranking person in the State after the President of the Republic. As a result, when de Gaulle resigned in 1969 and when Pompidou died in office in 1974, the President of the Senate, Alain Poher on both occasions, assumed the position of interim President of the Republic. In practice, though, this is a purely formal title. Indeed, on such occasions the President of the Senate is explicitly forbidden from using certain presidential powers, such as dissolving the National Assembly or calling a referendum. In practice, the institution's most important constitutional and legal power is the power of appointment. The President of the Senate has the right to make appointments to, for example, the Constitutional Council, the High Council of the Judiciary, and the agencies that regulate both the stock market and the broadcasting sector. The President also plays a role in making appointments to the Monetary Policy Council of the Bank of France. Like the equivalent power of the President of the Republic (see Chapter 4), the power of appointment can only be exercised at pre-programmed intervals. All the same, it does give the President of the Senate a real opportunity to shape the composition and the direction of these institutions. What is more, given that the right has an in-built Senate majority, it means that there is guaranteed right-wing representation on all of them.

More generally, the Senate plays a key role in passing legislation. That said, the upper chamber's role is nonetheless limited in this regard. Nominally at least, the Senate has the same powers as the National Assembly. That is to say, the Senate must approve a bill before it becomes law. So, in the 1999–2000 parliamentary session the Senate sat for a total of 107 days. It passed over 50 bills and more than 60 international conventions. During the course of these debates a total of more than 5,500 amendments were proposed, of which more than 3,000 were passed. All told, the Senate is a very active institution. The fact remains, though, that the Senate is subordinate to the National Assembly and, by extension, the government. This is because in the cases where the Senate and the National Assembly disagree about a particular piece of legislation, the lower house has the final say. In essence, the two houses have to agree an identical wording for each bill.[4] If no agreement has been reached by the time a bill has been considered at least twice by each house, the government can call a conference committee (*commission mixte paritaire*, or CMP) comprising seven representatives from each of the two chambers.[5] If the CMP agrees a final version, the bill is then returned to each house for approval. However, if no such agreement is possible, the government can ask the National Assembly to have the final say (Article 45-4). In the last resort, therefore, a left-wing government with a majority in the National Assembly can overcome an intransigent right-wing Senate. The 1999–2000 parliamentary session was a case in point. The government called a CMP on twenty-three occasions, only seven of which resulted in an agreed text between representatives of the two houses. In other words, the National Assembly had the last word sixteen times.

Over and above the basic legislative process, the Senate has two other main powers. The first relates to the Constitutional Council. Since 1974 a bill can be sent to the Constitutional Council if a request to this end is made by either sixty Senators or sixty deputies (Article 61-2). This reform greatly increased the power of the legislature and, in particular, the party groups opposed to the government in each house of the legislature (see Chapter 7). Prior to this time, only the President of the Republic, the Prime Minister, and the Presidents of the two parliamentary houses enjoyed this prerogative. As a result, while the President of the Senate did use this power to some effect on a limited number of occasions—indeed, the Council's landmark decision in 1971 was the result of a request by Alain Poher—in practice government bills were rarely sent to the Council at all. Since 1974, though, the opposition has used Article 61-2 to harass the government on a regular basis. So, for example, in the 2000–1 session alone thirteen bills were sent to the Council by the Senate. It must be appreciated that the Council is not obliged to strike down all or even part of the bill on these occasions. All the same, the Constitutional Council has emerged as an important check on executive power and when the left has been in government the role of the Senate by virtue of Article 61-2 has been important in this regard.

The Senate's other main power relates to 'organic laws' and constitutional amendments. Organic laws are hybrid creatures. They are separate from both 'ordinary' laws, which comprise the vast bulk of legislation, and bills to amend the Constitution. Instead, organic laws flesh out the details of the existing Constitution, indicating, for example, the number of deputies and Senators and the rules that organize their activities. In this context, the key point to note is that organic laws relating to the Senate have to be passed in identical terms by both houses (Article 46-4). What this means is that an opposition Senate can, in effect, veto government-inspired amendments. So, for example, when the Jospin government changed the regulations relating to the *cumul des mandats* (see below), the reform applied only to the National Assembly. The Senate refused to agree the government's proposals. In a similar way, bills to amend the Constitution itself must also be passed in identical terms by both chambers (Article 89-2). Only then can they be submitted for approval either by a referendum or by the vote of a three-fifths majority at a special parliamentary congress. Again, an opposition Senate has the power to veto government amendments of this sort. Admittedly, this is a negative power. Nonetheless, it is an important one. In particular, it means that the Senate can only be reformed by these means if the upper house itself agrees to the change.[6] In the same way that turkeys rarely vote for Christmas, the Senate rarely agrees to reform itself.

The National Assembly

There are 577 deputies. They are directly elected for a five-year term by a two-ballot majority-plurality system. The electoral system is similar to the one used for presidential elections (see Chapter 4). The country is divided into single-member constituencies. To be elected at the first ballot a candidate must win more than 50 per cent of the valid votes cast, providing that more than 25 per cent of the registered electorate has cast a vote. If no candidate is elected at the first ballot, then a second ballot takes place one week later. Here, the candidate with the most votes is elected. The key point to note is that for presidential elections only the top two candidates at the first ballot are allowed to proceed to the second ballot. By contrast, for legislative elections any candidate who wins more than 12.5 per cent of the registered electorate is entitled to proceed to the second ballot. That said, in practice most second-ballot contests end up pitting one candidate against another and, more often than not, a left-wing candidate against a right-wing candidate. (See Table 6.2 for the party groups in the National Assembly after the 2002 election.)

The composition of the National Assembly does not faithfully represent the party political preferences of the country as a whole. Using the deviation from proportionality standard (Taagepera and Shugart 1989; Machin

TABLE 6.2	Party groups in the National Assembly after the 2002 election	
Party group		**Seats**
Union for a Popular Movement		365
Socialist		141
Union for French Democracy		29
Communist and Republican		22
Non-affiliated		20
Total		577

1993), it is clear that in party political terms the electoral system over-represents some parties and under-represents others (see Table 6.3). For example, in 2002 the figures indicate that over a quarter of all National Assembly seats were won by parties that were not entitled to them on the basis of their share of the first-ballot vote. In particular, the electoral system over-represents large parties and under-represents both small parties and parties that are either unable or unwilling to form alliances with other groups. For instance, in 2002 the right-wing UMP party won 33.4 per cent of the votes cast at the first ballot, but in the end won 63.3 per cent of the seats in the National Assembly. By contrast, the Greens won 4.4 per cent of the vote, but only 0.5 per cent of the seats. Most strikingly of all, the National Front won 11.1 per cent of the vote, but gained no seats what-soever. In normative terms, it may or may not be a good thing that the electoral system prevents the extreme right from being able to voice its opinions in parliament. What is incontestable, though, is that from a comparative perspective the French electoral system is beaten only by the British system in terms of the deviation from proportionality that it pro-duces (Machin 1993: 630). This leads to a constant debate about reforming the system. In the past, governments have manipulated the system to suit their own ends. For example, in 1985 the Socialists introduced a proportional system so as to minimize their predicted losses at the 1986 elections only for the right to revert to the old system a year later in anticipation of sweeping gains.[7] In recent years, the Greens have been the most vociferous proponents of a proportional system. However, their allies, the Socialists, who generally profit from the current system, have

TABLE 6.3	Deviations from proportionality in National Assembly elections, 1958–2002	
Election	By party	By governing coalition
1958	32.4	26.6
1962	31.4	20.5
1967	17.6	11.8
1968	28.1	28.1
1973	18.6	17.8
1978	14.9	15.0
1981	20.3	12.9
(1986 PR)	10.7	5.3
1988	17.4	12.1
1993	38.7	38.1
1997	24.8	14.3
2002	28.9	14.9

Source and method of calculation: Machin (1993: 629). Figures for the 1997 and 2002 elections calculated by the author.

been able to ignore their demands, while the right, who also gain from the status quo, have little incentive to change the current system.

Like the Senate, another feature of the composition of the National Assembly concerns the large number of deputies who hold other elected offices. In relation to the National Assembly, the *cumul des mandats* has come about for two reasons. First, politicians have wanted to gain experience at the local level in order to further their ambitions at the national level. Thus, local government has become a training ground for deputies. Secondly, parties have had the habit of 'parachuting' favoured candidates in areas where they have no personal or political background. If they are elected, these candidates have then sought or been encouraged to seek election at the local level so as to build up a network of local support. For both reasons, multiple office-holding by deputies has been rife. Indeed, it has increased over time (Augé 2001: 20). In 1956, 42 per cent of all deputies held at least one local elected office as well (Mény 1993: 131). In the 1997–2002 legislature this figure had risen to 97 per cent (see Table 6.4 for the figures following the 2002 election). This situation was subject to a number of criticisms: first, that it weakened the checks and balances between central and local government; secondly, that it presented deputies with a conflict of interests and encouraged absenteeism in the National Assembly;

and, thirdly, that it rendered parliamentary reform irrelevant because of the high levels of absenteeism that it was said to cause (ibid. 132–4). In 1985, the Socialists changed the law and in effect limited the number of elected offices that could be held simultaneously to two. In 2000 the Socialists reformed the rules again to try to encourage deputies to focus on their responsibilities to the National Assembly. However, as in the upper house, multiple office-holding in the lower house is still the norm. Indeed, it is likely to remain so, especially in the situation where the various levels of local government have been and will be given more powers. In this context, it becomes even more important for deputies to build a local-level profile for themselves.

There are, therefore, certain similarities between the National Assembly and the Senate in terms of the composition of the two chambers. That said, the lower house is unquestionably the more important of the two in terms of policy-making. By virtue of the fact that it has the last word in the parliamentary process, the National Assembly is the main focus of political attention in this regard. However, it would be wrong to conclude that the National Assembly has free rein when it comes to passing legislation. On the contrary, as a general rule the National Assembly only passes the laws that the government of the day wants it to pass (see below). In short, the government controls the legislature. This is in stark contrast to the Fourth Republic (1946–58). Here, governments were regularly defeated in the

TABLE 6.4	Multiple office-holding by deputies after the 2002 legislative elections
Office	Number
Mayors	264
Deputy mayors	52
Municipal councillors	383
Presidents of General Council	19
Vice-Presidents of General Council	54
General councillors	191
Presidents of Regional Council	3
Vice-Presidents of Regional Council	18
Regional councillors	85
Members of the European Parliament	4

Source: www.assemblee-nationale.fr (accessed 8 Aug. 2002).

lower house and the system was disparagingly called a *régime d'assemblée* by some observers. The onset of the Fifth Republic changed all that. The combination of disciplined majority governments and institutional rules ensures that in relation to the government the lower house is now best described as little more than a 'loyal workhorse' and a 'poor watchdog' (Frears 1990). In terms of institutional rules, the reasons for the weakness of parliament lie in the restricted domain of parliamentary activity, the constraints on the powers of the National Assembly within this domain, and the limited capacity of the lower house to hold the administration to account.

The 1958 Constitution restricted the parliamentary domain in two respects. First, as noted in Chapter 3, Article 16 gives the President the right to assume emergency powers when there is a serious and immediate threat to the political system. In short, it gives the President the right to bypass parliament altogether. This Article has only been used on one occasion. The fact remains, though, that in times of crisis the President can assume full law-making powers. Secondly, even when there is no emergency, the areas in which parliament can legislate are restricted. Article 34 sets out the so-called 'domain of the law'. Within this domain parliament has the right to pass laws. Outside it the Prime Minister issues decrees (*décrets règlementaires*) that have the force of law (Article 37-2). True, the parliamentary domain includes most of the policy areas that would usually be associated with the legislative process (civil liberties, social security, education, defence, and so on). All the same, it excludes others (foreign affairs, for example). As a result, in 1991 the Prime Minister issued 680 decrees of this sort (*Pouvoirs* (1993), 64: 47). Overall, the 1958 Constitution places significant limitations on the areas in which parliament, and its most important element, the National Assembly, can pass legislation.

More importantly still, even within the domain of the law, there are severe restrictions on the power of the National Assembly. In general terms, the creation in 1958 of the Constitutional Council meant the end of parliamentary sovereignty (see Chapter 7). Parliament has the right to pass legislation within the terms of Article 34, but this legislation must itself conform to the provisions of the Constitution as a whole. More specifically, the 1958 Constitution introduced a raft of measures that shifted the balance of legislative power quite deliberately and explicitly towards the government (see Box 6.2). The net effect of these measures is that in theory at least the government can oblige the National Assembly to examine any bill that it wants, when it wants (Article 48). It can accept or reject any parliamentary amendment that it wants—the package vote (Article 44). It can pass legislation as quickly as it wants (Article 45). In fact, in the absence of an opposition majority, the government can pass any bill that it wants in whatever form it wants (Article 49-3). In practice, governments may want to avoid abusing their powers or at least being seen to be doing so (see below). At the same time, generally speaking, governments are not slow to call upon the constitutional weapons at their disposal in order to facilitate their legislative programme.[8] So, for example, in the 1999–2000 session, the government used the package vote procedure on three occasions. What is more, over and above the constitutional situation the standing orders of the National Assembly further reinforce the position of the executive. Assuming that it has the support of at least a relative majority of deputies in the lower house, the government will also enjoy a majority on all committees and commissions and it will be able to elect the President of the National Assembly and a majority of parliamentary officials (vice-presidents, *questeurs*, secretaries). The result is that the government

BOX 6.2	Constitutional restrictions on the powers of the National Assembly
Article 28:	Sets a maximum of 170 days a year for parliamentary sessions
Article 38:	Allows parliament to authorize the government to legislate by decree
Article 40:	Prohibits any amendment that reduces public income or increases public spending
Article 42:	States that the discussion of a bill must begin by first examining the text proposed by the government
Article 44:	Allows the government to refuse to consider any parliamentary amendment that has not previously been examined by a parliamentary committee. The government can call for a package vote (*vote bloqué*) on a bill containing the amendments that it selects
Article 45:	Allows the government to declare a bill to be urgent to quicken its passage through parliament
Article 47:	Limits the time parliament can discuss the budget to 70 days. After this time, the PM can pass the budget by decree
Article 48:	Allows the government to set the parliamentary timetable
Article 49:	Allows the government to declare a bill a matter of confidence. The bill is automatically passed unless a motion of no-confidence is passed by an absolute majority of deputies

will be able to shape the internal organization and functioning of the Assembly.

Having said all that, there is no doubt that, like the Senate, the National Assembly is a very active chamber. For example, in the 1999–2000 parliamentary session alone (1 October 1999–30 September 2000), the National Assembly sat for 104 days; it passed 117 laws and treaties; and it tabled more than 12,000 amendments of which nearly 4,800 were passed. In reality, though, much of this activity was devoted to governmental business. This does not mean that deputies had no influence, that their input was completely ignored, or that their time and effort was utterly wasted. After all, at worst the National Assembly has an important role to play in legitimizing government legislation. It simply means that the government is well placed to control the parliamentary process and that the National Assembly spends most of its time examining the government's legislative priorities.

In a similar fashion, the National Assembly has few powers to bring the government to account even if it wanted to do so. This can be seen in a number of ways. First, even though deputies are extremely motivated when it comes to asking questions, governments have rarely been troubled by this aspect of the accountability process. So, for example, in the 2000–1 session deputies asked nearly 1,000 questions in the parliamentary chamber itself and lodged a further 11,500 written questions. Moreover, contrary to certain parliamentary practices, there is usually a good attendance at the twice-weekly session of questions to the government. This is, of course, encouraged by the fact that the ritual is shown live on television. All the same, questions are a very imperfect form of control. Oral questions add little to the ongoing political debate that takes place outside the parliamentary arena. Written questions are the subject of carefully considered governmental replies. Overall, the number of questions has increased over time (Nguyen Huu 1981), but it is doubtful whether the same is true for the quality of accountability over the same period. Secondly, the role of parliamentary committees is quite limited. There are only six permanent, or standing, committees that scrutinize proposed legislation. They are all large, unwieldy organizations that operate as mini-parliaments where the government has a majority and party discipline is the norm. The same is largely true for the other main type of parliamentary committee, the committees of inquiry, which investigate one-off policy-related matters. In the 2000–1 parliamentary session, two such committees were formed, one investigating issues concerning contaminated animal feed and the other examining the causes of flooding in the country. These committees have an investigative role and they often come up with important policy recommendations. The key point, though, is that the government still has to approve any recommendations that the committee might make and can choose to ignore them. Thus, while the committees undoubtedly do good work, they have little or no independent decision-making power. The government is still the main actor.

All told, the constitutional and legal position of the National Assembly remains quite weak. It is certainly true that in recent years a number of reforms have been passed designed to increase the importance of parliament in the system. For example, there is now an annual debate on the social security funds; there is a permanent committee, modelled on the US Congressional Budget Office, whose aim is to increase the National Assembly's influence over the budgetary process; there has been the introduction of the so-called 'simplified examination procedure' that allows the National Assembly to spend more time examining the most important aspects of legislation by cutting back the amount of time spent on peripheral issues; there has been a constitutional amendment (Article 88) to try to improve parliamentary control over European legislation; an amendment that once a month allows the Assembly to set the parliamentary timetable rather than the government; and a further amendment (Article 28) establishing a single nine-month parliamentary session (October–June) that allows the legislature to follow the government's work more closely over the course of the year. All of these reforms have strengthened the statutory position of parliament. The problem is that, at bottom, the parliamentary process is still only one aspect of a wider party political game. For the most part, though, this game has weakened the position of parliament in the system. This is the issue to which we shall now turn.

Party politics and the parliamentary game

There is a basic problem with much of the established work on the French parliament. This is because most of this work assumes that the basic units of analysis are the government on the one side and the legislature on the other. If this assumption is made, then naturally the fundamental issue is to examine the extent to which one institution can control the other. Can the executive control the legislature or does parliament have the capacity to influence the government's policy programme? However, this assumption is flawed. The parliamentary game is not a game between the executive and the legislature. Instead, the parliamentary game is primarily a game between competing political parties and competing coalitions of parties where the main aim is to win office and pass policy. According to this view of the world, parliamentarians are only interested in government policy to the extent that it increases their party's chance of gaining power. In this context, parliament is weak not because of constitutional constraints, but because of the basic preferences of deputies and Senators. If parliamentarians placed a greater importance on parliament's independent policy-making role, then they would be able to shape the passage of legislation whatever the restrictions placed upon them by the 1958 Constitution. However, they do not. They value office and policy more highly. The net result is that government deputies will invariably support government legislation and opposition deputies will oppose it. In this context, and assuming that the government has a majority, parliament has little independent influence. Moreover, even when the government does not have a majority, it will use the restrictive legislative procedures at its command and deputies will continue to follow the party line. If we view parliamentary politics in this way, then the basic issue is to examine how party politics shapes the functioning of parliament. What is the impact of competition between the majority and opposition parties? What is the effect of party relations within the majority party or coalition of parties? These questions are the main focus of the rest of this chapter.

The majority vs. the opposition

The parliamentary game is a game between, on the one hand, the government and the government's supporters in parliament and, on the other hand, the opposition parties and their supporters in parliament. This situation has a profound impact on parliamentary politics. The most noticeable effect is that the government's supporters have little incentive to allow the opposition to have any influence over the legislative process. This is because there are likely to be basic policy disagreements between the government and the opposition. More importantly, it is because the opposition will most likely try to make political capital out of any such influence. As a general rule, therefore, the government and the government's supporters will want to oppose opposition amendments and reforms because they believe that these will weaken the government's position.[9] The net result, though, is that the influence of parliament is weak. The government and the government's supporters have no good reason to allow the opposition to establish an independent policy-making role for itself. By the same token, they have no good reason to allow the opposition to scrutinize the business of government for fear that the uncovering of any mistakes will be politically costly.

This way of viewing the parliamentary game is important because since 1958 governments have typically been supported by a highly disciplined majority in the National Assembly. As Table 6.5 demonstrates, governments have rarely been backed by anything less than a comfortable majority of seats in the lower house. In fact, governments have failed to enjoy *de facto* majority support for only one period (1988–93)[10] and on certain occasions have enjoyed the equivalent of super-majority support (most notably 1968–73 and 1993–7). At the same time, while it is certainly the case that deputies do occasionally fail to support or even vote against government policy in the legislature, generally speaking party loyalty is very strong. For the reasons outlined above, it is virtually unknown for majority deputies to defeat government legislation. Indeed, Huber (1992: 680) shows that from 1981 to 1986 the majority Socialist government won 99.2 per cent of all votes in parliament and passed 100 per cent of its legislation. Moreover, a government has been brought down by a parliamentary vote on only one occasion and that was in exceptional circumstances concerning the proposed introduction of the direct election of the President in October 1962 (see Chapter 4). All told, majority governments are safe in office and can be sure of being able to pass their legislative programme. Inevitably, though, this means that parliament will be seen as little more than a governmental 'voting machine', or, as Laurent Fabius, a former President of the National Assembly, put it rather more poetically, 'a theatre of shadows' (in *Le Monde*, 6 September 1991: 6).

Typically, then, the majority dominates the opposition and the independent policy-making impact of parliament is weak. However, this situation does not always apply. For example, left-wing governments have always faced a right-wing majority in the Senate (1981–6, 1988–93, and

TABLE 6.5	Government support in the National Assembly, 1959–2002			
Year	Government	Government seats in the National Assembly	Total number of seats in the National Assembly	Government support in National Assembly (%)
1959	Right	429	552	77.7
1962	Right	268	482	55.6
1965	Right	268	482	55.6
1967	Right	242	487	49.7
1968	Right	354	487	72.7
1969	Right	387	487	79.5
1973	Right	268	490	54.7
1974	Right	302	490	61.6
1978	Right	277	491	56.4
1981	Left	329	491	67.0
1984	Left	285	491	58.0
1986	Right	286	577	49.6
1988	Left	272	577	47.1
1993	Right	473	577	82.0
1995	Right	473	577	82.0
1997	Left	319	577	55.3
2002	Right	365	577	63.3

Source: Adapted from Thiébault (2000: 499) and updated by the author.

1997–2002). On these occasions, the government has found that it has to negotiate with the Senate majority more than it might otherwise have liked to. Indeed, what is perhaps significant about the figures for the 1999–2000 parliamentary session was that as many as seven CMPs resulted in an agreed text between representatives of the two houses (see above). All the same, what is noticeable about these periods is that governments have had recourse to Article 45-4 (which gives the National Assembly the final say over legislation) much more frequently than when there have been right-wing majorities in both the upper and lower house. So, for example, one study showed that in the period 1969–73, when relations between the majority in the National Assembly and the Senate were good, 85.2 per cent of all legislation was agreed between the two houses without recourse to a conference committee and Article 45-4 was used only 3.4 per cent of the time (Tsebelis and Money 1995: 107). By contrast, from 1981 to 1985, when

the left held power in the lower house, the corresponding level of agreement was little more than 30 per cent, and 26.2 per cent of all legislation
was approved by the National Assembly alone (ibid.). These figures show
that in the first instance the real source of parliament's capacity to shape
the decision-making process is the relationship between the majority and
the opposition. They indicate that when the majorities in the two houses
have been the same the upper house has had more influence over the final
content of legislation. However, when the majorities have been opposed,
even though the Senate has maintained some degree of influence, governments have resorted to using Article 45-4 more frequently and the Senate
has been less influential.

A similar point applies to the National Assembly. On occasion, the government has enjoyed only a fragile majority in the lower house. On these
occasions, the government has used the constitutional powers at its disposal in order to minimize the influence of the opposition over the legislative process. This point can be illustrated very well by examining the use of
Article 49-3 of the Constitution (Elgie 1993a). This article allows the government to make one of its own bills an issue of confidence. When it does
so, the bill is considered to be passed unless one-tenth of the total number
of deputies in the National Assembly table a motion of no-confidence
within 24 hours and an absolute majority of deputies vote for the motion
48 hours later. If no motion is tabled, or if one is tabled but fails to be
supported by an absolute majority of deputies, then the bill is passed.
There have been occasions, particularly in the periods 1981–6 and 1986–8,
when governments have resorted to Article 49-3 as a way of speeding up
the legislative process. All the same, this article was used particularly frequently when the government's majority was fragile (see Table 6.6). Most
notably, from 1988 to 1993 the Socialist government was twelve votes short
of a majority.[11] During this period, the various Prime Ministers used
Article 49-3 on thirty-nine separate occasions. A motion of no-confidence
was tabled on fourteen occasions and the government survived every
single vote.

Observers usually claim that Article 49-3 is one of the reasons why the
parliament of the Fifth Republic is weak. To a degree, this is true. After all,
the figures for the 1988–93 period show that this article helps to allow
minority governments to stay in office and continue to legislate. More
importantly, though, these figures are testimony to the importance of

TABLE 6.6	The use of Article 49-3, 1959–2002		
Government	Is there a government majority?	Are there problems within the majority?	Number of times Article 49-3 used
Debré (1959–62)	Yes	Yes	4
Pompidou (1962–8)	Yes	Yes	6
Couve, Chaban, Messmer, Chirac (1968–76)	Yes	No	0
Barre (1976–81)	Yes	Yes	8
Mauroy (1981–4)	Yes	No	7
Fabius (1984–6)	Yes	No	4
Chirac (1986–8)	Yes	No	8
Rocard (1988–91)	No	No	28
Cresson (1991–2)	No	No	8
Bérégovoy (1992–3)	No	No	3
Balladur (1993–5)	Yes	No	1
Juppé (1995–7)	Yes	No	2
Jospin (1997–2002)	Yes	No	0

majority/opposition relations in explaining why parliament is so weak. In the 1988–93 period, the government survived in office because at the time the opposition comprised a multitude of political forces, including communists, centrists, the right, and a hotchpotch of non-aligned deputies. In this context, even though the government failed to enjoy a majority, the communists were usually unwilling to vote with the centrists and the right for fear that they would be punished by the Socialist party at the next election. Even then, when the communists were willing to do so the government was able to buy off a sufficiently large number of non-aligned deputies to avoid being dismissed from office. So, yes, Article 49-3 helped to keep the government in place, but the real reason why the government was able to survive was because of the particularities of the relationship between the majority and the opposition.[12] The National Assembly could have dismissed the government. Instead, the various parliamentary party groups for reasons of their own chose not to do so.

The majority vs. the majority

The parliamentary game, then, is at bottom a party political game. In this context, just as parliament's influence is affected by the relationship between the majority and the opposition, it is also affected by the politics of the majority. In particular, the role of parliament is at least partly determined by both the relationship within the party (or parties) of the majority and the relationship between the various parties of the majority when there is a coalition government. Moreover, when the right has enjoyed a majority in the National Assembly, coalition politics have also affected the relationship between the lower house and the Senate. Let us take each case in turn.

The presence of government majorities in the National Assembly and the absence of any incentives for the majority to cooperate with the opposition mean that the most likely source of parliamentary influence lies within the majority itself. This is because even if the basic parliamentary game is a majority vs. opposition game rather than a government vs. parliament game, a distinction still has to be made between, on the one hand, government Ministers and, on the other, the government's supporters in parliament. The former will be responsible for proposing and drafting legislation. However, the latter may well wish to shape the content of that legislation either prior to its presentation to parliament or during the discussion in parliament. The basic conflict between the two groups may be policy-related: there may be different interpretations as to which policy options should be chosen. Equally, the conflict may be personal or party political: a Minister belonging to one party faction may be opposed by parliamentary colleagues belonging to another faction. Whatever the motivation, there is good reason to believe that deputies belonging to the majority may wish to influence government-prepared legislation. What is more, to the extent that the government may wish to keep good relations with its supporters in parliament and that cooperating with its own supporters is likely to be less electorally damaging than cooperating with the opposition, then the government may be favourably disposed to working with the representatives of its own party in the National Assembly.

In fact, there is good evidence that such cooperation has occurred. For example, in the period 1988–93 it was an almost annual occurrence for the government and Socialist party representatives to meet to discuss the contents of the budget and particularly its fiscal component before the Finance Bill was presented to parliament. On the government side, those attending the meeting usually included the Prime Minister, the Budget and Finance Ministers, and the Minister for Parliamentary Relations. On the party side, the participants invariably included the First Secretary of the Socialist party, the party's Budget Secretary, and representatives from the National Assembly's finance committee. At the meeting, the two sides would present their different policy priorities and the government would regularly change the details of its proposed budget in order to meet at least some of the demands of the party representatives.[13] Thus, there is clear evidence that parliamentarians have been able to influence public policy choices, even if this influence has occurred outside the cut and thrust of the parliamentary chamber itself.

That said, there are limits to the extent to which governments will make concessions to their party's parliamentary representatives. There is always the risk that the public will see such concessions as a sign of governmental weakness. Moreover, there is also the risk that the opposition will try to exploit the differences between the government and its supporters in parliament. In this way, governments may have to trade off the benefits to be gained from keeping its parliamentary supporters happy with the costs incurred from making concessions to them. As a result, in the cases where the costs are deemed to outweigh the benefits it is not unusual for governments to use restrictive parliamentary procedures against their own supporters. Again, the explanation of this seemingly paradoxical situation relates to the importance of party politics. For example, in the period 1985–6 Prime Minister Laurent Fabius used Article 49-3 because he did not want the Socialists to appear divided in the run up to the 1986 elections. Indeed, a similar motivation lay behind Rocard's use of this article on at least a couple of occasions in the late 1980s. He was willing to use Article 49-3 so as to avoid any dissent amongst members of the Socialist parliamentary party. The head of government feared that if the parliamentary debate were to be prolonged, then he would have to accept too many concessions from the party. Thus, Rocard invoked Article 49-3 and was able to maintain the wording of the bill as he wanted (Elgie 1993a: 22–3). It is clear, then, that the politics of the majority can impact on the role of parliament in the system. The majority party may be able to influence government legislation. However, the government will not give majority deputies a blank cheque.

A similar point applies to coalition governments. On these occasions, the influence of majority deputies can be very small indeed. This is because coalition policies are often the result of highly complex negotiations between leading representatives of the coalition partners. These policies, and the hard-fought compromises that they represent, are then embedded in the proposed legislation that the government presents to parliament. In this context, it is vital that the parliamentary majority is not given the opportunity to propose potentially destabilizing amendments that might unpick these sometimes fragile political deals. As a result, governments will resort to restrictive legislative procedures so as to maintain the original wording of the bill and the cohesion of the coalition. So, for example, Huber (1992) has found that there is a correlation between the use of Article 44-3 and the existence of coalition government. The so-called package vote (*vote bloqué*) allows the government to request a single vote on the text of all or any part of a bill containing only the amendments that the government has selected. In this way, the government can ensure that the original deal is secure. Another example concerns the government's use of Article 49-3. What needs to be explained about the numbers in Table 6.6 is not so much why Article 49-3 has been used so frequently by minority governments, but why it has been used so much by majority governments as well. At least part of the answer to this question lies in the politics of coalition government. If Article 44-3 is used to maintain hard-fought coalition deals, then Article 49-3 is used to pass legislation when no such deals have been forthcoming. For example, one of the periods when Article 49-3 was used most frequently was between November 1979 and January 1980 under Raymond Barre's premiership. During this period, Barre headed a UDF/RPR coalition which had a comfortable majority in the lower house. However, such was the rivalry between the two groups in anticipation of the 1981 presidential elections that Barre, who was allied to the UDF group, found that he could not rely upon the support of the RPR. Matters came to a head during the passage of the 1980 budget, when the Prime Minister refused to accept certain RPR amendments to the bill. In retaliation, the RPR announced that it would abstain, leaving only the UDF voting in favour of the bill and Barre without a majority. Thus, Barre used Article 49-3 as a way of staying in power and passing legislation in the context of an extremely problematic coalition situation.

A final example of the importance of party politics concerns the relationship between the National Assembly and Senate. For much of the Fifth Republic there has been a right-wing majority in both houses of parliament (1958–81, 1986–8, 1993–7, 2002–   ). However, this majority has never been homogeneous. In particular, there were underlying tensions between the gaullist and the non-gaullist components of the majority. These tensions were at their most acute in the period 1963–9 as a result of the Senate's failure to provide unequivocal support for de Gaulle's decision to hold a referendum on the direct election of the President in 1962 (Grangé 1981). The result was that the government used the restrictive constitutional procedures at its disposal against its own majority in the upper house. So, for example, from 1963 to 1968 seventy-two bills were subject to CMPs but only forty resulted in an agreed text by representatives of the two houses (ibid. 39). Similarly, during the same period the government requested a package vote in the Senate on seventy-one occasions and was defeated fifty-six times. In short, during this period the Senate was the main opposition within the majority. At times, this situation meant, as Grangé (ibid.) put it, that the Senate 'no longer participated in the life of the regime'. That said, on occasion the Senate was able to use its position to influence the course of events. So, for example, the Senate's opposition to de Gaulle's ill-fated 1969 constitutional reform was at least one reason for its defeat. Moreover, as noted above, in 1971 the path-breaking decision of the Constitutional Council was the result of a request by the then President of the Senate, Alain Poher (see Chapter 7). In the main, simultaneous right-wing majorities in the National Assembly and the Senate have allowed the upper house to have some influence in the decision-making process. However, when the relationship between the government and the upper house has been problematic, then the former has not hesitated to use its constitutional powers to constrain the latter.

Conclusion

This chapter has highlighted the importance of the interaction between institutions and actors in the policy-making process. The French parliament is weak. It is tempting to account for the weakness of parliament by referring solely to the constitutional restrictions that were placed on the legislature at the beginning of the Fifth Republic. This explanation, though, would be misleading. There is no question that the constitutional restrictions on the legislature fundamentally affect the politics of the legislative process. The existence of Article 49-3, the *vote bloqué*, and the CMP all help to structure the government's choices. Moreover, there is no doubt that without them the government's position would on occasions be less secure and that legislation would be more difficult to pass. However, the French parliament is not weak merely because of the existence of these constitutional restrictions and others like them. Instead, parliament is weak because of the competition between party politics. The parliamentary game pits the majority against the opposition. The aim of the majority (including the government) is to stay in power, pass legislation, and win the next election. This means that the majority has little or no incentive to cooperate with the opposition. True, when the majority's position is weak, then the government is grateful for the constitutional restrictions that are placed on parliament. The bottom line, though, is that even with these restrictions parliamentarians could amend government legislation and hold the government truly accountable if they really wished to do so. They choose not to do so because their first loyalty is to the majority or the opposition rather than to parliament. To the extent that the ordering of these loyalties is unlikely to change in the near future, then parliament will remain weak. What this means is that in contrast to many of the other topics examined in this book the legislature has been subject to very little institutional change since 1958. Moreover, there is very little prospect of any such change in the foreseeable future.

KEY TERMS

- Senate
- National Assembly
- Executive dominance
- Parliamentary rules
- Party discipline

NOTES

1 Studies pointing out the deficiencies of the parliamentary system include Belorgey (1991), Birnbaum, Hamon, and Troper (1977), and Masclet (1982).

2 All deputies, general councillors, and regional councillors are included in the electoral college. However, the same is not true for municipal councillors. On the one

hand, in communes with less than 9,000 people, only a proportion of the members of the town council are included and an election takes place to decide who will represent the council. On the other hand, in communes with more than 30,000 people, supplementary places are available.

3 The result of this reform was that departments electing three or more Senators must now use a proportional system. This means that more than 70% of Senators are now elected proportionally.

4 A diagrammatic overview of this highly complex process can be found in Tsebelis and Money (1995).

5 The government can call a CMP after just one reading if it formally declares the passage of a bill to be 'urgent' (Article 45-2).

6 The Senate can also be reformed if the Prime Minister proposes a referendum and the President agrees (Article 11). In this case, the Senate's approval is not necessary. However, during the most recent period of 'cohabitation' when Jospin wanted to reform the upper house this procedure was ruled out. Leaving aside the question of whether or not the public would agree to any such reform (in 1969 de Gaulle's plans to restructure the Senate and reorganize local government were defeated in a referendum), for much of this period President Chirac's closest institutional ally was the President of the Senate, Christian Poncelet, and so the Prime Minister knew that the President's support for a referendum proposal would not be forthcoming. Consequently, Jospin's desire to reform the Senate had to proceed by other, much more limited, means.

7 In fact, the left benefited from the two-ballot majority system at the 1988 election.

8 See the figures in Keeler (1993).

9 Frears (1981: 60) does give some examples of occasions when the government has been willing to accept opposition amendments.

10 On the other occasions when governing parties have failed to enjoy the support of more than 50% of people in the National Assembly, they have enjoyed the *de facto* support of a sufficient number of non-aligned deputies to make up the numbers in this regard. It might also be noted that there is disagreement about how to classify the 1959–62 period. For the purposes of this chapter, Thiébault's (2000: 499) classification will be adopted.

11 In the period 1986–8 the government had only a three-seat majority. As a result, Article 49-3 was used to speed up legislation but also to prevent any risk of defeat.

12 For a fuller analysis of this period, see Huber (1996).

13 For a detailed account, see Elgie, (1993*b*: 89–98).

....

GUIDE TO FURTHER READING

Huber, J., *Rationalizing Parliament: Legislative Institutions and Party Politics in France* (Cambridge, Cambridge University Press, 1996).
An excellent book.

Williams, P., *The French Parliament 1958–67* (London, George Allen & Unwin, 1968).
This classic book charts the decline of the French parliament's power.

7

···

The Judiciary

Overview

This chapter outlines the French judicial system. There are three distinct elements to this system: constitutional law, administrative law, and civil and criminal law. This chapter examines the main institutions in each of these areas. In addition, it also notes the role of various courts at the European level. It shows how each element of the judicial system has increased in importance and strengthened the rule of law. It also shows how political actors continue to use various elements of the judicial system to promote their own interests.

Introduction

Textbooks on constitutional theory state that there are three branches of government: legislative, executive, and judicial. They go on to state that there must be a separation of powers between the three branches so as to avoid the possibility of tyranny and dictatorship. In some countries, most notably the USA, the system of separation of powers has been backed up by a series of checks and balances. Here, each of the three branches of government has the power to limit the other two. The result is a system that is sometimes criticized for failing to provide the capacity for leadership, but one that protects the varied interests that make up US society. In France, the situation has been very different. The French version of the separation of powers created a distinct inequality between, on the one hand, the legislative and executive branches of government and, on the other hand, the judicial branch. The former, as expressions of the will of the people, were superior to the latter. In short, the judiciary had authority but the executive and legislature had power.[1] The result was the belief that the government should control the judiciary. This situation, though, has changed. There has been a growing belief that governments act arbitrarily if they are not checked. In short, the ideational foundations of the relationship between the executive and the judiciary have changed. The result is that over the course of the last thirty years the rule of law has been strengthened and the judiciary has emerged as an independent counterweight to the government. All the same, the judiciary is still a key component of the political game. The majority and the opposition continue to use certain elements of the judiciary to protect and promote their own interests.

The Constitutional Council

There are three distinct elements to the French judicial system: constitutional law, administrative law, and civil and criminal law (see Table 7.1). The Constitutional Council operates within the domain of constitutional law where it is the highest constitutional authority in the land. The Council does not deal with civil or criminal cases. It simply determines whether bills, treaties, and so forth conform or not to the Constitution. The Constitutional Council has always been a highly politicized institution. Over time, the position of the Council has changed. In 1958 it was designed to support the executive and act as a check on parliament. However, in the 1970s it emerged as a significant political actor in its own right and started to issue rulings that embarrassed the government. What is more, in the 1980s and 1990s it was systematically used by both right- and left-wing opposition forces to counteract the power of the government of the day. As a result of these developments, the Constitutional Council has been accused of being a party political rather than an independent institution. More recently, it has been associated with scandal and has seen its once highly positive public image somewhat tarnished.

The Constitutional Council comprises nine appointees, three of whom are chosen by the President of the Republic, three by the President of the National Assembly, and three by the President of the Senate.[2] Once appointed, strict rules govern the activities of its members. For example,

TABLE 7.1	The organization of the French judicial system		
	Constitutional law	Administrative law	Civil and criminal law
Court of highest instance	Constitutional Council	Council of State Court of Accounts	Court of Cassation
Court of appeal	n/a	Administrative Courts of Appeal	Courts of Appeal, Courts of Assizes
Court of first instance	n/a	Administrative Tribunals, Regional Courts of Account	*tribunaux de grande instance*, *tribunaux d'instance*, *tribunaux de police*, *tribunaux correctionnels*, and others

they cannot serve in either the government or parliament (Article 57-1) and, since a 1995 reform, they cannot hold any other elected office. They have to swear to perform their functions with 'full impartiality' (Ordinance no. 58-1067 of 7 November 1958, Article 3-2) and they have to desist from engaging in any activity that might compromise the independence of the Constitutional Council's functions (Decree no. 59-1292, 13 November, 1959, Article 1). In addition, its members serve for a non-renewable nine-year term (Article 56-1). This means that they have absolutely no incentive to try to ensure that they are reappointed once their mandate expires. Overall, a set of rules was devised to try to make the members of the Constitutional Council as independent from political influence as possible.

All the same, the Constitutional Council has always been a politicized institution. For example, members of the Council have been appointed at least in part because of their political leanings. That is to say, right-wing Presidents have made right-wing appointments, while Socialist Presidents have made left-wing appointments. (For the political composition of the Council since 1959, see Table 7.2.) Over the years, the political composition of the Council has varied. In the early years of the Fifth Republic the Constitutional Council was very loyal to the gaullist administration. By the mid-1990s there was a left-wing majority on the Council that caused a number of problems for the incumbent right-wing government. By 2001 the right once again had a very solid majority and some of the Council's rulings, such as its decision in January 2002 to strike down the restrictions that had been placed on companies who wanted to make employees redundant, were distinctly embarrassing for the left-wing government at the time. (For the members of the Constitutional Council in 2002, see Table 7.3.) All told, there is no doubt that the Constitutional Council is institutionally independent. All the same, there is also no doubt that it has often been criticized by members of the political elite either for being subservient to the government or for being too critical of it (see below). That said, until recently the public had a very positive opinion of the Council and this was at least partly because the Council had shown that it could act as a counterweight to a potentially overbearing executive.

The Constitutional Council is headed by a President. (For a list of Presidents since 1959, see Table 7.4.) The President is chosen from among the Council's nine members by the President of the Republic (Ordinance no. 58-1067 of 7 November 1958, Article 1-2). The presidency of the Constitutional Council is a highly esteemed position. Over the years, though, it has been the subject of some political controversy. In the early years of the

TABLE 7.2	The political composition of the Constitutional Council, 1959–2001	
Date	Left	Right
1959–81	0	9
1983	2	7
1986	4	5
1987	3	6
1988	3	6
1989	5	4
1992	6	3
1995	5	4
1996	5	4
1997	5	4
1998	5	4
1999	4	5
2000	3	6
2001	2	7

Source: Adapted and updated from Wright (1999: 115).

TABLE 7.3	Members of the Constitutional Council, 2002		
Name	Appointed by	Political leaning	Leaves office
Yves Guéna	Pres. of Senate	Right	2004
Michel Ameller	Pres. of the NA	Right	2004
Pierre Mazeaud	Pres. of the Rep.	Right	2004
Monique Pelletier	Pres. of the Rep.	Right	2004
Simone Veil	Pres. of Senate	Right	2007
Jean-Claude Colliard	Pres. of the NA	Left	2007
Olivier Dutheillet de Lamothe	Pres. of the Rep.	Right	2010
Dominique Schnapper	Pres. of Senate	Right	2010
Pierre Joxe	Pres. of the NA	Left	2010

Republic, the first two Presidents of the Constitutional Council were extremely loyal to General de Gaulle. Indeed, Gaston Palewski admitted once he had left office that when de Gaulle was in power it was difficult for him to interpret the Constitution in any way other than that of the person who had actually written it.[3] There was further controversy in 1986 when President Mitterrand appointed a former Minister and close political associate, Robert Badinter, as President. There is no doubt that Badinter was supremely well qualified for the position. However, the difficulty arose from the fact that his appointment only came about when the outgoing President, Daniel Meyer, stepped down after just three years in office immediately prior to an election which the right was universally expected to win. In this way, Mitterrand was accused of politicizing the Constitutional Council by ensuring that it would have a Socialist President for a further nine years at least. More recently, the Council was also the subject of a great deal of comment during the presidency of Roland Dumas. After his appointment, Dumas was at the centre of corruption charges for events that had occurred during his time as Foreign Minister. The evidence against him was considerable and of a highly embarrassing nature. All the same, Dumas at first refused to resign. In the end, he was obliged to stand down and was later convicted. In the meantime, though, the Constitutional Council remained loyal to the President, but at the expense of great criticism (for example, Montebourg 2000: 225–30) and the loss of at least some of its institutional credibility. More than that, in January 1999 the Constitutional Council declared that the President of the Republic was effectively immune from prosecution during his term of office. Indeed, it did so even though it was not called upon to make any such pronouncement. In this context, there was the suspicion (ibid. 231–6) that Dumas and Chirac, who was himself the subject of corruption investigations at the time, had made a secret 'pact' (ibid. 236) to support each other in the face of their difficulties. The existence of any such agreement was impossible to prove. All the same, there is little doubt that the accusations tarnished the reputation of the Constitutional Council.

There are two main aspects to the Constitutional Council's work. The first relates to elections. The Constitutional Council is the supreme authority on matters relating to presidential and parliamentary elections as well as referendums. In this context, for example, the Council is responsible for publishing the official results of all elections, for ensuring that election campaigns are conducted fairly, and for guaranteeing that presidential candidates keep within campaign spending limits. This is numerically the most significant aspect of the Constitutional Council's work. In the period 1958–99 the Council made 2,173 decisions in this regard (**www.conseil-Constitutionnel.fr/francais/fra1.htm**—accessed 16 January 2002). Indeed, on occasion, some of these decisions were somewhat controversial, particularly when the Council annulled the election of certain deputies on the basis of procedural irregularities. For the most part, though, the first aspect

TABLE 7.4	Presidents of the Constitutional Council, 1959–2002		
Name	Appointed by	Political leaning	Term of office
Léon Noël	de Gaulle	Right	1959–65
Gaston Palewski	de Gaulle	Right	1965–74
Roger Frey	Pompidou	Right	1974–83
Daniel Mayer	Mitterrand	Left	1983–6
Robert Badinter	Mitterrand	Left	1986–95
Roland Dumas	Mitterrand	Left	1995–9
(Yves Guéna)[a]	(interim Pres.)	(Right)	(1999–2000)
Yves Guéna	Chirac	Right	2000–

[a] In March 1999, Dumas suspended his activities because of ongoing criminal investigations against him. As the oldest member of the Council, Guéna served as the interim President. He was formally appointed to this post in March 2000.

of the Council's work has been relatively uncontentious. The second aspect of the Council's activities is more open to political controversy. The Constitutional Council is the supreme constitutional authority in the land. True, the Council's decisions can in effect be challenged at the European level. However, in a domestic context, the Council's ruling on all matters constitutional is final.

In relation to this aspect of its work, the Constitutional Council operates within certain quite specific constraints. First, the Council only considers certain matters, (see Table 7.5). All organic laws, meaning laws that flesh out the details of the 1958 Constitution, are submitted to the Council automatically (Article 61-1). The same is true for amendments to the rules governing parliamentary proceedings (ibid.). In addition, the Council can be petitioned to rule on an international agreement before it comes into force (Article 54). Moreover, the Council can be called upon by the Prime Minister to decide whether a reform should come under the heading of the 'domain of the law' for discussion by parliament (see Chapter 4), or whether it should be classed as a *règlement* to be dealt with by a ministerial decree (Article 37-2). Most importantly, though, the Council is called upon to judge legislation (Article 61-2). To the extent that bills invariably set the majority against the opposition, this aspect of the Constitutional Council's work means that its judgments are seen, rightly or wrongly, to be inherently political in nature. In this context, the Constitutional Council is usually criticized when its rulings appear systematically to favour either one side or the other.

Secondly, the Constitutional Council has no appellate power. That is to say, it does not have the power to decide for itself which bills, treaties, or rules it wants to examine. Instead, it can only examine the items that are sent to it. However, unlike the situation in the United States, individual citizens do not have the right to petition the Council, even though a reform to this end was proposed in June 1990 at the behest of Robert Badinter and with the support of President Mitterrand. Instead, the power to request the Constitutional Council to issue a ruling is restricted to a very small set of people: the President of the Republic, the Prime Minister, the President of the National Assembly, the President of the Senate, and, since 1974, sixty deputies, or sixty Senators (Article 61-2).[4] (Figures for petitions, or *saisines*, from the various authorities can be found in Table 7.6.) Even then, Presidents rarely petition the Council for fear that they will be seen to

TABLE 7.5	The activity of the Constitutional Council, 1958–2000				
	1958–74	1975–85	1986–96	1997–2000	Total
Laws	9	165	166	34	374
Organic law	20	28	29	6	83
Parliamentary rules	21	11	23	3	58
Treaties	1	2	2[a]	6	11
Article 41	8	3	0	0	11
Article 37-2	82	62	35	8	187
Congress	1	0	0	1	2
New Caledonia	n/a	n/a	n/a	1	1
Total	142	271	255	59	727

[a] Deputies and Senators have only been allowed to petition the Council in relation to international agreements since 1992 following a constitutional amendment.

Source: Adapted from **www.conseil-constitutionnel.fr** (accessed 15 Jan. 2002).

be acting in a partisan manner. They tend merely to send international treaties to the Council, reinforcing their position as the leading figure in high politics (see Chapter 4). By contrast, Prime Ministers frequently petition the Council. This is because they are involved in the nitty-gritty of the decision-making process and cannot avoid making partisan decisions. A limit to the power of the various petitioners is that they may only refer a bill to the Council immediately after it has been passed by parliament and before it becomes law. Thus, if a bill is not submitted to the Constitutional Council before this time, then it cannot be declared unconstitutional. The only way for a law to be sanctioned once it has been promulgated is if a case is taken to the European Court of Justice or the European Court of Human Rights. This is a sign of the Europeanization of the French judicial system, but in practice the number of constitutional issues that have been affected in this way is very small.

Thirdly, the Council bases its decisions on the Constitution of the Fifth Republic. Here, though, it must be appreciated that the text of the 1958 Constitution also contains references to two other documents: the 1789 Declaration of the Rights of Man and the Preamble of the 1946 Constitution of the Fourth Republic. The former contains a list of basic human rights, such as the right to liberty and free speech. The latter complements this list by referring to the so-called fundamental (but unenumerated)

TABLE 7.6	Sources of Constitutional Council petitions, 1959–2000				
	1958–74	1975–85	1986–96	1997–2000	Total
President	0	2	1	3	6
PM	109	92	71	18	290
President NA	15	8	12	3	38
President Senate	18	10	13	1	42
60 deputies	n/a	106	85	20	211
60 Senators	n/a	53	73	13	139
New Caledonia	n/a	n/a	n/a	1	1
Total	142	271	255	59	727

Source: www.conseil-constitutionnel.fr (accessed 15 Jan. 2002).

principles recognized by the laws of the Republic and makes explicit mention of a number of 'political, economic, and social' rights, such as the right to work and the right to trade union membership. So, in fact, there are three constitutional documents. These comprise the so-called 'bloc de constitutionnalité' that was established by the Council's now famous judgment in 1971 (see below).

Fourthly, when passing judgment on a bill, the Constitutional Council can decide, in the space of a month, or eight days if the government declares a matter to be urgent, one of four things: (*a*) whether all of the bill is constitutional; (*b*) whether the bill is constitutional subject to certain interpretations as outlined by the Council; (*c*) whether a section of the bill is unconstitutional; or (*d*) whether all of the bill is unconstitutional. In the case of (*a*) and (*b*) the bill can immediately become law. However, in the case of (*c*) and (*d*), the bill, or at least the offending elements of it, fail to become law. In this case, the government has to decide whether to abandon the censured items, or redraft them in a way that might be acceptable to the Council were it to be called upon again to give a judgment.

The decision to create a Constitutional Council in 1958 was another of the measures that aimed to make a complete break with the Fourth Republic (see Chapter 1). In particular, it was deliberately designed to limit the powers of parliament. The Fourth Republic was founded on the principle of parliamentary sovereignty, meaning that parliament could pass a law on any matter it wanted. As noted in Chapter 6, the Fifth Republic ended this principle by rigidly defining the areas in which parliament could make laws (Article 38) and by allowing the Prime Minister to issue decrees (*règlements*) in all other areas (Article 37-1). In this context, the Constitutional Council was designed to act as the institution that would decide whether parliament had the right to pass a law in a particular area, or whether the Prime Minister had the right to issue a decree. In other words, de Gaulle assumed that deputies would want to ignore the limitations imposed upon them by Article 38 and would try to legislate in all areas. Thus, he envisaged that the Council would patrol the boundaries between the law-making powers of parliament and the decree-issuing powers of the Prime Minister. Moreover, in this regard the General had no illusions about the Council's role. He expected it to rule in favour of the government.

Over the years, though, the Constitutional Council has gradually evolved in such a way that it now plays almost exactly the opposite role from the one that de Gaulle originally planned. In this regard, there are two key dates: 1971 and 1974. In 1971 the Council ruled against the government for the first time. Prior to this time, the Council operated in exactly the way that de Gaulle had envisaged. The Council was called upon to arbitrate between the government and parliament on seven occasions and on each occasion it came down on the side of the former. Moreover, in November 1962 the Council declared that it did not have the power to strike down the law that established the direct election of the President, despite the fact that the referendum which preceded the law appeared to have been held in rather dubious constitutional circumstances (see Chapter 4). In these ways, then, the Constitutional Council was seen to be subservient to the government. However, in 1971 matters changed considerably. The Council decided that a bill which the government had drawn up and which parliament had passed was unconstitutional. This judgment was a breakthrough not only because it was the first time that the Constitutional Council had ruled against the government, but also because the Council based its judgment on the argument that there was the right to free association. This was important because the right to free association is not to be found in the text of the 1958 Constitution, but in the Preamble to the 1946 Constitution. In this way, the Council expanded not just the nature of its activity by ruling against the government, but also the scope of its rulings by identifying the 'bloc de constitutionnalité' on which its judgments would henceforth be made.

The other major change to the Council's role came in 1974. At the behest of the new President, Valéry Giscard d'Estaing, a constitutional reform was passed that allowed sixty deputies or sixty Senators to refer bills to the Council. This was a major change because it meant that from this point on the opposition was able to petition the Council.[5] As a result, the number of bills referred to the Constitutional Council increased dramatically. In the 1958–73 period, only nine bills had been sent to the Council, seven of which were partially struck down as unconstitutional, but only one of which was a governmental bill (the 1971 decision). By contrast, from 1974 to 1980 there were 66 referrals to the Council and from 1981 to 1990 there were a further 183 referrals. Moreover, of the 249 referrals during the period 1974–90, 238 were made by parliamentarians and only eight by the three Presidents and the Prime Minister (all figures from Stone 1994: 449). By the same token, after the 1974 reform the number of bills that the Constitutional Council considered to be unconstitutional increased as well. In the period 1974–81, fourteen bills, the majority of which were government texts, were declared to be either partially or wholly unconstitutional. In the period 1981–7, this figure rose to forty-nine bills, again the majority of which concerned government legislation. All in all, the 1974 reform made the Constitutional Council much more central to the decision-making process. It became a real check on the government.

The influence of the Constitutional Council can be seen in a number of ways. For example, the Council has played the role of gatekeeper on issues relating to the relationship between France and Europe (Harmsen 1993). At times it has paved the way for greater European integration. This can be seen in a 1975 decision when the Council indicated that the administrative courts and the criminal courts were responsible for determining whether there was a clash between European law and domestic law. While this decision meant that the Council washed its hands of such a responsibility, it also meant that these other courts had the flexibility to decide such matters for themselves. It can also be seen in a 1976 decision when it ruled that the introduction of direct elections to the European Parliament did not violate the Constitution. At other times, though, the Council has been more circumspect. In 1992 the Council decided that various elements of the Maastricht Treaty on European Union did not conform to the

Constitution. As a result, a constitutional amendment was required in order for the Treaty to become law.[6]

In general terms, though, the Council's influence has been felt the most when it has ruled consistently against the government of the day. In this regard, it was in the period after the Socialists came to power in 1981 that the Council started regularly to make the headlines. From 1981 to 1986, the right-wing opposition in parliament systematically referred any major bill to the Council in the hope that the right-wing majority there would declare the government's legislation unconstitutional. On several occasions this is precisely what happened. Most notably, in 1982, the Council declared part of the government's nationalization bill to be unconstitutional because insufficient financial compensation had been provided for the owners of the companies that were about to be taken under State control. By the mid-1980s, though, the Socialists had a stronger presence on the Council. Indeed, during the second period of cohabitation (1993–5), they were in a majority. As a result, the Constitutional Council made a number of key rulings against the right-wing government. Most notably, it struck down one of the major provisions of the government's immigration bill which limited the right to asylum. This meant that the government was obliged to pass a constitutional reform in order to bring about this change. Finally, in the period 1997–2002 the Council was again very active. During this period, the right-wing Council struck down a number of pieces of government legislation, including part of the bill that was designed to provide greater powers to the Corsican Assembly and that was seen as a key element of the ongoing peace process on the island.

All told, over the years the role of the Constitutional Council has become increasingly important and for two reasons. First, the Council has been a driving force in the increased importance of the rule of law. When governments draft legislation, they are now aware that they have to remain within the block of the Fifth Republic's constitutional law. This is known as 'auto-limitation', or 'the government's exercise of legislative self-restraint resulting from anticipation of a referral to and an eventual negative decision of the Council' (Keeler and Stone 1987: 175). Governments can still miscalculate the Council's reaction to a particular issue, but the opportunity for them to act arbitrarily has been reduced. Secondly, the Council has emerged as one of the main ways in which the opposition can check the law-making power of the majority (see Chapter 4). The

Constitutional Council is not merely concerned with the technical aspects of legislation; it is an integral part of the game between the opposition and the majority. In this respect, rather like the situation with regard to the dual executive and the legislature (see Chapters 4 and 6 respectively), the influence of the Council varies as a function of the configuration of party politics. At times, the opposition has used the Council to weaken the position of the executive. On other occasions, the Council has supported the majority and reinforced the position of the executive. In this context, the situation after the 2002 elections is clear. The right-wing Raffarin government will have to take cognizance of the Council's previous decisions and the body of constitutional law that it has established. All the same, the left-wing opposition will not be able to use the right-wing Council to challenge the position of the government. Overall, therefore, the Raffarin government is well placed.

The administrative courts

As noted in Chapter 5, the administration has long been a key element of the French State. In this context, an elaborate system of administrative law has developed. The basic aim of this system is to ensure that the State and its representatives act within the law. The highest administrative courts are the Council of State (*Conseil d'État*) and the Court of Accounts (*Cour des comptes*). These institutions, it should be noted, are State institutions and they are staffed by civil servants. This is a function of the French version of the separation of powers, which is based on the principle that the judiciary should be separate from the executive. The net result is that actions taken by State officials are themselves judged by State officials. This is one of the reasons why Councillors of State (*conseillers d'État*) and the auditors in the Court of Accounts are some of the most prestigious State officials in the country. They have the responsibility for passing judgment on their peers. Thus, they occupy positions at the very top of the French administrative system. Both institutions have a very long history. The Council of State was founded in 1799, while the Court of Accounts was created by Napoleon Bonaparte in 1807, although its origins date back to the Middle Ages. Unlike the Constitutional Council, neither the government nor the opposition is in a position to use these institutions to try to damage the government of the day. Instead, their increasing importance lies in the fact that in recent years they have both played a significant role in the development of the rule of law. In this way, they have constrained the room for manoeuvre of successive governments.

The Council of State

The Council of State is the highest administrative institution in the land (see Table 7.1). Technically, the Prime Minister, as the head of the administration (Article 20), is the President of the Council of State. However, this is merely a formal title. In practice, the Council of State is headed by a Vice-President who is appointed by the President of the Republic in the Council of Ministers. The current Vice-President, Renaud Denoix de Saint Marc, was a former General Secretary of the Government (see Chapter 4). In January 2000 there were nearly 300 people in the Council of State.[7] Together they constitute one of the so-called *grands corps* of higher civil servants (see Chapter 5) and their talents are in great demand. Indeed, at any one time, around one-third of all Councillors of State are working on secondment to other public- and private-sector institutions. These people have the right to return to the Council of State at any time. However, such is their expertise that many Councillors of State choose to pursue a successful administrative, commercial, or political career outside the Council itself. One of the main reasons why Councillors of State are in such demand is because the vast majority of them are recruited directly from the highly prestigious administrative training school ENA (see Chapter 5). That said, approximately one-third of all Councillors of State are external, or *tour extérieur*, appointments. There is the suspicion that some of these latter appointments are politically motivated. Indeed, in a recent book, Lionel Jospin's most senior political adviser revealed that during the 1997–2002 period of cohabitation such appointments were governed by the principle: two for the Prime Minister and one for the President (Schrameck 2001: 112). All the same, the Council of State does not really exhibit a consistent left- or right-wing bias. Unlike the Constitutional Council, the Council of State is not part of the game between the majority and the opposition. Its role does not vary as a function of the configuration of party politics. Instead, the Council of State is important because it helps to guarantee the rule of law in the French system.

The Council of State has two main functions. The first is to act as the government's main legal and constitutional adviser. In some cases, the Council's advice is obligatory. So, Articles 38 and 39 state that all regular government bills as well as bills designed to allow the government to legislate by ordinance have to be examined by the Council of State before they are considered by the Council of Ministers and sent to parliament; Article 37 states that certain government decrees also have to be examined by the Council; finally, by virtue of a 1992 constitutional amendment Article 88-4 indicates that the Council of State has to decide whether certain European Union decisions fall within the domain of the law, in which event they have to be examined by parliament. In other cases, the government can simply call upon the Council's advice if it feels the need to do so (see figures in Table 7.7). So, for example, in 1989 the government asked for the Council's advice on the politically and socially sensitive issue of whether pupils were allowed to wear religious head scarves in school. In both cases, the Council makes a judgment as to the constitutionality of the text, its administrative implications, and the extent to which it conforms with laws already in existence. In relation to Article 39, it should be noted that, even if the government is obliged to seek the Council's advice, it is under no obligation to accept the Council's advice. So, if, for political reasons, the government decides to press ahead with a measure that the Council of State has deemed to be juridically problematic, then it has the absolute right to do so.[8] Of course, if it does so, the government runs the risk of being censured by the Constitutional Council if it has the same opinion of the offending measure as the Council of State. Moreover, even if

TABLE 7.7	The advisory activity of the Council of State, 1998–2000		
Type of decision	1998	1999	2000
Laws and ordinances (Articles 38 and 39)	125	97	112
Decrees (Article 37)	547	557	617
Other decrees	758	523	583
Non-obligatory governmental advice	14	18	29
Total	1,444	1,195	1,341

Source: www.conseil-etat.fr/ce-data/actus/chiffre1.htm – accessed 23 Jan. 2002.

the bill becomes law, the government may find that at a later date the issue in question is the subject of a legal challenge that requires a ruling by the Council of State in its capacity as a court of appeal for administrative law. The bottom line, though, is that while the Council of State clearly plays a major role as the government's main adviser on legal and constitutional matters, the government retains the right to determine the content of proposed legislation for itself.

The Council of State's second function is to act as the highest administrative court in the land. In France, litigation implicating the State or a representative of the State is processed through a system of administrative courts. In general terms, this system is organized hierarchically.[9] The court of first instance is called an Administrative Tribunal (*Tribunal administratif*). There are thirty-six such tribunals, twenty-eight of which are situated in various cities throughout mainland France. If a case cannot be resolved at this level, it will be heard by an Administrative Court of Appeal. These courts were established in 1987 so as to ease the workload of the Council of State. There are currently seven such appeal courts in mainland France. Finally, if a case is still not resolved, then the highest court of appeal is the Council of State itself. However, it should be noted that the Council does not hear the details of the case again. The Council's role is merely to determine whether previous judgments contained errors of law. Whatever its judgment, the Council's decisions are sovereign. That is to say, they are binding upon the State and the administration generally. In some cases, it may still be possible to appeal to a higher jurisdiction at the European level. Within France, though, in the domain of administrative law the Council of State is supreme.

A large number of cases involving the State are filed each year. (For figures, see Table 7.8.) For the most part, though, they relate to relatively insignificant issues, including, for example, compensation claims where injury has been caused while a person is on public property, and cases where a person believes that planning permission has been unjustly refused. All the same, the courts also deal with some extremely sensitive matters. For example, the Council of State has to decide the cases where the refusal to grant a visa is being contested, or where a deportation order is being challenged. Indeed, 5,058 of the 8,817 new cases filed with the Council of State in 1999 concerned such matters (Latournerie 2000: 404). Given that immigration and asylum issues have been so salient in France over the last decade, it is inevitable that the Council will be drawn into the political domain in this regard. The Council has also played a particularly important role in the gradual Europeanization of the French political process over the years. In this context, the Council was relatively slow to accept the supremacy of European law over French law (see Harmsen 1993: 82–5). In 1968, the Council of State ruled to this effect in the so-called 'semolina' judgment (*Syndicat général des fabricants de semoules en France*, March 1968), which was subsequently confirmed in a 1979 decision (*Union démocratique du travail*, 22 October 1979). Thereafter, the Council gradually relaxed its opposition (Guyomarch, Machin, and Ritchie 1998: 69–70). In fact, though, it was only in 1989 that the Council of State finally accepted the primacy of European over domestic legislation (*M. Nicolo*, October 1989) and gave effect to Article 55 of the Constitution, which had appeared to indicate that this was the case all along. Again, what is clear is that even though the Council of State is not a politicized institution, its decisions nonetheless have profound political consequences for the functioning of the State, the administration, and the political process generally.

The Court of Accounts

The Court of Accounts is an integral part of the system of administrative law. It is not attached to any government department and its members have the status of judges. The Court is headed by a First President who is appointed in the Council of Ministers. The current incumbent, François Logerot, was appointed in March 2001 after a long career in the Court and periods of secondment to other public-sector institutions. Overall, there are around 200 members of the Court of Accounts and, like Councillors of

TABLE 7.8	The activity of administrative courts, 1999		
	Administrative Tribunals	Administrative Courts of Appeal	Council of State
New cases	117,427	16,056	8,817
Cases resolved	112,198	11,390	7,581

Source: Latournerie (2000: 402–3).

State, together they constitute one of the *grands corps* within the French administration. The junior members of the Court are recruited from ENA, even though the government does have the opportunity to make outside appointments to some of the more senior grades. Members of the Court cannot be removed from office and, like the Council of State, while the Court of Accounts is undoubtedly one of the elite institutions of the French administration, it is not seen as a party political body. Its influence does not vary as a function of party politics. It is important because it is an essential element of the rule of law in the French system. In this regard, it serves to constrain the decision-making freedom of governments even further.

The Court of Accounts has two functions. The Court's main role is to judge the legality of public-sector accounts. So, for example, it has the responsibility for overseeing the work of all State-sector institutions, including the administration, the social security funds (since 1950), and nationalized industries (since 1976). In 1999, the Court had responsibility for verifying a total of 931 sets of accounts (*Rapport public, 2000*, at **www.ccomptes.fr**—accessed 29 January 2002). In addition to the Court of Accounts itself, the 1982 decentralization reform established a set of Regional Courts of Account. Their role is to ensure the regularity of the accounts of local authorities. In 1998, the Regional Courts were responsible for judging 69,760 sets of accounts (ibid.). The decisions of the Regional Courts may be appealed to the Court of Accounts proper. Furthermore, the decisions of the Court of Accounts itself may be appealed to the Council of State. Thus, the Court of Accounts may be deemed to be inferior to the Council of State in this regard.

In relation to this function, the basic role of the Court is to protect the financial rights of citizens. Here, two points are worth noting. The first is that the Court of Accounts has an essentially retrospective focus. That is to say, the Court only examines the accounts of public-sector organizations after they have been prepared. So, while it may be the case that the Court's decisions discourage fraud and encourage accounts to be presented properly, the Court always acts after the event. Moreover, it sometimes acts quite a considerable time after the event. Indeed, in 1999, 7.5 per cent of the total number of accounts still to be judged dated back more than ten years (**www.ccomptes.fr**—accessed 29 January 2002). The second point is that the number of illegalities discovered by the Court is relatively small. In

1999, the Court issued only fourteen fines in cases where public-sector accountants were judged to have behaved irregularly and only nine cases were transmitted to the criminal courts for prosecution proceedings to begin. In part, these figures testify to the professionalism and honesty of French public servants. All the same, there have been criticisms that government officials have not been held sufficiently accountable for the management (or mismanagement) of public funds (see, for example, Mény 1987: 286).

The second main function of the Court of Accounts is to comment on the management of public funds and to help parliament and the government in controlling the use of such funds. Indeed, the Court has a constitutional responsibility in this latter regard (Articles 47 and 47-1). Here, the highest-profile aspects of the Court's work are the annual reports that it presents to parliament. It produces a report on the implementation of the budget, a report on the financing of the social security funds, and a report on the management of the public purse generally. In addition, it also produces a large number of reports on specific topics throughout the course of the year. The Court's annual report is widely debated in the media because it invariably contains some almost unbelievable examples of how public money is wasted. For example, in its annual report for 1999 the Court reported that it had been unable to determine the precise number of people employed by the State, so complicated, ambiguous, and downright opaque were the conditions under which some officials were employed. In addition, it also found that 14 per cent of the total police force was not engaged in policing. This figure included members of the police orchestra and people working in the offices of the police unions. It also included people who were engaged in what amounted to full-time sporting activities on behalf of the service. Similarly, in its annual report for 2000 the Court criticized the cost to the State of hosting the 1998 football World Cup, around 10 billion francs (1.5 billion euro), while a host of public-sector institutions, such as the employment agency, were also accused of a lack of 'rigour' in their budgetary and auditing processes. Overall, it would seem reasonable to suggest that the Court's reports have had a certain impact on public perceptions of the French State. True, as one writer is no doubt correct to point out (Mény 1987: 287), the reports are written in a legalistic rather than a public-oriented tone and this lessens their impact. All the same, the Court's relentless pursuit of waste and mismanagement has helped to dent the once seemingly impregnable reputation of the French public service.

The civil and criminal courts

In contrast to the Council of State and the Court of Accounts, the civil and criminal courts are a basic component of the political game. Over the years, they have been controlled by the government of the day. In short, governments have used their powers to thwart potentially controversial judicial investigations. In recent times, though, representatives of the civil and criminal courts have tried to assert their independence and certain judges have been instrumental in prosecuting a number of very high-profile cases of political corruption. The net result is that, unlike the situation with the Constitutional Council, the opposition is not in a position to use the civil and criminal courts as an instrument against the majority. However, governments have been able to use their powers to influence the work of the courts and avoid political embarrassment. To the extent that the civil and criminal court judges have been able to resist this pressure, they have emerged as an important element of the rule of law.

The system of civil and criminal courts is organized hierarchically. Most small-scale civil cases are heard in a so-called *tribunal d'instance*, while the more important cases go directly to a *tribunal de grande instance*. There are 473 *tribunaux d'instance* throughout the country and 81 *tribunaux de grande instance*. Similarly, criminal cases are heard by *tribunaux de police* or *tribunaux correctionnels* in the case of more serious charges. In addition, there are equivalent institutions that deal with more specific issues, such as the 277 *conseils de prud'hommes* that hear matters relating to labour law and the 191 *tribunaux de commerce* that deal with aspects of commercial law. If a case remains contested after it has been judged by any of the courts at this level, it can be heard by one of the 35 Courts of Appeal (*cours d'appel*) across the country. Thus, in principle any case has the right to be heard twice. Moreover, in criminal cases, the Courts of Assizes (*cours d'assises*), of which there is one for every department, consider the most serious crimes. The highest court of appeal in this system is the Court of Cassation (Cour de cassation). Like the Council of State in relation to administrative law (see above), the Court of Cassation does not hear the facts of a case from scratch. Instead, the role of the Court is simply to decide whether lower-level courts have applied the law correctly. In this sense, the Court of Cassation judges the judges, and this helps to account for the very senior status of the members of the Court. Whatever it decides, the Court's judgment is final, although its decisions can be appealed to the European courts. Finally, it should be noted that there are special courts relating to Ministers and the President. The Court of Justice of the Republic meets to hear cases involving Ministers and the High Court of Justice is responsible for matters relating to the President (see Box 7.1).

The Court of Cassation has the capacity to play an important role in the

---

BOX 7.1   **The High Court of Justice and the Court of Justice of the Republic**

The High Court of Justice

Article 67 of the 1958 Constitution makes reference to the High Court of Justice (HCJ). The HCJ is composed of an equal number of deputies and Senators. Article 68 states that the role of the Court is to judge the President in cases where the head of State is accused of high treason. No President has ever been accused of such a crime and so to date the Court has never met.

The Court of Justice of the Republic

Article 68-1 states that government Ministers are legally responsible for the decisions that they take during their time in office. This means that they may be found guilty of a crime or a misdemeanour and face punishment. If they are accused of such a crime, then they are tried by the Court of Justice of the Republic (CJR). Article 68-2 indicates that any such accusation must be made through the criminal court system. As the court of final instance, the Court of Cassation decides whether or not there is a case to be heard. If there is, then the CJR is convened. The CJR is composed of six deputies, six Senators, and three judges from the Court of Cassation. The CJR was established by a constitutional amendment in 1993.

In 1999, there was a high-profile trial involving a former Prime Minister, Laurent Fabius, and a former Minister and junior Minister for Health, Edmond Hervé and Georgina Dufoix respectively. The trial took place because in the mid-1980s they were in office when decisions were made concerning the State's policy on blood transfusion. The policy subsequently resulted in a considerable number of people being given blood transfusions that were contaminated with the Hepatitis C and the HIV viruses. As a result, some of these people died. The three politicians were accused of complicity to poison and the trial took place in March 1999. In the end, Fabius and Dufoix were cleared of all charges. However, Hervé was found guilty on two counts, but was not punished.

system. It has made various decisions that have affected France's relationship with Europe. For example, it was very quick to give effect to the Constitutional Council's 1975 judgment concerning the relationship between domestic law and European law. Only a few months after the Council's ruling, in its so-called Vabre decision (Harmsen 1993: 81–2), the Court of Cassation emphasized the primacy of European law over French law. This was a landmark ruling and pre-dated the Council of State's decisions in this regard by more than a decade (see above). In addition, the Court of Cassation has been drawn into the political process as the highest court of appeal in various cases of political corruption. In these cases, the Court has invariably upheld the prosecution. It has not tended to hand out last-gasp reprieves for desperate politicians.

In this context, the most important judicial actors in relation to political life are individual judges themselves. In this regard, the organization of the French system of justice is very different from both the British and American systems. In France the magistrature is composed of various types of judges. In general terms a distinction can be made between judges who hear cases and make decisions and judges who prosecute cases. (In France, judges prosecute cases, not the police.) The judges who hear cases can be divided into two basic types. The first simply preside over mainly civil cases in a manner that is recognizably similar to the role of judges in Britain and the USA. The second, who are known as examining or investigating magistrates (*juges d'instruction*), are involved in criminal cases. They have a very different role. Their job is to decide whether a prima facie case can be made for prosecution.[10] Thus, they have to investigate the facts of a case, interviewing witnesses, gathering evidence, and so forth. If they decide that there is such a case to be heard, then they call upon a prosecuting judge to bring the matter to a trial. As we shall see, *juges d'instruction* have played an important role in cases of political corruption. By contrast, the judges who prosecute cases are collectively known as the *parquet*. The main role of the *parquet* is to begin formal criminal proceedings. A key point to note is that even if a *juge d'instruction* considers that a prima facie case can be made, the *parquet* has to decide whether or not prosecution proceedings can actually begin.

In France, then, the organization of the civil and criminal courts and the role of judges are both very different from their British and American counterparts. A further difference can be found in the relationship between judges and the government. In France, judges are classed as civil servants. This means that they are subordinate to their immediate political superior, the Minister of Justice (sometimes known as the Garde des sceaux or the Chancellerie). In this context, a variety of measures has been put in place to ensure the independence of the judiciary. For example, judges who hear cases are appointed for life. They can only be dismissed if they have been found guilty of wrongdoing. Moreover, issues relating to promotion, remuneration, and disciplinary proceedings are decided by the Higher Council for the Magistrature (Conseil supérieur de la magistrature or CSM). Over the years, though, judges have been controlled by the government of the day. For example, the 1958 Constitution states that the President of the Republic is 'the guarantor of the independence of the judicial authority' (Article 64) and that in this regard the President is merely 'assisted by' the CSM. In 1993 a constitutional amendment was passed to try to make the CSM more independent of the government, most notably by increasing the representation of judges. However, politicians still sit on the CSM and make appointments to it. What is more, even though the CSM makes recommendations in regard, for example, to judicial appointments, the government is not obliged to accept these recommendations. Indeed, it was revealed that in 1997 the government had refused seven of the fifteen recommendations made by the CSM in relation to appointments to the *parquet* (Jean 1999: 22). This more than fuelled the suspicion that judicial appointments are sometimes politically motivated. Finally, the relationship between the government and the *parquet* is particularly important. The members of the *parquet* are, in effect, State prosecutors. In practice, this means that they can be given orders by the Minister of Justice. Most notably, the Minister maintains the right to order the *parquet* not to begin prosecution proceedings or to drop them once they have begun. In other words, the final decision as to whether or not to prosecute a case lies with the government.

In recent times, the political aspect of this system has focused on the relationship between the *juges d'instruction* and the *parquet*. The *juges d'instruction* play a key role because they have the capacity not just to embarrass the government by investigating a case but also to create the conditions for a successful prosecution. In some senses, they are in a strong position in relation to the political class. They work alone. They may not receive orders as to how a case should progress. They cannot be removed from a case, unless they commit procedural irregularities. They also have powers to compel witnesses to testify, to seize documentation, and so forth. In this context, several *juges d'instruction* have gained a considerable reputation for themselves while investigating the corrupt affairs of politicians. For example, judge Renaud Van Ruymbeke successfully investigated the illegal financial practices of the Socialist party in the so-called Urba affair. These investigations led to the conviction of a high-profile former Budget Minister and Treasurer of the party, Henri Emmanuelli. Another judge who gained a similar reputation was Eric Halphen. He investigated the allegations of illegality that surrounded the gaullist party in Paris and the surrounding region and he made some startling accusations about an alleged system of secret and illegal party political financing in the capital (Halphen 2002). This was a particularly sensitive matter because it implicated a number of very senior political figures, not the least of whom was Jacques Chirac himself, who was mayor of Paris for nearly two decades prior to his election as President.

Even though the *juges d'instruction* have some important powers, they have often found it very difficult to carry out their work effectively. Members of the political class have often used their influence and resources to frustrate investigations. So, for example, Judge Halphen eventually resigned his position in disgust at the general lack of progress he was making. Another *juge d'instruction*, Laurence Vichnievsky, who helped to investigate the so-called Elf affair involving Roland Dumas, indicated that she no longer thought that investigating judges could carry out their role properly (Vichnievsky 2002). These experiences are not unique. By virtue of the fact that they play such a key role, *juges d'instruction* have been subject to tremendous criticism from the political class. Many politicians who have found themselves under investigation have claimed that their right to be treated as innocent until proved guilty has been violated. Indeed, in some cases, there is no doubt some truth in this point. For example, the former Finance Minister, Dominique Strauss-Kahn, was under investigation for more than a year before he was finally cleared of any wrongdoing. In the meantime, his political career suffered. The fact remains, though, that on occasion *juges d'instruction* have found it very difficult to investigate certain political matters as fully as they would have liked. Worse than that, one newspaper quoted an anonymous message that a judge received in January 2001. It read: 'Have a happy birthday, you might not celebrate any more' (*Libération*, 15 January 2002).

One of the reasons why *juges d'instruction* have found it difficult to carry out their work properly is because of the relationship between the executive and the *parquet*. The *parquet* has to make two key decisions: whether to open criminal proceedings and launch an investigation; and whether to close an investigation once it has started. In recent years, both types of decision have been the source of great controversy. In relation to the decision as to whether to begin proceedings, one such case concerned the former Prime Minister Alain Juppé. He was accused of using his influence in the Paris town hall to acquire low-cost accommodation for himself and his son in some of the most prestigious areas in the capital. However, no investigation was initiated. For the outspoken Socialist deputy Arnaud Montebourg, this was at least partly the work of the then Minister of Justice, Jacques Toubon, who, was, of course, appointed to his post by . . . Alain Juppé (Montebourg 2000: 77). In the end, in the face of what appeared to be an open-and-shut case, the *parquet* simply decided to drop the matter, even though it did take the highly unusual step of suggesting that it would be best for Juppé to move out of his luxury apartment as soon as possible. In terms of whether to close an investigation once it has started, there have been a number of striking examples in recent times. For example, one of the reasons why Van Ruymbeke's work in the Urba case was so celebrated was because one of the previous *juges d'instruction*, Thierry Jean-Pierre, had been summarily dismissed from the case on the orders of the Socialist Minister for Justice on the same day that he was searching the headquarters of the party for incriminating evidence. However, the most bizarre incident was no doubt the occasion when the aforementioned Jacques Toubon chartered a helicopter to obtain the signature of a member of the *parquet* so that an investigation into the corruption allegations relating to the wife of the then mayor of Paris, Jean Tiberi, could be stopped. This would be unusual in itself, but the judge was on holiday in the Himalayas at the time! There is no doubt that these examples reflect badly on the *parquet*, and, of course, they, and plenty of others like them, have helped to discredit the political class generally. That said, it must not be thought that the *parquet* is always a willing participant in these affairs. The *parquet* would like to be independent. However, its members have not always had the opportunity to be so.

There is no doubt, therefore, that governments have used their powers to protect their supporters. Increasingly, though, governments have found that their reputation has been damaged by trying to cover up examples of political corruption. The public has sanctioned governments that have ignored the rule of law. This was particularly true for the Socialists in the period 1988–93, when a number of party representatives found themselves under investigation. As a result, governments have tried to improve their image by increasing the independence of the judiciary. For example, as noted previously, in 1993 a constitutional amendment was passed that reinforced the independent nature of the CSM. Similarly, in 1997 Prime Minister Jospin announced that the Minister for Justice would no longer issue orders to the *parquet* regarding individual cases and that the government would accept all of the recommendations of the CSM in relation to appointments. Moreover, with the initial support of President Chirac, the government proposed a constitutional amendment designed to break the link between the Minister for Justice and the *parquet* once and for all. The reform proposal was passed by both houses of parliament. However, 24 hours before parliament was due to meet in Congress for the final vote on the amendment, Chirac stopped the process. This was an abrupt about-turn from a person who had once been in favour of the reform. Perhaps the decision was understandable, though, because the President's party and indeed the President himself probably stood to lose the most from any such change. After all, the latter part of Chirac's first term in office was plagued by continuing allegations about the corrupt practices with which he and his closest associates had supposedly been involved (see Chapter 1). This example suggests that even though the independence of the judiciary has increased, it is still subject to political manipulation.

European courts

In recent years, European courts have had an increasing impact on the French judicial system. In particular, the European Court of Justice has emerged as an important institution in the relationship between France and the EU. In addition, the European Court of Human Rights has also begun to assert its influence. A key point is that, rather like the situation with the Council of State and the Court of Accounts, neither the government nor the opposition is able to use either of the two European courts to promote their own interests. Instead, these courts are important because they have helped to strengthen the rule of law in the political system as a whole. Governments still try to maximize their room for manoeuvre, but the development of the European courts has made the decision-making process that much more difficult for domestic political leaders.

The European Court of Justice (ECJ) ensures respect for EU law across member States. The Court has jurisdiction in three main areas (Hix 1999: 106–7). First, it can hear actions brought against member States by the European Commission and/or other member States in regard to Treaty obligations and EU law. Secondly, it has the power to review the actions of EU institutions. In this domain, cases can be brought to the ECJ by private citizens and member States as well as by various European institutions themselves. Thirdly, member State courts can ask the ECJ to make a ruling on aspects of EU law. In effect, this makes the ECJ the highest tier of judicial authority in national judicial systems. The supremacy of EU law over domestic law was established in a landmark judgment in 1964. In the *Costa* v. *ENEL* case, the ECJ ruled that 'By creating a Community of unlimited duration . . . member states have limited their sovereign rights . . . and have thus created a body of law which binds both their individual citizens and themselves' (case 6/64 ECR 585). In this chapter we have already seen that courts in France were perhaps rather slow to acknowledge the supremacy of European law over domestic law and, as we shall see, France remains rather slow at implementing the ECJ's decisions. Even so, the ECJ is an important part of the French judicial process and in the end France does have to implement ECJ judgments.

The main importance of the ECJ in the domestic context is twofold. It has the power to decide for itself whether or not existing French law is compatible with EU law. Also, by virtue of its decisions, it has the power to shape the decisions of the courts in France. As we have already seen in this chapter, French courts increasingly make reference to ECJ decisions when making their own judgments. For example, in 2000 the Paris Court of Appeal drew upon an ECJ decision when ruling that it should be easier for credit institutions based in other EU countries to grant mortgage loans in France. This decision served to liberalize the credit market and, by extension, reduce the degree of State regulation (see Chapter 3). In addition,

French courts explicitly ask the ECJ to make a ruling about the applicability of EU law in France. In 2000 the Courts of Appeal, the Council of State, and the Court of Cassation requested that ECJ make a ruling on 12 occasions out of a total of 224 requests from the 15 member States as a whole (COM[2001]309). Even though in this particular year this proportion was slightly lower than the figure for both the UK and Germany and even though it was also lower than the equivalent French figure for certain previous years, it still illustrates the ongoing impact of the ECJ on the French system of law, and in this regard France is no different from any other member State country (see Table 7.9).

The bottom line is that French governments are more constrained now than they were previously. They have to amend existing legislation so as to take account of ECJ rulings. Also, they have to draft new legislation in such a way that it stays within the boundaries of EU law, because if they fail to do so they are aware that they will have to comply with the ECJ's judgments when the matter comes to court. That said, there is no doubt that French governments try to maintain as much influence as possible for as long as possible. For example, France has a record of implementing ECJ decisions rather more slowly than most other countries. The European Commission monitors the extent to which member States are applying EU law in their own jurisdictions, and in its 2001 report the Commission found that by the end of 2000 France had failed to implement twenty-seven ECJ judgments, one of which dated back to 1991 (COM[2001]309). This compares with an equivalent figure in the same year of six ECJ judgments in the case of Germany and just three for the UK. So, in this regard

TABLE 7.9	Number of requests made by selected national courts to the ECJ, 1990–2000										
	1990	1991	1992	1993	1994	1995	1996	1997	1998	1999	2000
Germany	34	50	62	57	44	51	66	46	49	49	47
France	21	24	15	22	36	43	24	10	16	17	12
UK	12	13	15	12	24	20	21	18	24	22	26
Total	142	186	162	204	203	251	256	239	264	255	224

Source: (COM[2001]309).

at least, France is not a very good European. In the end, though, it always has to comply.

In addition to the ECJ, the European Court of Human Rights (ECHR) has also become increasingly important. The Convention for the Protection of Human Rights and Fundamental Freedoms was drawn up in 1950 and came into force in 1953. Over time, the number of countries that have agreed to abide by the Convention has increased. Currently, forty European countries are signatories to the Convention. Contracting States and, importantly, their citizens can lodge a case with the Court if they feel that their rights have been violated. The ECHR is the institution that applies the Convention and decides whether or not the claim is well founded. One problem is that the Court's decisions can be difficult to police. There is a strong moral pressure on States to uphold the Court's rulings, but the ECHR does not have the same institutional capacity as the ECJ to implement its decisions.

The Convention for the Protection of Human Rights and Fundamental Freedoms was ratified by France in 1974, but French citizens were only given the right to petition the Court in 1981. What is clear is that since this time France has been pursued very actively in the ECHR. In 2001, no fewer than 1,117 cases were formally opened against France. This figure was greater than the equivalent figure for almost any other contracting country. Indeed, only Russia had more cases opened against it in the same year (see Table 7.10). That said, this figure needs to be placed in context. As Table 7.10 shows, only a small number of cases opened against France are declared admissible. By contrast, in 2001 Turkey and, especially, Italy had a much larger number of cases declared admissible, Greece had a greater proportion of cases declared admissible of the ones that were opened, while Russia was still not fully integrated into the system in regard to the admissibility of cases. A similar picture emerges if we examine the judgments made by the Court in the same year (see Table 7.11). In this context, France was found to have violated the Convention in a larger number of cases than any other country except Italy and Turkey. Even so, the comparison is slightly misleading because, as mentioned previously, countries like Russia are not fully part of the system. Moreover, the figures for the number of judgments tell us nothing about the nature of the cases brought or the significance of the judgments made. In this latter regard, France stands out because a high proportion of the cases taken to the ECHR relate to Article 6 of the Convention, which guarantees the right to a 'fair trial' and, in particular, the right to a fair trial 'within a reasonable time'. In fact, 60 per cent of the total number of cases declared admissible against France and 40 per cent of all the cases giving rise to a violation judgment relate to this clause of the Convention (Abraham 2001: 148). Thus, the ECHR has clearly identified a general problem within the French legal system. In the Court's opinion, it takes too long for certain cases to be brought before

TABLE 7.10	Cases taken to the ECHR in selected countries, 2001		
	Applications registered	Applications struck off	Applications declared admissible
France	1,117	891	51
Germany	714	527	8
Greece	193	96	32
Italy	590	265	341
Poland	1,763	1,411	26
Russia	2,108	1,253	2
Turkey	1,059	384	90
UK	474	529	34
Total	20,578	8,989	739

Note: The figures for applications struck off and those declared admissible may include applications registered in the previous year.

Source: Council of Europe, European Court of Human Rights, Survey of Activities, 2001.

TABLE 7.11	ECHR judgments against selected countries, 2001	
	Cases giving rise to at least one violation	Total cases judged
France	32	45
Germany	13	17
Greece	14	21
Italy	359	413
Poland	17	20
Russia	—	—
Turkey	169	229
UK	19	33
Total	682	889

Source: Council of Europe, European Court of Human Rights, Survey of Activities, 2001.

the French courts. This is an important matter, but if we exclude from these figures the violation judgments relating to this particular issue then France's record before the ECHR is not quite as bad as might at first appear.

Whatever the interpretation of the figures, there is no doubt that the ECHR poses an increasingly difficult problem for the French government. For example, in recent times law and order has been a major political issue in France. Governments have wanted to be seen to be tough on crime. However, they are faced with ECHR judgments indicating that reforms should be introduced to speed up the judicial process. Such reforms may be right and proper, but if the government were to introduce them it would run the risk of being accused by the opposition of being soft on crime. Thus, the government may try to avoid embarrassment by delaying the implementation of difficult decisions, while the opposition may try to embarrass the government by calling upon it to implement such decisions as soon as possible. Again, therefore, we see the relationship between the courts and politics. Unlike the Constitutional Council, the majority and the opposition cannot manipulate either the ECHR or the ECJ to suit their own ends. Even so, the judgments made by both of these Courts are both technical and political in nature. In other words, like the national courts, the European courts do more than just strengthen the rule of law. They also affect the wider party political situation.

Conclusion

Two main observations should be made about the relationship between the judiciary and politics in France. The first is that the role of the judiciary has changed over time. There is an increasing emphasis on the rule of law. This change has come about because of the creation and development of the Constitutional Council, the work of the Council of State and the Court of Accounts, the investigative activity of the *juges d'instruction*, and the role of the European courts. The result is that governments can longer act quite as arbitrarily as they used to do. They have to take account of the body of constitutional law that has been established by the Constitutional Council. They have to respond to the decisions of the Council of State and the reports of the Court of Accounts. They have to be aware that political corruption may lead to a damaging investigation by a *juge d'instruction*. They have to implement the decisions of the European authorities. In short, governments, and elected representatives generally, no longer have quite the same freedom that they once had. They are constrained by a more independent and active judiciary. The second observation is that political actors have nonetheless continued to use the judiciary as an instrument in a wider political game. For example, both the majority and the opposition have used the Constitutional Council to try to promote their own political interests. The result is that the role of the Council has varied as a function of the party political situation. When the opposition has had a majority on the Council, then the government has been constrained. When the government has had a majority, then its position has been strengthened. In relation to *juges d'instruction*, the situation is different. Here, the opposition is relatively powerless. However, governments have intervened to try to shape the outcome of investigations and prevent potentially damaging political revelations. Overall, the judiciary has established itself as a check on the government. Even so, the impact of the judiciary still varies as a function of the configuration of wider political forces.

KEY TERMS

- Constitutional Council
- Administrative Courts
- Criminal Courts
- European Courts
- Rule of law

NOTES

1 In legal terms a public 'power' derives its authority from the people. By contrast an 'authority' is merely delegated the right to act in a particular area by the State.

2 It should be noted that all former Presidents of the Republic have the automatic right to sit on the Council when they leave office. This means that former President Valéry Giscard d'Estaing has been eligible to take his place since he lost the presidency in 1981. However, Giscard has consistently declined to do so.

3 Cited by another former member of the Council, François Luchaire (**www.conseil-constitutionnel.fr/divers/temoignages/luchaire.htm**—accessed 15 Jan. 2002).

4 A 1998 constitutional amendment also allowed various authorities in New Caledonia to petition the Council in relation to laws passed by the island's Assembly.

5 Since 1974, the Council has been petitioned by members of the parliamentary majority in this way on only nine occasions and these have mostly concerned ethical issues that have cut across party lines. Examples include the bill on abortion in 1975 and the bill on bioethics in 1994 (**www.conseil-constitutionnel.fr/textes/jan2000.htm**—accessed 16 Jan. 2002).

6 The amendments were passed by a parliamentary congress in June 1992. It was only then that President Mitterrand decided that a referendum should be held to ratify the Treaty. Thus, the Maastricht referendums was totally superfluous in law. It was a purely political decision.

7 Source: **www.conseil-etat.fr/ce-data/aquoi/conseta1.htm**—accessed 23 Jan. 2002.

8 The Council of State's recommendations are secret, so there is no way of identifying the cases where the government has ignored the Council's advice. However, off-the-record interviews have suggested that this practice does occur, albeit rarely.

9 Certain issues go directly to the Council of State. This is the case, for example, for litigation concerning visas and deportation.

10 The decision to begin the investigation can be made by the *parquet* or by an alleged victim. The *juge d'instruction* cannot decide independently to begin investigations.

GUIDE TO FURTHER READING

ABRAHAM, H., *The Judicial Process: An Introductory Analysis of the Courts of the United States, England and France* (Oxford, Oxford University Press, 1998).
A good comparative introduction.

BELL, J., *French Constitutional Law* (Oxford, Clarendon Press, 1992).
A good overview of constitutional law.

——BOYRON, S., and WHITTAKER, S., *Principles of French Law* (Oxford, Oxford University Press, 1998).
A more general introduction to French law.

STONE, A., *The Birth of Judicial Politics in France: The Constitutional Council in Comparative Perspective* (Oxford, Oxford University Press, 1992).
An excellent book that traces the development of the Constitutional Council.

—— *Governing with Judges: Constitutional Politics in Europe* (Oxford, Oxford University Press, 2000).
A comparative overview of the interplay of courts and politics.

8

Local Government

Overview

The chapter begins by briefly outlining the normative principles upon which centre–periphery relations in France were based. It then examines, first, the role of the main actors and institutions at the central level and, secondly, the equivalent actors and institutions at the sub-central level. The aim is to emphasize the degree of institutional change in this area over the last twenty years.

Introduction

The French system of local government is, at once, profoundly affected both by the historical context within which it has operated for more than 200 years and by the modern-day political environment which is the source of new constraints and, perhaps above all, new opportunities. The historical context of centre–periphery relations in France is clear: the centre was supposed to dominate the periphery and, following the Revolution, the system of local administration required the equal provision of services throughout the national territory. The modern-day political situation is equally clear: the centre is no longer designed to control the periphery and the new system of local governance means that inevitably there is more and more variation in the delivery of services across the country as a whole. In this way, the study of local government reflects some of the most basic issues with which this book has been concerned: it demonstrates the ongoing impact of the past on contemporary French politics; it illustrates the challenges with which the country is now faced; it shows how political actors have changed the institutional environment in which they operate as a response to these challenges; it points to some of the ways in which the new institutional framework of centre–local relations in France has affected the behaviour of political actors in the country. In essence, France maintains a predominantly centralized system of local government. All the same, many of the established precepts on which the system was developed have been challenged. Consequently, local authorities now have more freedom than ever before to act independently. As a result, there is less institutional and policy uniformity across the system than was previously the case.

The normative principles of centre–periphery relations

The French system of centre–periphery relations was based on two normative principles: that the centre should control the periphery and that there should be equal treatment of citizens across the national territory. The belief that the centre should control the periphery has its origins in the *ancien régime* prior to the Revolution, but found its most complete expression during the early years of the nineteenth century under the Napoleonic Empire when the process of centralization was completed. The belief that there should be equal treatment of citizens across the national territory is a product of the Revolution itself.

The first normative foundation of centralization was the fear that local autonomy would undermine the very integrity or at least the political stability of the national territory. In this context, it should be remembered that in geographical terms France is only a relatively recent creation. Indeed, the area of what is now commonly known as the French Hexagon is merely the end result of the incremental accumulation of various towns and regions over an extremely long period of time. For example, Corsica was purchased from Genoa in 1768 and the Savoie only became part of France as late as 1860. More than that, some of these towns and regions, and other areas besides, have not always consistently been part of the French national territory. Here, the best example is the Lorraine area in the east of the country, which moved between French and German control as a function of wartime victory and defeat. Against this background, there was a long-standing fear that peripheral areas were susceptible to secession and/or conquest. As a result, centralization appeared to be a rational response to threat of territorial disintegration. In addition, over and above the issue of whether peripheral areas were likely to secede or be seized, there was a similar fear that the periphery was essentially rebellious. There was a sense that the 'provinces' were politically unreliable and unstable. Moreover, there was a feeling that if rebellion was allowed to take hold in one area, then it might spread elsewhere. So, centralization also seemed to be a rational response to issues relating to internal security. Overall, the only way of ensuring the integrity and stability of the national territory, it was argued, was to rule from the centre.

The second normative foundation of centralization was the belief that local autonomy was an essentially anti-national concept. In Chapter 3, it was noted that the system of State-centred decision-making in France was based on the *jacobin* idea that the State represented the common good, or the national interest. This belief legitimized the notion that the State should take responsibility for public policy-making and that such responsibility should not be left to partial or sectoral interests, such as political parties or pressure groups. By the same token, there was also a belief that only a highly centralized State could properly represent the national interest. Just as political parties and pressure groups were con-sidered to be necessarily self-interested, so too were local actors because their primary concern was for the local area. In this context, if local actors were given the autonomy to pursue these interests, so the argument went, then the national interest would suffer. Thus, in order to promote the national interest, the centre needed to control the periphery. Indeed, it is more appropriate to say that from the early nineteenth century onwards France had a system of local administration rather than a system of local government. In other words, the basic task of people in positions of responsibility at the local level was simply to implement decisions taken in Paris.

The force of these two normative principles has weakened over the years. The threat of secession receded. Moreover, even though French poli-tics remains volatile and unpredictable, the fear that the periphery was an essentially rebellious place has also diminished. By contrast, the experience of revolutionary and imperial politics had shown that the centre was a potentially repressive and undemocratic force. Thus, its power had to be diluted. In addition, a system of local *notables* developed. These were people who were highly influential at the local level, for example as mayors of large towns, but who were also elected to the national parliament and often held office in government. This form of multiple office-holding is known as the *cumul des mandats* (see Chapter 6). The development of the *cumul des mandats* led to an intermingling of central and local interests. The *notables* could be relied upon to defend the Republic in the localities, while they were also in a position to represent the interests of periphery at the centre. The result was a more entrenched and secure Republic, but also pressure for a greater degree of local autonomy. The first decentralization reforms were passed in 1871 and 1884 during the early years of the Third Republic. There was also a gradual increase in the degree of functional or administrative decentralization in the period after 1944, even if the centre still dominated the periphery. However, the most important changes occurred when the Socialists won power in 1981. In the period 1982–4 the Minister of the Interior and Decentralization, Gaston Defferre, was able to pass a suite of reforms that President Mitterrand himself called 'la grande affaire' of his term of office. The real extent of decentralization is still debated (see Elgie and Griggs 2000: ch. 4). However, there is little doubt that the Defferre reforms fundamentally changed the nature of centre–periphery relations in France.

In sum, the normative principles that underpin the contemporary system of French local government are now much more varied than was previously the case. For example, it is certainly true that the belief that only a highly centralized State can properly represent the national interest is still held by a certain section of the population. Indeed, this is one of the main preoccupations of the 2002 presidential candidate, former Minister of the Interior, and leader of the Pôle républicain, Jean-Pierre Chevènement. Even so, there is now a broad degree of consensus that decision-making needs to reflect the tremendous degree of economic, social, and cultural variation that occurs across the set of regions, cities, towns, and villages of France as a whole. Within this section of the political class, though, there is disagreement over whether there is a need for another major set of decentralization reforms, or whether the current system is basically sound. In general terms, the Greens, and perhaps the Socialist party too, would appear to be more favourable to such reform than the other parties. However, in recent times President Chirac has also emphasized the need for further decentralization reforms. Indeed, the same is true for the Prime

Minister who was appointed after the 2002 presidential election, Jean-Pierre Raffarin. As a result, the likelihood is that in the years to come the issue of decentralization will remain politically salient. Indeed, one of the first tasks of the Raffarin government was to prepare a new decentralisation reform. The rest of this chapter identifies the main actors and institutions that operate within the French system of centre–periphery relations.

Actors and institutions: the central level

There are three main categories of actors and institutions that represent the interests of the central State. These are: Ministers and Ministries; prefects; and the State's deconcentrated services.

Ministers and Ministries

As befits the highly compartmentalized State structure in France (see Chapter 5), a number of Ministers and Ministries have responsibility for local affairs. Over the years, the titles of some of these organizations have changed. However, in general terms it is useful to identify four main actors: the Ministry of the Interior; the Ministry for Local Development; the Ministry for State Reform; and both the President and the Prime Minister.[1]

The most prominent organization with responsibility for local affairs has long been the Ministry of the Interior. In the past, the Ministry of the Interior was synonymous with France's highly centralized system of local administration. This was partly because the Ministry has responsibility for the work of the prefectoral system. As we shall see below, prefects were the main agents of the State in each of the local departments and, prior to the 1982 decentralization reforms, their main role was to ensure that local authorities faithfully implemented the policies of the central government. It was also because the Ministry has responsibility for the police. As a result, in conjunction with prefects and the government information-gathering services (*les renseignements généraux*), the Ministry had a major role to play in maintaining law and order at the local level. This led to the Ministry being portrayed in popular mythology at least as a repressive force that maintained the dominant position of the centre by force if necessary. In recent times, though, the role of the Ministry of the Interior has changed somewhat. It is certainly the case that some recent Ministers have continued to have a very traditional, *jacobin* view of centre–periphery relations. For example, in July 2000 Jean-Pierre Chevènement resigned from his post in protest at the government's decision to allow the Corsican Assembly the right to amend national legislation to suit its own needs. That said, the fact that in 1981 Gaston Defferre held the title Minister of the Interior and Decentralization minimized the risk that the government's decentralization reforms would be vetoed or at least delayed. In fact, the vast majority of the Ministry's activity is now focused on basic law and order issues, including cross-border problems, such as drug trafficking, illegal immigration, and terrorism, as well as matters relating to crime, internal security, and delinquency at home. Overall, even though the Ministry of the Interior maintains a general responsibility for the institutional architecture of centre–periphery relations, there is now much less of a preoccupation with keeping the potentially rebellious periphery in check. Moreover, as we shall see, the role of prefects has changed considerably. They are no longer the agents of what was commonly portrayed as a fundamentally repressive State.

A second organization with responsibility for local affairs has been the Ministry for Local Development. This organization has its origins in the context of the general concern for national planning that began in the immediate post-war period (see Chapter 3). By the early 1960s, there was a desire to focus attention on local development more specifically. In 1963, this led to the creation of an interministerial agency, the Delegation for Local Development and Regional Action (DATAR), and then, in 1967, a Ministry for Planning and Local Development. Over the years, the precise title, location, and status of the Ministry have varied.[2] Even so, the Ministry has consistently been involved in trying to promote the economic development of areas outside Paris. On occasions, this aspect of its work has brought it into conflict with the Ministry of the Interior. This was particularly true in the period 1997–2000 when the Green Minister for Local Development and the Environment, Dominique Voynet, was opposed to many of the principles of the Minister of the Interior, Jean-Pierre Chevènement. Indeed, in 1999 both Ministers presented local government reforms that were underpinned by quite different ideas, with the pro-European, regionalist-oriented Voynet being pitted against the anti-European, *jacobin* Chevènement. Whatever the particularities of the relationship, given that the essential mission of the Ministry for Local Development has been to increase the economic performance of relatively deprived areas, it has often been viewed rather more favourably than the Ministry of the Interior by local decision-makers.

Another institution with a concern for centre–periphery relations has been the Ministry for State Reform. This Ministry was particularly active during the Jospin government from 1997 to 2002. However, similar organizations existed previously. For example, during much of the 1960s there was a Ministry for Administrative Reform. Indeed, the Minister at the time, Louis Joxe, was responsible for the creation of DATAR. During the Jospin government, one key aspect of the work of the Ministry for the Public Service and State Reform was to implement the government's policy of deconcentration, or the transfer of public-sector institutions and employees from Paris to elsewhere (see below). More generally, the Ministry has been concerned with principles of new public management (see Chapter 5). In this context, as part of the desire to ensure the most efficient delivery of public services, the Ministry addressed a number of issues that affected centre–periphery relations, including the provision of public services at the local level.

The final set of actors who have a major role at the central level comprises the President and the Prime Minister. Outside 'cohabitation' the President is expected to exercise policy leadership (see Chapter 4). As a result, a number of centre–local initiatives have been associated with the President of the day. This is particularly true for the failed referendum on local government in 1969 under de Gaulle, the creation of regional administrative units in the early 1970s under Pompidou, and the decentralization laws of the early 1980s under Mitterrand, even if these were piloted extremely skilfully by Gaston Defferre. As noted above, President Chirac has recently emphasized the need for further decentralization reforms. Indeed, in December 1998, during the last period of 'cohabitation', he made a major speech at Rennes in which he promised to reinvigorate local democracy. This pledge was reiterated during the 2002 election campaign and the issue has already become a central theme of his second term of office. In addition, the Prime Minister is also an important actor. In Chapter 4, we saw that the Prime Minister is expected to coordinate the policy-making process. Given that issues regarding centre–periphery relations cut across ministerial boundaries, Prime Ministers have been obliged to provide a certain coherence to government policies in this regard. This was perhaps most notably the case for

Debré and Pompidou in the 1960s. Moreover, during the most recent period of 'cohabitation', Prime Minister Jospin established a working group, headed by the former head of government, Pierre Mauroy, which produced a long report with dozens of recommendations for reform (Mauroy 2000). The fact that the group failed to establish cross-party support for the report was one of the reasons why its main proposals were never implemented. However, Prime Minister Raffarin has already prepared a major set of reform that will lead, all being well, to a constitutional amendment in 2003.

Prefects

The origins of the prefectural system can be found in the so-called *intendants* of the *ancien régime*. The present-day prefectural system was established by Napoleon Bonaparte in 1800. The basis of this system was the presence of a government-appointed prefect in every French department (the equivalent of a British county—see below). There are now ninety-six mainland prefects and four prefects in overseas departments. Within the various mainland departments, there are also 326 deputy prefects (*sous-préfets*) as well as thirteen deputy prefects in the overseas departments.

The prefectural system was deliberately designed to ensure that the centre controlled the periphery. There was both an administrative and a political aspect to the work of prefects in this regard (de Montricher 2000). In the first place, prefects were charged with ensuring the implementation of government policy in the localities. They were charged with the overall maintenance of law and order at the local level and they had responsibility for reporting information about the localities back to Paris on a regular basis. They also came to be responsible for coordinating the work of the deconcentrated services of the various government Ministries (see below). Secondly, the prefect was officially designated as the executive of the departmental council (or general council—see below). This power, the so-called power of tutelage (or *la tutelle*), meant that they had a *de facto* veto over actions proposed by the departmental authority. The prefect was also responsible for implementing the departmental council's decisions once they had been agreed. Indeed, prefects had the power to dismiss councils if they felt the need arose. Overall, then, the basic role of the prefect was to ensure internal stability and policy uniformity. Thus, the prefectural system was a direct expression of the normative foundations on which the system of centre–periphery relations as a whole was based.

A key aspect of the prefectural system was that prefects were, and still are, appointed by the President of the Republic in the Council of Ministers on the advice of the Minister of the Interior. This situation has meant that over the years there has been a politicization of the prefectural system. In his comprehensive study, Rouban (2000: 538–41) identified three key periods in this regard. First, in the early, and turbulent, years of the Third Republic (see Chapter 1) there was a very high turnover of prefects as governments appointed people whom they felt could be trusted. So, for example, in 1873 there were 40 new appointments, in 1877 there were 73 changes, and in 1879 and 1880 there were a further 49 new faces. Secondly, during the Vichy and Liberation periods there was another wave of nominations. So, the Vichy government dismissed a total of 40 prefects, while the Liberation governments made no fewer than 66 appointments in 1944 and 1945. Finally, there was a particularly high rate of change in the 1980s. In the first three months of the 1981 Mauroy government, the prefect was changed in 58 departments. Moreover, in a similar period of the 1986 Chirac administration and the 1993 Balladur government 23 and 36 changes were made respectively.[3] Previously (the Vichy period aside), there was a distinct republican logic that legitimized these changes and others. The prefect was the agent of a government that was responsible to the legislature which had been elected by the people (Grémion 2000: 555). In the 1980s and 1990s, though, it is difficult to see the high turnover of prefects as anything more than part of a French-style spoils system—a patronage power that successive governments were happy to use for their own partisan ends.

There is no doubt that in the past the prefectural system was considered to be part of a set of political institutions that were deliberately designed to create a highly centralized system of government. All the same, various writers have suggested that prefects were more integrated into the local system of politics than the formal organization of power would have appeared to suggest (Worms 1966). For example, as part of a general model of centre–periphery relations, Grémion (1976) argues that there was always a high degree of interaction between the prefect and local *notables*. This was because prefects found it easier and more efficient to work with local representatives than to oppose them. The result was that prefects often defended the interests of their local interlocutors in meetings with officials in Paris. They became an ally of local *notables* rather than an enemy. Thus, one sub-prefect was quoted as saying: 'At the same time as they control local authorities, the Ministry of the Interior and prefects respond to the needs and worries of locally elected representatives. All the main problems that the latter have to deal with end up at the prefecture and then the Place Beauvau [the site of the Ministry of the Interior in Paris]. The people who exercise control, who first and foremost are meant to impose rules on local authorities, cannot ignore their difficulties and rapidly transform themselves into the role of spokespersons for them' (quoted in Grémion 1976: 182). In other words, there is evidence that in practice the French system was somewhat less centralized than the formal set of institutional arrangements might have suggested.

Whatever the informal relationship between prefects and local *notables* might have been, there is no doubt that over the years the nature of the system has changed. For example, in 1964 prefects were also appointed at the regional level. There are now twenty-two regional prefects in mainland France and four regional prefects overseas. Moreover, when the left won power in the early 1980s, they were given the title 'commissaires de la République', only for the term 'prefect' to be reinstated when the right returned to office in 1986. More fundamentally, the 1982 decentralization reforms were explicitly designed to reduce the power of prefects. To this end there were several high-profile changes. For example, the prefect was no longer officially designated the chief executive of the departmental council. Instead, this responsibility was now incumbent upon the president of the departmental council, who was an elected representative. This reform strengthened the democratic credentials of local government. In addition, the prefect no longer enjoyed the power of tutelage. The prefect lost the power to veto council decisions before they were implemented. Instead, the prefect can now only call them into question after they come into force, such as by referring them to the regional courts of accounts (see Chapter 7). This reform strengthened the rule of law across the system. More generally, the prefect has now come to play a major role as a policy coordinator at the local level. For instance, the prefect is closely involved in the negotiation of regional development plans (see below). Indeed, the same point applies to the contracts that the State draws up with town councils and departmental councils. Overall, what is clear is that prefects are now much less preoccupied with maintaining uniformity across the national territory and are more concerned with coordinating the work of central and local actors in their own geographical area. In short, there has been a shift from a 'military model' of the prefect to a 'managerial model' (Rouban 2000).

The State's deconcentrated services

The State's deconcentrated services may be defined as 'the different State administrations that are located on the national territory, or indeed abroad, with a view to carrying out the work of the central administrations' (Quermonne 1991: 118). There is a clear split within French Ministries between the central administration and these deconcentrated services (or *services extérieurs* as they were known until 1992). Moreover, there is a hierarchical relationship between the two with the former being superior to the latter. This means that the central administration controls matters relating to the recruitment, promotion, and dismissal of people working outside Paris. It also means that the centre defines the areas in which the deconcentrated services can operate. There are various estimates as to the percentage of civil servants who work in the various organizations that comprise the State's deconcentrated services. However, it is safe to say that the figure is somewhere between 90 and 98 per cent. So, while there is little doubt that the most senior civil servants in the central administration have the potential to be important political actors (see Chapter 5), the role of the officials who work for the State outside the central administration in Paris should also be noted.

The deconcentrated services of French Ministries, like their central administration counterparts (see Chapter 5), are organized on a functional basis. That is to say, individual administrative units have responsibility for specific elements of the Ministry's work. These units are usually located in the main town of a department (often called *directions départementales*). The nature of these services can be illustrated by using the example of the so-called *Directions départementales de l'équipement* (or DDEs). They had a long-standing responsibility for road-building and town-planning. They were staffed by highly skilled scientific technocrats from the Roads and Bridges *corps* (see Chapter 5) and they had a major influence on the infrastructural development of the geographical area in which they operated. In so doing, however, they often forged close relations with local authorities. After all, local representatives were usually the ones who lobbied most forcefully for new roads to be built and so forth. The net result of this organization, though, was a highly compartmentalized system and an absence of joined-up government. There was conflict, or at the very least a lack of coordination, between the deconcentrated services of different Ministries—for example, DDEs wanted to make sure that there was money for road-building in their area rather than, say, agriculture. There was also conflict between the different territorial units carrying out the same function—DDEs in different areas competed with each other to make sure that their own road-building projects were approved. Finally, there was conflict between the central administrative units of individual Ministries and their deconcentrated services. The central administration often felt that the deconcentrated services had been captured by local interests.

Against this background, there have been repeated attempts to improve the coordination of government policy over the years. In the post-war period, particularly with the 1964 administrative reform, attempts were made to introduce regionally based deconcentrated services. Their role was to coordinate the work of the various departmental services in the region. Prefects were also charged with coordinating the work of the State's deconcentrated services (see above). More importantly still, the 1982 decentralization reforms transferred many of the functions that were previously carried out by the State's deconcentrated services to local authorities. This meant that officials who used to be employed by government Ministries were now employed by local councils. Arguably, this made it easier to coordinate policy because the responsibility for both making decisions and implementing them was concentrated in a smaller area and in smaller units.

In recent times, the issue of deconcentration has remained prominent. In 1992, the Cresson government issued what is called a 'deconcentration charter' (in the same spirit as John Major's Citizen's Charter in the UK). The deconcentration charter was part of the general reform of the State that was under way at the time. More specifically, it was an attempt to bring decision-making closer to the people and to do so in a way that helped local economic development. The 1992 law stated that the central administration was only responsible for matters that were national in nature, or for matters that were not able to be delegated to an authority at a local level. By implication, everything else should be carried out by units that operated as close as possible to the point of service delivery. Thus, it was an attempt to close the gap between the elite in Paris and citizens throughout the rest of the country. More than that, the Cresson government and subsequent governments have actively pursued the policy of physically transferring organizations from the Paris region to the provinces. This is part of an attempt to improve the quality of life of public-sector employees. It is also supposed to have the effect of bringing economic resources to less well-off areas. In the period 1991–2000 inclusive, a total of 35,200 public-sector employees were scheduled for transfer and around 20,000 transfers actually took place (source: www.citep.gouv.fr—accessed 9 May 2002). In short, the long-standing belief that administrative resources should be concentrated at the centre has been successfully challenged.

Actors and institutions: the sub-central level

There are three main categories of actors and institutions at the sub-central level. These are: communes, departments, and regions.[4]

Communes

The commune is the most basic administrative unit of local government. This does not mean, though, that it is the least important. There is no official hierarchy across the three main tiers of French local government. Communes, departments, and regions all have equal status. Moreover, some communes are so large, such as Paris, Marseille, Lyon, Bordeaux, and Lille, that the person who heads the elected council (the municipal council) is likely already to be or will almost inevitably become an important national political figure. For example, Jacques Chirac was the mayor of Paris 1977–95. The most noticeable feature of this element of the French system of local government is the sheer number of communes. In 1999, there was a grand total of 36,565 communes in mainland France. Inevitably, this means that the vast majority of communes are extremely small (see Table 8.1). In 1999, only 874 communes had more than 10,000 inhabitants (the size of a small town). By contrast, 1,006 had fewer than

50 inhabitants. Given that every commune elects a municipal council and that the municipal council in even the smallest commune comprises a minimum of nine councillors, it is hardly surprising that there are more than 500,000 municipal councillors in France. There is no doubt, therefore, that the communes are an important expression of democracy in the French system as a whole. They do bring representative government close to the people. However, there are doubts as to whether the communes constitute the most efficient way of organizing a system of local government. They are, perhaps, an expensive luxury.

There are elections to municipal councils every six years. The last set of elections was in 2001. The electoral system is extremely complicated. There is a two-ballot system. In communes with more than 3,500 inhabitants, parties usually run a list of candidates. If a list wins more than 50 per cent of the valid votes cast, then that list automatically wins 50 per cent of the council seats. The remaining seats are then distributed across all the lists that won more than 5 per cent of the vote, including the winning list once again, on a proportional basis. If no list wins more than 50 per cent of the valid votes cast, then there is a second ballot. Here, only those lists that won more than 10 per cent of the votes cast at the first ballot can stand again. At

TABLE 8.1	The number and size of communes in mainland France
Number of inhabitants	Number of communes
0–99	3,911
100–499	17,124
500–999	6,759
1,000–1,999	4,133
2,000–2,999	1,530
3,000–4,999	1,259
5,000–9,999	975
10,000–29,999	633
30,000–49,999	129
50,000–99,999	76
100,000–299,999	31
Over 300,000	5
Total	36,565

Source: Ministère de l'intérieur, Direction générale des collectivités locales, *Les Collectivités locales en chiffres*, Paris, La Documentation française, 2001: 14.

this ballot, the list with the most votes (even if this figure is less than 50 per cent) automatically wins 50 per cent of the council seats. The remaining seats are then distributed in the same way as described above. Overall, then, it is a majoritarian system with a dose of proportionality. The proportional element was included in the 1982 decentralization reforms. In addition, as part of the 1999 parity reforms, lists now have to include an equal number of male and female candidates. This was an attempt to increase the representation of women in local government (see also Chapter 6).

The most important person within the commune is the head of the municipal council, the mayor. The mayor is elected by the council. However, the person elected is invariably the head of the victorious list. Thus, municipal elections are often highly personalized. At the head of the competing lists, there will be rival candidates for the post of mayor. Thus, there is what amounts to the *de facto* direct election of the mayor. This is one of the reasons why the mayors of large towns can command attention at the national level and why established politicians often seek election at the local level as mayor. For example, in 2000 Martine Aubry resigned her post as a senior government Minister so that she could prepare her campaign for the municipal elections in Lille the following year. She was successful and replaced the outgoing mayor, former Prime Minister Pierre Mauroy. For his part, Mauroy had come to prominence in the 1970s precisely because of his success in this important town in the north of the country. Indeed, following the 2002 elections, a total of 264 deputies simultaneously held the post of mayor and a further 52 held the post of deputy mayor (see Chapter 6). It might also be noted that 128 Senators also held the position of mayor in the 2002 Senate (source: **www.senat.fr/listes/index.html**— accessed 16 May 2002). The position of mayor is so important because the mayor is the chief executive of the commune. This means that the mayor is responsible for implementing the decisions of the municipal council. In fact, this means that the mayor is responsible for showing leadership at the communal level. The council usually ratifies decisions prepared by the municipal executive. In addition, the mayor is also the head of the commune's administrative services. This means that the mayor is officially responsible for the employment, promotion, and dismissal of municipal employees.

The municipal council carries out many of the basic tasks of service delivery commonly associated with local government. For example, the commune is responsible for maintaining the record of births and deaths and the electoral register, and carries out a range of similar information-collection tasks. The mayor (or an assistant) also performs civil marriage ceremonies. (A civil ceremony is obligatory in France, even if there is a religious ceremony as well.) The municipal council looks after meals for certain pensioners and organizes child-care facilities. The council is also charged with the upkeep of local roads. This is a particularly costly task. The commune has responsibility for the construction, maintenance, and equipment of primary schools. The commune has also traditionally looked after issues relating to waste management. Over and above these basic tasks, the various decentralization reforms of the 1980s transferred the responsibility for certain functions from the State's deconcentrated services to the communes (see above). Thus, communes became responsible for town-planning. They were also given more responsibilities for cultural affairs. Indeed, this has been one of the areas where the activity of municipal councils has increased rapidly in recently years (see below). Finally, communes have the opportunity to intervene more directly in issues relating to economic development. The net result is that both in terms of brute numbers and in relation to departments and regions municipal councils have large numbers of employees (see Table 8.2). Indeed, in 1999 32.4 per cent of total spending at the communal level went on council workers.[5]

The funding for municipal councils comes from a variety of sources (Gohin and Cabannes 2000: 62–7) (see Table 8.3). The largest proportion, around 50 per cent, comes from taxation. Strictly speaking, municipal

TABLE 8.2	The local public administration (*fonction publique locale*), 2000	
	Total no. of employees	%
Regional and departmental institutions	245,136	14.5
Municipal institutions	1,145,442	67.9
Intercommunal institutions	122,822	7.3
Other	174,351	10.3
Total	1,687,751	100.0

Source: Ministère de l'intérieur, Direction générale des collectivités locales, *Les Collectivités locales en chiffres*, Paris, La Documentation française, 2001: 108.

councils do not impose their own sales taxes or income tax. Instead, the vast majority of their income in this regard comes from direct taxes, which are established at the national level (such as the *taxe d'habitation* and the *taxe professionnelle*). However, communes do have the power, within strict limits, to set the rate of these various taxes in their own area. As a result, some areas have been able to attract industry by reducing the rate of local business taxes. Another large proportion, around 25 per cent, takes the form of a transfer payment from central government. A roughly equivalent percentage is raised from service charges. In addition, there is the option to borrow money, but only up to a certain percentage of their assets.

In this context, in recent years the system of municipal councils has been characterized by three main features. First, there has been a drive to decrease the number of communes, or, at least to decrease the number of administrative units at the communal level. This is the policy of inter-communality. Laws passed in 1992 and 1999 encouraged communes to cooperate with each other. Moreover, the 1999 law strengthened the legal basis of the cooperation, furthered the potential for the powers of municipal councils to be shifted to the intercommunal level, and increased the fiscal powers of the resulting institutions. By the beginning of 2002, a total of 2,174 intercommunal organizations with their own fiscal powers had been created. Thus, even if the number of communes has not decreased, there is greater potential for intercommunal cooperation and policy efficiency. Secondly, municipal councils generally enjoy a greater degree of autonomy than was previously the case. For example, John and Cole

TABLE 8.3	Income by the different levels of local government in France, 1999 (in billions of euro)			
	Region	Dept.	Commune	Intercommunal organization
Income from taxes	6.94	22.31	36.94	5.58
Non-fiscal income (transfers, borrowing, etc.)	5.75	15.66	36.53	16.20
Total	12.69	37.96	73.48	21.78

Source: Ministère de l'intérieur, Direction générale des collectivités locales, *Les Collectivités locales en chiffres*, Paris, La Documentation française, 2001: 43.

(2000) stress the varied nature of policy networks across different policy sectors. A similar point is made by Le Galès (2001). Both sets of writers suggest that there is now a more varied set of actors (both public and private) and a greater variety of instruments (partnerships, programmes, contracts, and so forth) involved in municipal policy-making than there used to be. As a result, in some policy areas, such as culture and urban planning and property development, municipal councils now have more room in which to manoeuvre than was previously the case. In short, there is now greater differentiation across communes than before. Thirdly, even if municipal councils enjoy a greater degree of autonomy than before, the State remains a key actor in the relationship between the centre and the municipalities. The smallest communes remain heavily dependent on the State's deconcentrated services. They do not have the resources to employ large numbers of council workers, so they rely on the State to carry out functions on their behalf. Similarly, even though the larger communes employ large numbers of council workers, they are faced with such severe social problems that they are unable to tackle them effectively by themselves. Thus, they look to the centre for assistance. Moreover, even within their own sphere of competence, municipal councils are largely dependent on the grant they receive from the central government. In this sense, the system of municipal government remains fundamentally centralized.

Departments

The departmental system was established in 1790 in the period immediately following the Revolution. At the time, the boundaries of the departments were determined so that no point was more than one day's ride on horseback from the main town in the department. Over the years, the number of departments has fluctuated. There are now 100 departments, 96 of which can be found in mainland France. Initially, the role of the departmental council was purely administrative. Indeed, following the creation of the prefectural system in 1800, there was no doubt that the most important figure at this level of the system was the prefect (see above). However, in 1871 elections to departmental councils—otherwise known as general councils (*conseils généraux*)—were permitted. These historical roots mean that the French have a strong attachment to their own department. However, there is a growing feeling among parts of the political and technocratic class that the department is an increasingly outmoded level of local government.

There are elections to departmental councils every three years. The term of office for departmental councillors is six years. This means that elections are staggered, with one half of the council's members being elected every three years.[6] The basic constituency unit in each department is known as the canton (and elections to the departmental council are known as cantonal elections). Each canton returns one councillor. Elections are held under the two-ballot majority system, similar to the one used for National Assembly elections (see Chapter 6). The number of cantons does vary from one department to another, but in general terms rural areas are over-represented. In other words, departments with high population densities (around Paris, for example) do not necessarily have a much greater number of councillors than departments in less populated areas. There is, thus, a basic conservative bias to the departmental system. This bias is reflected in elections to the Senate, where departmental councillors are one of the core electoral constituencies and where the right has an in-built majority (see Chapter 6).

The president of the departmental council has generally been considered to be a less important position than the mayor of a large town or city. In the past, the same person often held both posts. However, now that the number of elected offices people can hold simultaneously has been reduced (the *cumul des mandats*), most deputies have chosen to hold the post of mayor or president of the regional council at the expense of other posts. Thus, at the end of the 1997–2002 legislature, only nineteen deputies also held the position of president of the departmental council (see Chapter 6). In 1979, when the right was also in power, the equivalent figure was twenty-four (Hayward 1983: 34).[7] There are various reasons for this trend. The main factor is that there is now more scope for policy creativity at the level of large towns and regions (see below) than at the departmental level. Indeed, one writer has argued that following the decentralization reforms in the 1980s and 1990s towns have been extending their policy influence, regions have been appropriating their institutional territory, but departments have been forced merely to defend or preserve their traditional functions (Michel 1998: 165). Overall, there is a sense that departments are neither small enough to be in direct contact with citizens (like communes), nor large enough to provide economies of scale (like regions). In other words, they are an increasingly inefficient unit of administration.

The income received by departments comes from the same sorts of sources as for communes (see Table 8.3). As a result, there is a heavy reliance of transfers from the central State. Departmental councils carry out a range of essential tasks and they account for a considerable proportion of total local government expenditure (see Table 8.4). The main area of the department's activity comprises social affairs. Indeed, in 1983 a number of tasks in this domain were transferred to departments from the State's deconcentrated services. So, departments are now explicitly responsible for public health issues, such as vaccinations, as well as matters relating to social policy, such as the provision of low-cost council housing. Around 40 per cent of the department's recurrent expenditure occurs in this area. In addition, departments have an important role to play in terms of rural and local development. For example, they promote tourism in the local area. They are also charged with the upkeep of main roads. In this domain and others, they often work closely with small communes providing infrastructural services which would be too costly for individual communes to fund for themselves. Finally, departments are responsible for certain educational and cultural matters. For instance, the 1982 decentralization reforms entrusted departments with the construction and maintenance of *collèges*, or post-primary schools. They also have duties in relation to areas as varied as public libraries and the protection and maintenance of historic monuments. The bottom line is that departments deliver a range of basic services. All the same, and in contrast to communes (see above), only 10.6 per cent of all departmental expenditure goes

TABLE 8.4	Spending by the different levels of local government in France, 1999 (in billions of euro)			
	Region	Dept.	Commune	Intercommunal organization
Day-to-day spending	5.64	24.32	50.15	11.53
Investment spending	7.06	13.38	22.46	12.30
Total	12.70	37.70	72.61	23.84

Source: Ministère de l'intérieur, Direction générale des collectivités locales, *Les Collectivités locales en chiffres*, Paris, La Documentation française, 2001: 43.

towards employing council workers. Thus, while municipal councils have a very direct impact on the lives and livelihoods of the people in the immediate local area because they employ so many council workers, the same point is not quite so true for departmental councils.

In fact, the position of departments has been increasingly criticized in recent times. In particular, the geographical organization of the departmental system has been ridiculed. After all, very few people would set out on horseback from the main town in the department any more. More generally, there is a feeling that the functions of departmental councils could be transferred to municipal councils and regional councils without any major difficulties. Altogether, the department, some believe, now represents an anachronistic element of the French system of local government. Partly as a result, there has been somewhat less opportunity for policy innovation at the departmental level. At the same time, there is no doubt that departments remain a popular level of government. One writer reports the findings of a survey which showed that 78 per cent of people supported the departmental structure, while only 14 per cent opposed it (Grémion 1992: 59). Moreover, support for the department was even stronger in rural areas, where 85 per cent of people in communes with fewer than 2,000 inhabitants supported the departmental structure (ibid.). In fact, even the recent Mauroy report acknowledged that the debate over the most appropriate role for the department was largely confined to the political elites in Paris and was of little interest to the public at large (Mauroy 2000: 43). In short, even if departments are now perhaps the poor relation among the set of sub-central units of government, it would be a very brave government that decided to abolish them.

Regions

In contrast to communes and departments, regions are a relatively recent creation. While in some senses regionalism has a long history (Deyon 1998), governments only began to pay particular attention to the regional level in the period after the Second World War (see Mény 1974). Equally, in some regions, such as Brittany, there was an increasing sense of cultural identity during the same period. The result was a growing sense of the need for administrative and representative institutions at the regional level (Quermonne 1991: 118–21). For example, in 1963, the regional development agency, DATAR, was created (see above). In 1969, President de Gaulle held a referendum, one element of which was the proposal to create a new (but unelected) level of regional government. The referendum was defeated and de Gaulle resigned (see Chapter 4). However, in 1972 a similar reform was passed by de Gaulle's successor, President Pompidou. This reform was largely symbolic. It established a set of (at that time unelected) regional councils with very few powers. Moreover, the geographical organization of the regions was deliberately designed to frustrate micro-nationalist movements, by placing departments with a common cultural identity in separate regional areas. All the same, the 1972 reform provided a foundation for regional government. This tier of government was enhanced with the 1982 decentralization reforms. These reforms provided for the direct election of regional councils and transferred a number of important policy-making responsibilities to the regional level. Since this time, regions have emerged as important political actors. Moreover, a sense of regional identity has quickly developed among the population at this level. All told, if there is to be further decentralization in the near future, the chances are that regions will benefit from the resulting situation.

There are twenty-one regions in mainland France. There are elections to regional councils every six years. The first set of elections was held in 1986. Previously, the department was the basic electoral constituency. At this level, there was a form of fairly pure proportional representation for each party list. In 1998, the net result of this system was not just the absence of a single-party majority in any region, but a highly fragmented form of party political representation that made coalition-building of any reasonable sort extremely difficult. Indeed, in some cases, notably the Centre and the Rhône-Alpes councils, local right-wing politicians preferred to reach an agreement with representatives of the extreme right rather than see the left gain control of the council (see Chapter 2). As a reaction to these outcomes, the electoral system was reformed in 1999 and the next set of regional elections in 2004 is scheduled to be held under a two-ballot system similar to the one used for municipal elections. Here, the region itself will be the electoral constituency. If a party list wins more than 50 per cent of the votes cast at the first ballot, then that list will win 25 per cent of the total number of council seats with the rest being distributed proportionally among all the parties that won more than 3 per cent of the votes cast (including the winning list again). If no party wins more than 50 per cent, then there is a second ballot in which the seats are distributed in the same way, even if the winning list wins less than 50 per cent of the vote. At the second ballot, only lists which won more than 5 per cent of the votes cast at the first ballot can stand again. Overall, the hope is that moderate parties or coalitions will manage to win a majority of council seats and that extreme parties will not be called upon to make up the numbers.

The key actor at the regional level is the president of the regional council. The president is the head of the executive of the regional council and, thus, is responsible for the council's budget. The president is also the head of the council's administrative services. In the last decade, this position has become highly sought after. At the end of the 1997–2002 legislature, seven National Assembly deputies simultaneously held this post as well (source: **www.assemblee-nationale.fr/qui/statistiques.asp**—accessed 14 May 2002), even though the figure fell to just three following the 2002 election (see Chapter 6). In addition, nine people simultaneously held the position of Senator and president of the regional council. Again, this is an indicator of the growing importance attached to this office. Indeed, Jean-Pierre Raffarin made his name as president of the Poitou-Charentes region prior to his appointment as Prime Minister in May 2002.

Regional councils carry out a small number of specific tasks. For example, following the 1982 decentralization reforms, regions have responsibility for the upkeep and maintenance of secondary schools. They have duties in relation to tourism and culture. They also have responsibility for professional training and apprenticeship policies in the local area. In reality, though, the success of regional governments in some of these areas has been quite limited. For instance, in the area of professional training and apprenticeships regions have not been able to have the impact that they might have expected (Bernard-Steindecker 1998). In fact, regions have been most successful in the areas where they have somewhat more general policy competences. Notably, regions came to prominence in the 1980s and 1990s when the European Union decided to administer its so-called structural funds through units of government at the regional level. More importantly still, in France the 1982 decentralization reforms gave regions an overarching responsibility for economic development at the sub-national level. Amongst other things, regions are involved in the development of infrastructure projects, economic assistance, and environmental issues. This area of responsibility has been underpinned by a series of

State–Region Planning Contracts (*contrats de plan État–région*). These began in 1989 and the fourth generation of such contracts was negotiated in 1999 between the State, the regional prefect, regional councillors, and other local actors. These negotiations identified the main economic development needs of the various regions for the period 2000–6. These priorities were then enshrined in law and funding was promised. The effect of these contracts has been to establish a privileged relationship between the State and the regions in France. Moreover, it has allowed regions to identify their own priority issues and to seek funding for them. In short, it has allowed leaders at the regional level to show a degree of policy leadership.

In the future, regions are likely to become an even more important focus of political attention. They are large enough to provide economies of scale in terms of planning and development. At the same time, the public has quickly developed a sense of regional identity and a positive appreciation of the role played by regional councils (Dupoirier 1998: 197–200). Partly as a result, a number of regions have established international links. For example, the relationship between the Rhône-Alpes region and equivalent areas in Germany, Italy, and Spain has been well documented elsewhere (Dunford 1995: 167–8). Equally, Jean-Pierre Raffarin at the head of the Poitou-Charentes region was a key actor in the development of the so-called Atlantic Arc that links areas in a variety of different States on the western periphery of Europe. In a different context altogether, regions have also emerged as an important partner for communes and departments in the development and financing of projects at the sub-regional level. Altogether, it is certainly true that regions are hampered by the fact that they still do not have the same level of resources as those enjoyed by either municipal councils or departments. Moreover, the nature of the *contrats de plan* means that the central State still has to approve and fund the projects that regions wish to propose. All the same, regions have shown a great deal of creativity and innovation. They can provide an efficient link between the local policy area and both the national and the European policy area. This strategically important position bodes well for their future development.

Conclusion

There is a sense in which the normative foundations of the French system of local government were always rooted more in myth than reality. Certainly for the last 100 years or more, it was never the case that the centre totally dominated the periphery. Even prior to the 1982 decentralization reforms, the dominant intellectual view of centre–periphery relations in France was that they were characterized by a 'beehive' (Crozier and Thoenig 1975) or 'honeycomb' of informal networks based on a system of mutual interdependence between central State and local actors, most notably prefects and mayors. After the reforms, a similar system is still in place. This has led one influential writer to talk about the 'interlocking' nature of contemporary political society based on both cooperation and competition (Mabileau 1998: 54). Other people have talked about the emergence of local governance, where policy-making is the result of interactions between a wide range of public and private actors (Cole and John 2001; Le Galès 1995). By the same token, it would be wrong to think that before the Defferre reforms there was complete uniformity of service delivery across the range of local government units. In particular, there were, and there remain, considerable differences between small and large communes. Overall, this gap between theory and practice was nicely summed up by one writer who stated: 'the law of the Republic is the same for everyone and in principle guarantees *equality*, but it is flexible enough to take into account the individual habits of each local territory, the place where *liberty* has its roots and can be found; the mix of the two, the general and the specific, the far and the near, creates a *fraternity*, which is another way of saying that people "want to live together"' (Merle 2000: 269).[8]

Whether or not the normative principles of centre–periphery relations were rooted in reality, it is clear that there has been a change in the very foundations of centre–periphery relations over the course of the last twenty or more years. In particular, the left and the right have embraced the belief that decentralization is a good thing. The left became convinced of the need for reform in this area when for more than twenty years following the creation of the Fifth Republic it found itself out of government at the central level. During this time, it maintained support at the local level, but its representatives there had very few prerogatives. The

Defferre decentralization reforms were the result. For its part, the right was sceptical of the 1982 reforms. However, the fact that so many of its most senior political figures simultaneously held office at the local level meant that they were able to enjoy the benefits of greater local autonomy for themselves directly and came to support the call for further reform. Indeed, the Raffarin government has made decentralization one of its top priorities. Equally, the belief in the need for uniform service delivery has also weakened. Political actors on both the left and the right have acknowledged that uniformity is both costly and unnecessarily bureaucratic. Moreover, they have used their new-found powers to develop their local area and, by extension, their own personal reputations and political careers. Thus, the idea of decentralization has taken root and along with it an acknowledgement that diversity is both politically inevitable and economically more efficient.

That said, the traditional ideational foundations of French centre–periphery relations still have a force. There have to be limits to decentralization and the delivery of public services must be safeguarded. For example, even though Jacques Chirac has promoted the policy of decentralization, he has opposed the idea that Corsica should enjoy a greater degree of autonomy in return for an end to political violence on the island. Equally, the President has been more than equivocal in his support for minority languages and ethnic cultures in France. For Chirac, and many like him who are attached to the so-called republican tradition, France is composed of citizens, not communities. Thus, decentralization is considered to be a good thing to the extent that it allows greater freedom for the citizens of the Republic. However, decentralization should be opposed if it runs the risk of creating separate sub-cultures that threaten the one and indivisible nature of the Republic. In this sense, centralization is still very present in the minds of key political actors as a response to the fear of territorial and/or cultural fragmentation. The same point applies to policy uniformity. There is a general belief that autonomy and local experimentation is a good thing. At the same time, there is a worry that autonomy creates inequality. For example, the mayors of large towns may be in a position to bring benefits to their area. However, people who live in small communes in rural communities may end up being left behind. In short, the traditional republican beliefs still have a resonance. Moreover, these beliefs are common to the majority of both the left and the right.

There are differences of emphasis between the various political parties. However, there is a basic commonalty of beliefs. In this regard, the key point is that the issue of centre–periphery relations is just one aspect of a much wider political situation.

....

KEY TERMS

- Centralisation
- Decentralisation
- Multi-level governance

- Equality
- Diversity

....

NOTES

1 In addition, there is usually a Minister for the Overseas Departments and Territories (DOM-TOM). However, this organization will not be considered here.

2 Following the 2002 presidential election, the Ministry was retitled the Ministry for the Civil Service, State Reform, and Local Development.

3 It might be noted that the same pattern was not followed during the Jospin government when only five changes were made during the equivalent period in 1997 (Rouban 2000: 541).

4 In addition, there are three overseas territories (French Polynesia, Wallis and Futuna, and the French Southern and Antarctic Lands), as well as three collectivities with a special status (New Caledonia, Mayotte, and Saint-Pierre-et-Miquelon). These areas will not be considered in this chapter.

5 Source: Ministère de l'intérieur, Direction générale des collectivités locales, *Les Collectivités locales en chiffres*, Paris, La Documentation française, 2001: 59.

6 In 1990, the staggered election procedure was abandoned, only for it to be reinstated in 1994.

7 In 2002, there were also 34 people who simultaneously held the position of Senator and president of the departmental council. To the extent that the Senate is a less dynamic and important institution, this figure is perhaps another indicator of the extent to which the departmental level is seen to be less important than either the municipal level or the regional level.

8 Emphasis in the original.

GUIDE TO FURTHER READING

COLE, A., and JOHN, P., *Local Governance in England and France* (London, Routledge, 2001).

Excellent comparative study of the contemporary system of local government.

LE GALÈS, P. (ed.), *Cities in Contemporary Europe* (Cambridge, Cambridge University Press, 2000).

A comparative analysis of the development of cities.

——and LEQUESNE, C. (eds.), *Regions in Europe* (London, Routledge, 1998).

Comparative study of European regions including France.

LOUGHLIN, J., and MAZEY, S. (eds.), *The End of the French Unitary State? Ten Years of Regionalization in France (1982–1992)* (London, Frank Cass, 1990).

Good overview of the early years of regional government.

SCHMIDT, V., *Democratizing France: The Political and Administrative History of Decentralization* (Cambridge, Cambridge University Press, 1990).

A comprehensive survey of the Defferre decentralization reforms.

9

....

Conclusion

The Fifth Republic was founded on a distinct set of normative principles. There was the idea that political life was characterized by left/right competition. There was the conviction that the State was a legitimate and mobilizing force. There was the belief that strong presidential government was needed to restore the country's national standing both at home and abroad. There was the feeling that highly trained experts should provide policy leadership. There was the notion that only a highly centralized system could ensure the continuance of some of the most basic republican principles. Over the years, these principles have been challenged. They have been challenged for a variety of interrelated reasons: social change, ideological reform, political corruption, Europeanization, globalization, and no doubt many other factors too. Whatever the reason, the changing beliefs and preferences of political actors have helped to bring about institutional change. The role of the State has been called into question. There has been an increase in judicial independence. The legitimacy of so-called policy experts has been undermined. There has been an ongoing process of decentralization. Within this revised institutional framework, the political process operates very differently now from before. The State is less purposive. The President is less able to bring about change. The government is challenged by a wider variety of forces than was previously the case. The bottom line is that the political system of the Fifth Republic has changed and Table 9.1 tries to capture the degree of change in the various areas covered in this book.

Within this general context, two main points need to be made. The first observation is that the degree of institutional change has not been uniform across all areas. In some domains the extent of change has been considerable. This is particularly the case for the State, the judiciary, and local government. It also applies to the structure of party competition. By

TABLE 9.1	The changing political system in France from the 1980s onwards		
Area	Degree of change	Nature of change	Comments
Party system	Great	Ideological division between left and right is less great. Greater number of parties.	Left/right divide is still salient. More fragmented system.
State	Great	Privatization. Deregulation. Liberalization. NPM reforms. Independent agencies.	More fragmented and multi-level system. But public-service ethos still strong.
Executive	Moderate	Cohabitation. Five-year presidential term.	Presidential power is dependent on parties. Five-year term should reinforce party basis of presidential power. Desire for presidential leadership is still present.
Bureaucracy	Moderate	NPM reforms. Technocracy challenged.	System is still fragmented. Belief in need for reform is strong, but opportunity to implement reform is weak.
Legislature	Slight	Single session. Greater scrutiny of EU legislation, budget, and social security funds.	Legislature is dependent on party politics. Party member loyalties are to the majority/opposition.
Judiciary	Great	Rule of law more prominent. Greater role for Constitutional Council, *juges d'instruction*, and European courts.	Governments more constrained by domestic and European actors. But political actors still use judiciary for their own ends.
Local government	Great	Decentralization reforms. EU involvement at regional level.	More local autonomy. Less equality of public service delivery. But myth of the one and indivisible Republic is still present.

contrast, in other areas the degree of change has been much less great. There have been very few changes to the pattern of legislative politics. The bureaucracy has been difficult to reform, even if there have been some noteworthy developments. Equally, the President remains the predominant political actor within the executive. This is true despite the experience of cohabitation and at least partly because of the 2000 constitutional reform that reduced the President's term of office from seven years to five years. The varying degree of institutional change across these different areas means that generalizations about the French political system have to come with a health warning. There has not been a transformation from one type of system to another. More than that, we are not necessarily in a period of transition from one type of system to another. The old system was characterized as hierarchical, monocentric, and majoritarian. The State was believed to be purposive. The President was expected to exercise leadership. The centre dominated the periphery. By contrast, the new system is more multi-level, more pluralistic, and more proportional. The central government is challenged by local pressures and supranational influences—the State is being hollowed out. There is a wider range of significant actors—there are networks of governance containing a multitude of public and private actors. It is more difficult to concentrate power in the hands of a small set of political leaders and decision-makers—there is a greater opportunity for previously excluded forces to influence the political process. All the same, the old system was never quite as hierarchical, monocentric, and majoritarian as was sometimes believed. The State and the bureaucracy were always fragmented. The President was always dependent on the party political forces. There was always a competitive multi-party system. There was a honeycomb pattern of centre–local relations. What is more, the new system still exhibits certain hierarchical, monocentric, and majoritarian characteristics. The State is still a reference point for both left and right, even if representatives from both camps believe it needs to be reformed. The executive still controls the legislature and, after the 2002 elections, within the executive the President dominates the Prime Minister, even if the capacity for presidential leadership has been reduced. Political actors can still influence the judiciary, even if there has been a greater emphasis on the rule of law. Local authorities are still reliant on the centre for funding, even if the degree of local autonomy has increased. France can still influence European policies, even if it has to accept the basic logic of European integration. So, while we can say that there has been a hollowing-out of the French State and that a top-down system of government has been replaced by a more variegated system of governance, we have to acknowledge that some of the more traditional characteristics of the decision-making process are still easily identifiable. The political system has changed, but it is not unrecognizable from what went before.

The second observation is that in the context of this rather messy picture it becomes all the more important that we establish a clear framework for understanding the degree and direction of change in the French system. This book proposed a framework that focused on the interaction of institutions, actors, and ideas. To recap, we focused on institutions because institutional change is the outcome of a process of political competition and because institutions help to structure the ongoing nature of such competition. We focused on actors because institutions do not make decisions. Actors make decisions and they do so on the basis of their preferences and beliefs. We focused on ideas because ideas help us to understand why actors have the basic preferences and beliefs that they do. A framework of this sort is important because it allows us to provide more than just a description of events. Instead, it helps us to understand at least a little better why events occur in the way that they do. For example, the institutions of the State have been reformed because a wide range of political actors no longer believed that State-centred leadership was an appropriate model of political development. In turn, the new architecture of the State has made it more difficult for the President to exercise the same degree of policy leadership as was previously the case. A framework of this sort cannot explain every aspect of political life and it is not designed to do so. Moreover, even if it is appropriate for a study of this sort, it may not be appropriate for a different type of study. Whatever its limitations, hopefully it has helped us to provide a better understanding of why institutional reform occurs as it does and what the consequences of such reform can be.

Overall, the political system of the Fifth Republic combines a difficult mixture of the old and the new. The left is still opposed to the right, but now the ideological differences between the two main camps are much less wide. There is a general conviction that the State has to be reformed, but there is still the belief that there is a place for State intervention in the policy-making process and, certainly, there is a popular demand for it.

The President has increasing difficulty in exercising leadership, but, as the 2002 election showed very clearly, presidential elections are still the defining moment of the political regime and the public continue to want the President to be decisive and provide a coherent direction. There is undoubtedly a need for a set of institutional checks and balances and yet there is a fear of deadlock and stalemate. The public feels alienated from the central State, from Paris, from the political elite, but the public continues to look to the central State for assistance, it responds to a traditional republican rhetoric that emphasizes the national interest, and it votes for the same people who have been part of the political elite for more than thirty years in some cases. The net result is that political actors will continue to emphasize the traditional principles upon which the Fifth Republic was founded. At the same time, they will want to bring about change, even if they are constrained in the sort of change that they can bring about. This is the stuff of contemporary politics generally. It is certainly the stuff of politics in contemporary France.

REFERENCES

ABRAHAM, RONNY (2001), 'La France devant les juridictions européennes', *Pouvoirs*, 96: 143–60.

ARDANT, PHILIPPE (1991), *Le Premier Ministre en France*, Paris, Montchrestien.

ASKOLOVITCH, CLAUDE (2001), *Jospin*, Paris, Grasset.

AUGÉ, PHILIPPE (2001), 'La nouvelle législation sur le cumul des mandats électoraux et des fonctions législatives', *Regards sur l'actualité*, 270: 19–32.

BALLADUR, ÉDOUARD (1989), *Passion et longueur du temps*, Paris, Fayard.

——(1995), *Deux ans à Matignon*, Paris, Plon.

BELORGEY, JEAN-MICHEL (1991), *Le Parlement à refaire*, Paris, Gallimard.

BERGER, SUZANNE (1981), 'Lame Ducks and National Champions: Industrial Policy in the Fifth Republic', in William G. Andrews and Stanley Hoffman (eds.), *The Fifth Republic at Twenty*, Albany, State University of New York Press: 292–310.

BERNARD-STEINDECKER, CLAIRE (1998), 'La Région, acteur des politiques d'éducation et de formation', in Élisabeth Dupoirier (ed.), *Régions: la croisée des chemins. Perspectives françaises et enjeux européens*, Paris, Presses de sciences Po: 217–32.

BERT, THIERRY (2000), 'La réforme de Bercy: paralysie ou suicide collectif?', in Roger Fauroux and Bernard Spitz (eds.), *Notre État: le livre vérité de la fonction publique*, Paris, Hachette: 110–46.

BEVIR, MARK, RHODES, R. A. W., and WELLER, PATRICK (2002), 'Traditions of Governance: Interpreting the Changing Role of the Public Sector in Comparative and Historical Perspectives', *Public Administration*, 15/4 (forthcoming).

BIGAUT, CHRISTIAN (1997), *Les cabinets ministériels*, Paris, LGDJ.

BIRNBAUM, PIERRE, HAMON, FRANCIS, and TROPER, MICHEL (1977), *Réinventer le parlement*, Paris, Flammarion.

BRAUD, PHILIPPE (1992), 'La réactivation du mythe présidentiel: effets de langage et manipulation symbolique', in Bernard Lacroix and Jacques Lagroye (eds.), *Le Président de la République: usages et genèses d'une institution*, Paris, Presses de la Fondation nationale des sciences politiques: 377–97.

CARCASSONNE, GUY (1997), 'Les rapports du président français et du premier ministre', *Revue française d'administration publique*, 83: 397–409.

CAREY, JOHN M. (2000), 'Parchment, Equilibria, and Institutions', *Comparative Political Studies*, 33/6–7: 735–61.

CHARLOT, JEAN (1971), *The Gaullist Phenomenon*, London, George Allen & Unwin Ltd.

CHIRAC, JACQUES (1994), *Une nouvelle France: réflexion 1*, Paris, Nil.

COLE, ALISTAIR, and JOHN, PETER (2001), *Local Governance in England and France*, London, Routledge.

COLOMBANI, JEAN-MARIE (1998), *Le résident de la République*, Paris, Stock.

CROZIER, MICHEL, and THOENIG, JEAN-CLAUDE (1975), 'La régulation des systèmes organisés complexes: le cas du système de décision politico-administratif local en France', *Revue française de sociologie*, 16/1: 3–32.

DE BAECQUE, FRANCIS (1976), *Qui gouverne la France?*, Paris, Presses universitaires de France.

DECAUMONT, FRANÇOISE (1979), *La Présidence de Georges Pompidou: essai sur le régime présidentialiste français*, Paris, Economica.

DE GAULLE, CHARLES (1971), *Memoirs of Hope: Renewal 1958–62. Endeavour 1962–* , London, Weidenfeld & Nicolson.

DE MONTRICHER, NICOLE (2000), 'The Prefect and State Reform', *Public Administration*, 38/3: 657–78.

DENOIX DE SAINT MARC, RENAUD (1996), *Rapport au Premier ministre: le service public*, Paris, La Documentation française.

DERVILLE, JACQUES (1991), 'Les mutations inachevées du discours Socialiste', *Regards sur l'actualité*, May–June: 31–49.

DEYON, PIERRE (1998), 'Aux origines de la réforme régionale', in Élisabeth Dupoirier (ed.), *Régions: la croisée des chemins. Perspectives françaises et enjeux européens*, Paris, Presses de sciences Po: 21–34.

DUHAMEL, OLIVIER (1993), *La Gauche et la Vᵉ République*, Paris, Quadrige.

DUNFORD, MICK (1995), 'Rhône-Alpes: A Dynamic Region in an Age of Crisis', in Martin Rhodes (ed.), *The Regions and the New Europe: Patterns in Core and Periphery Development*, Manchester, Manchester University Press: 165–99.

DUPOIRIER, ÉLISABETH (1998), 'Les identités régionales', in Élisabeth Dupoirier (ed.), *Régions: la croisée des chemins. Perspectives françaises et enjeux européens*, Paris, Presses de sciences Po: 185–200.

DU ROY, ALBERT (2000), *Domaine réservé: les coulisses de la diplomatie française*, Paris, Seuil.

DUVERGER, MAURICE (1996), *Le système politique français*, Paris, Presses universitaires de France.

EDYE, DAVID, and LINTNER, VALERIO (1996), *Contemporary Europe: Economics, Politics and Society*, London, Prentice Hall.

ELGIE, ROBERT (1993a), 'From the Exception to the Rule: The Use of Article 49-3 of the Constitution since 1958', *Modern and Contemporary France*, 1/1: 17–26.

—— (1993b), *The Role of the Prime Minister in France, 1981–91*, London, Macmillan.

—— (1994), 'Christian Democracy in France: The Politics of Electoral Constraint', in David Hanley (ed.), *Christian Democracy in Europe: A Comparative Perspective*, London, Pinter: 155–67.

—— (1996), 'The Institutional Logics of Presidential Elections', in Robert Elgie (ed.), *Electing the French President: The 1995 Presidential Election*, London, Macmillan: 51–72.

—— (1997), 'Models of Executive Politics: A Framework for the Study of Executive Power Relations in Parliamentary and Semi-presidential Regimes', *Political Studies*, 45/2: 217–31.

—— (1999a), 'The Politics of Semi-presidentialism', in Robert Elgie (ed.), *Semi-presidentialism in Europe*, Oxford, Oxford University Press: 1–21.

—— (ed.) (1999b), *Semi-presidentialism in Europe*, Oxford, Oxford University Press.

—— (2000), 'Staffing the Summit: France', in B. Guy Peters, R. A. W. Rhodes, and Vincent Wright (eds.), *Administering the Summit:*

Administration of the Core Executive in Developed Countries, London, Macmillan: 225–44.

—— (2002), 'La cohabitation de longue durée: Studying the 1997–2002 Experience', *Modern and Contemporary France*, 10/3: 297–311.

—— and GRIGGS, STEVEN (2000), *Debates in French Politics*, London, Routledge.

—— and MAOR, MOSHE (1992), 'Accounting for the Survival of Minority Governments: An Examination of the French Case (1988–1991)', *West European Politics*, 15/3: 57–74.

FAVIER, PIERRE, and MARTIN-ROLAND, MICHEL (1990), *La Décennie Mitterrand*, i: *Les Ruptures (1981–1986)*, Paris, Seuil.

—————— (1991), *La Décennie Mitterrand*, ii: *Les Épreuves (1984–1988)*, Paris, Seuil.

—————— (1999), *La Décennie Mitterrand*, iv: *Les Déchirements (1991–1995)*, Paris, Seuil.

FREARS, JOHN (1981), 'Parliament in the Fifth Republic', in William G. Andrews and Stanley Hoffman (eds.), *The Fifth Republic at Twenty*, Albany, State University of New York Press: 57–78.

—— (1990), 'The French Parliament: Loyal Workhorse, Poor Watchdog', *West European Politics*, 13/3: 32–51.

FULDA, ANNE (1997), *Un président très entouré*, Paris, Grasset.

GAILLARD, JEAN-MICHEL (1995), *L'ENA, miroir de l'État: de 1945 à nos jours*, Paris, Éditions complexes.

GISCARD D'ESTAING, VALÉRY (1978), *Démocratie française*, Paris, Fayard.

GOHIN, OLIVIER, and CABANNES, XAVIER (2000), 'Compétences et ressources des communes', *Pouvoirs*: 55–68.

GRANGÉ, JEAN (1981), 'Attitudes et vicissitudes du Sénat (1958–1980)', *Revue française de science politique*, 31/1: 32–84.

GRÉMION, CATHERINE (1992), 'Région, département, commune: le faux débat', *Pouvoirs*, 60: 55–65.

—— (2000), 'Les paradoxes du corps préfectoral', *Revue francaise d'administration publique*, 96: 555–64.

GRÉMION, PIERRE (1976), *Le pouvoir périphérique: Bureaucrates et notables dans le système politique français*, Paris, Seuil.

GRUNBERG, GÉRARD, and SCHWEISGUTH, ÉTIENNE (1997), 'Vers une tripartition de l'espace politique', in Daniel Boy and Nonna Mayer (eds.), *L'Électeur a ses raisons*, Paris, Presses de la FNSP: 179–218.

GUYOMARCH, ALAIN, MACHIN, HOWARD, and RITCHIE, ELLA (1998), *France in the European Union*, London, Macmillan.

HALL, PETER (1986), *Governing the Economy: The Politics of State Intervention in Britain and France*, Cambridge, Polity Press.

HALPHEN, ÉRIC (2002), *Sept ans de solitude*, Paris, Denoël Impacts.

HANLEY, DAVID (1999), 'Compromise, Party Management and Fair Shares: The Case of the French UDF', *Party Politics*, 5/2: 171–89.

HARMSEN, ROBERT (1993), 'European Integration and the Adaptation of Domestic Constitutional Orders: An Anglo-French Comparison', *Journal of European Integration*, 17/1: 71–99.

HAYWARD, JACK (1982), 'Mobilising Private Interests in the Service of Public Ambitions: The Salient Element of the Dual Policy Style', in Jeremy Richardson (ed.), *Policy Styles in Western Europe*, London, George Allen & Unwin: 111–40.

HAYWARD, J. E. S. (1983), *Governing France: The One and Indivisible Republic*, 2nd edn., London, Weidenfeld & Nicolson.

HIX, SIMON (1999), *The Political System of the European Union*, London, Macmillan.

HOWORTH, JOLYON (1993), 'The President's Special Position in Foreign and Defence Policy', in Jack Hayward (ed.), *De Gaulle to Mitterrand: Presidential Power in France*, London, Hurst & Company: 150–89.

HUBER, JOHN D. (1992), 'Restrictive Legislative Procedures in France and the United States', *American Political Science Review*, 86/3: 675–87.

—— (1996), *Rationalizing Parliament: Legislative Institutions and Party Politics in France*, Cambridge, Cambridge University Press.

HUBSCHER, ANNIE PHILIPPE-DANIEL (1991), *Enquête à l'intérieur du Parti Socialiste*, Paris, Albin Michel.

HUCHON, JEAN-PAUL (1993), *Jours tranquilles à Matignon*, Paris, Grasset.

JEAN, JEAN-PAUL (1999), 'Les réformes de la justice', *Regards sur l'actualité*, 248: 17–36.

JOBERT, BRUNO, and MULLER, PIERRE (1987), *L'État en action: politiques publiques et corporatismes*, Paris, Presses universitaires de France.

JOHN, PETER, and COLE, ALISTAIR (2000), 'When do Institutions, Policy Sectors, and Cities Matter? Comparing Networks of Local Policy Makers in Britain and France', *Comparative Political Studies*, 33/2: 248–68.

JOSPIN, LIONEL (1991), *L'Invention du possible*, Paris, Flammarion.

—— (2002), *Le temps de répondre*, Paris, Stock.

KEELER, JOHN T. S. (1993), 'Executive Power and Policy-Making Patterns in France: Gauging the Impact of the Fifth Republic Institutions', *West European Politics*, 16/4: 518–44.

—— and STONE, ALEC (1987), 'Judicial-Political Confrontation in Mitterrand's France: The Emergence of the Constitutional Council as a Major Actor in the Policy-Making Process', in George Ross, Stanley Hoffman, and Sylvia Malzacher (eds.), *The Mitterrand Experiment: Continuity and Change in Modern France*, Cambridge, Polity Press: 161–81.

LATOURNERIE, MARIE-AIMÉE (2000), 'Reflections on the Development of French Administrative Courts', *European Public Law*, 6/3: 401–11.

LE GALÈS, PATRICK (1995), 'Du gouvernement local à la gouvernance urbaine', *Revue française de science politique*, 45/1: 57–95.

—— (2001), 'Urban Governance and Policy Networks: On the Urban Political Boundedness of Policy Networks. A French Case Study', *Public Administration*, 79/1: 167–84.

LEQUESNE, CHRISTIAN (1993), *Paris-Bruxelles: comment se fait la politique européenne de la France*, Paris, Presses de sciences Po.

LEWIS-BECK, MICHAEL S., and CHLARSON, KEVIN (2002), 'Party, Ideology, Institutions and the 1995 French presidential Election', *British Journal of Political Science*, 23: 489–512.

MABILEAU, ALBERT (1998), 'La Région à l'épreuve des relations intergouvernementales', in Élisabeth Dupoirier (ed.), *Régions: la croisée des chemins. Perspectives françaises et enjeux européens*, Paris, Presses de sciences Po: 53–64.

MACHIN, HOWARD (1993), 'Representation and Distortion in the

1993 French Election', *Parliamentary Affairs*, 46/4: 627–36.

MAIR, PETER, and VAN BIEZEN, INGRID (2001), 'Party Membership in Twenty European Democracies, 1980–2000', *Party Politics*, 7/1: 5–21.

MARCH, JAMES G., and OLSEN, JOHAN P. (1984), 'The New Institutionalism: Organizational Factors in Political Life', *American Political Science Review*, 78/3: 734–49.

MASCLET, JEAN-CLAUDE (1982), *Un député pour quoi faire?*, Paris, Presses universitaires de France.

MASSOT, JEAN (1979), *Le chef du Gouvernement en France*, Paris, La Documentation française.

——(1986), *La Présidence de la République en France: vingt ans d'élection au suffrage universel 1965–1985*, Paris, La Documentation française.

——(1997), *Chef de l'État et chef du Gouvernement: dyarchie et hiérarchie*, Paris, La Documentation française.

MATHIOT, PIERRE, and SAWICKI, FRÉDÉRIC (1999), 'Les membres des cabinets ministériels Socialistes en France (1981–1993): recrutement et reconversion. Première partie: caractéristiques sociales et filières de recrutement', *Revue française de science politique*, 49/1: 3–29.

MAUROY, PIERRE (2000), *Refonder l'action publique locale: rapport au Premier ministre*, Paris, La Documentation française.

MENDRAS, HENRI (1994), *La seconde Révolution française 1965–1984*, Paris, Gallimard.

MÉNY, YVES (1974), *Centralisation et décentralisation dans le débat politique français (1945–1969)*, Paris, Librairie générale de droit et de jurisprudence.

——(1987), 'France', in Donald C. Rowat (ed.), *Public Administration in*

Developed Democracies, London, Marcel Dekker: 273–92.

——(1993), 'Le cumul des mandats ou l'impossible séparation des pouvoirs', *Pouvoirs*, 64: 129–36.

MERLE, JEAN-FRANÇOIS (2000), 'Terroirs et territoires: les nouveaux horizons de l'État', in Roger Fauroux and Bernard Spitz (eds.), *Notre État: le livre vérité de la fonction publique*, Paris, Hachette: 269–303.

MICHEL, HERVÉ (1998), 'Government or Governance? The Case of the French Local Political System', *West European Politics*, 21/3: 146–69.

MILNE, LORNA (1997), 'The Myth of the President in French Political Culture', in John Gaffney and Lorna Milne (eds.), *French Presidentialism and the Election of 1995*, Aldershot, Ashgate: 23–41.

MONTEBOURG, ARNAUD (2000), *La machine à trahir: rapport sur le délabrement de nos institutions*, Paris, Denoël.

MOREL, LAURENCE (1996), 'France: Towards a Less Controversial Use of the Referendum', in Michael Gallagher and Pier Vincenzo Uleri (eds.), *The Referendum Experience in Europe*, London, Macmillan: 66–85.

NGUYEN HUU, PATRICK (1981), 'L'Évolution des questions parlementaires depuis 1958', *Revue française de science politique*, 31/1: 172–90.

PERRINEAU, PASCAL (1997), *Le symptôme Le Pen*, Paris, Fayard.

PFISTER, THIERRY (1985), *La vie quotidienne à Matignon au temps de l'union de la gauche*, Paris, Hachette.

PIASTRA, RAPHAËL (2000), 'Du pantouflage', *Revue du droit public*, 1: 121–51.

PICQ, JEAN (1995), *L'État en France: servir*

une nation ouverte au monde, Paris, La Documentation française.

POLLITT, CHRISTOPHER, and BOUCKAERT, GEERT (2000), *Public Management Reform: A Comparative Handbook*, Oxford, Oxford University Press.

PY, ROSELYNE (1985), *Le Secrétariat général du gouvernement*, Paris, La Documentation française.

QUERMONNE, JEAN-LOUIS (1991), *L'Appareil administratif de l'État*, Paris, Seuil.

RAFFARIN, JEAN-PIERRE (2002), *Pour une nouvelle gouvernance: l'humanisme en actions*, Paris, l'Archipel.

RÉMOND, RENÉ (1982), *Les droites en France*, Paris, Aubier Montaigne.

RIBAULT, ANNE (2001), 'Lessons from the French Experience in Public and Private Partnership', *Irish Banking Review*, Spring: 49–60.

ROCARD, MICHEL (1989), *Un pays comme le nôtre: textes politiques 1986–1989*, Paris, Seuil.

ROSANVALLON, PIERRE (1990), *L'État en France de 1789 à nos jours*, Paris, Seuil.

ROUBAN, LUC (1995), 'Public Administration at the Crossroads: The End of French Specificity?', in Jon Pierre (ed.), *Bureaucracy in the Modern State: An Introduction to Comparative Public Administration*, Aldershot, Edward Elgar: 39–63.

—— (1997), 'Douze ans de cabinets ministériels', *Regards sur l'actualité*, 236: 15–27.

—— (1998), *The French Civil Service*, Paris, La Documentation française.

—— (2000), 'Les Préfets et la construction de l'État républicain: du modèle militaire au modèle managérial', *Revue francaise d'administration publique*, 96: 531–44.

SCHMITTER, PHILIPPE (1974), 'Still the Century of Corporatism?', in Frédérick B. Pike and Thomas Strich (eds.), *The New Corporatism*, Notre Dame, Ind., University of Notre Dame Press: 85–131.

SCHRAMECK, OLIVIER (1995), *Les cabinets ministériels*, Paris, Dalloz.

—— (2001), *Matignon rive gauche, 1997–2001*, Paris, Seuil.

SÉGUIN, PHILIPPE (1985), *Réussir l'alternance: contre l'esprit de revanche*, Paris, Robert Laffont.

—— (1994), *Discours encore et toujours républicain de l'exception française*, Paris, Denoël.

SÉRÉNI, JEAN PIERRE, and VILLENEUVE, CLAUDE (2002), *Le suicide de Bercy*, Paris, Plon.

SHEPSLE, KENNETH A. (1986), 'Institutional Equilibrium and Equilibrium Institutions', in Herbert F. Weisberg (ed.), *Political Science: The Science of Politics*, New York, Agathon Press: 51–81.

—— and BONCHEK, MARK S. (1997), *Analyzing Politics: Rationality, Behavior, and Institutions*, New York, W. W. Norton & Company.

SHUGART, MATTHEW SOBERG, and CAREY, JOHN M. (1992), *Presidents and Assemblies: Constitutional Design and Electoral Dynamics*, Cambridge, Cambridge University Press.

SOWERWINE, CHARLES (2001), *France since 1870: Culture, Politics, Society*, New York, Palgrave.

STONE, ALEC (1994), 'Judging Socialist Reform: The Politics of Coordinate Construction in France and Germany', *Comparative Political Studies*, 26/4: 443–69.

SULEIMAN, EZRA N. (1984), 'From Right to Left: Bureaucracy and Politics in France', in Ezra N. Suleiman (ed.), *Bureaucrats and Policy-Making: A*

Comparative Overview, New York, Holmes & Meier: 107–35.

TAAGEPERA, REIN, and SHUGART, MATTHEW S. (1989), *Seats and Votes: The Effects and Determinants of Electoral Systems*, New Haven, Yale University Press.

THIÉBAULT, JEAN-LOUIS (2000), 'France: Forming and Maintaining Government Coalitions in the Fifth Republic', in Wolfgang C. Müller and Kaare Strøm (eds.), *Coalition Governments in Western Europe*, Oxford, Oxford University Press: 498–528.

THOENIG, JEAN-CLAUDE (1973), *L'Ère des technocrates*, Paris, Les Éditions de l'organisation.

THUILLIER, GUY (1982), *Les cabinets ministériels*, Paris, Presses universitaires de France.

TSEBELIS, GEORGE, and MONEY, JEANNETTE (1995), 'Bicameral Negotiations: The Navette System in France', *British Journal of Political Science*, 25: 101–29.

VEDEL, GEORGES (1993), *Rapport au Président de la République: propositions pour une révision de la Constitution. 15 février 1993*, Paris, La Documentation française.

VICHNIEVSKY, LAURENCE (2002), *Sans instructions*, Paris, Stock.

WILLIAMS, PHILIP (1968), *The French Parliament 1958–1967*, London, George Allen & Unwin Ltd.

WORMS, JEAN-PIERRE (1966), 'Le Préfet et ses notables', *Sociologie du travail*, 8/3: 249–75.

WRIGHT, VINCENT (1974), 'Politics and Administration under the French Fifth Republic', *Political Studies*, 22/1: 44–65.

——(1997), 'Introduction: la fin du dirigisme?', *Modern and Contemporary France*, 5/2: 151–3.

——(1999), 'The Fifth Republic: From the *Droit de l'État* to the *État de droit*?', *West European Politics*, 22/4: 92–119.

INDEX